mei → didnt do something this time

bu → normally dont do something

教材项目规划小组
Teaching Material Project Planning Group

严美华	姜明宝	王立峰
田小刚	崔邦焱	俞晓敏
赵国成	宋永波	郭　鹏

加拿大方咨询小组
Canadian Consulting Group

Dr. Robert Shanmu Chen

Mr. Zheng Zhining

University of British Columbia

Dr. Helen Wu

University of Toronto

Mr. Wang Renzhong

McGill University

荣获“优秀国际汉语教材奖”
Win the Award for Outstanding International Chinese Language Teaching Materials

中国国家汉办规划教材 

NEW PRACTICAL CHINESE READER

(2nd Edition)

2

新实用汉语课本

（第2版）

刘珣 主编

课本
TEXTBOOK

英文注释
Annotated in English

编　者：张　凯　刘社会　陈　曦
左珊丹　施家炜　刘　珣
英译审订：Jerry Schmidt　余心乐

北京语言大学出版社
BEIJING LANGUAGE AND CULTURE UNIVERSITY PRESS

图书在版编目（CIP）数据

新实用汉语课本：英文注释.2 /刘珣主编.
—2版. —北京：北京语言大学出版社，2010.2（2017.2 重印）
ISBN 978-7-5619-2895-0

Ⅰ. 新… Ⅱ. 刘… Ⅲ. 汉语—对外汉语教学—教材
Ⅳ. H195.4

中国版本图书馆CIP数据核字（2010）第200095号

书　　名：新实用汉语课本（第2版 英文注释）课本 2
中文编辑：王亚莉
英文编辑：侯晓娟
责任印制：汪学发

出版发行：北京语言大学出版社
社　　址：北京市海淀区学院路 15 号　　邮政编码：100083
网　　址：www.blcup.com
电　　话：国内发行 8610-82303650/3591/3648
　　　　　海外发行 8610-82300309/0361/3080/3365
　　　　　编辑部 8610-82303647/3592
　　　　　读者服务部 8610-82303653
　　　　　网上订购电话 8610-82303908
　　　　　客户服务信箱 service@blcup.com
印　　刷：北京联兴盛业印刷股份有限公司
经　　销：全国新华书店

版　　次：2010 年 12 月第 2 版　2017 年 2 月第 9 次印刷
开　　本：880毫米 × 1194毫米　1/16　印张：20.75
字　　数：372千字
书　　号：ISBN 978-7-5619-2895-0 /H.10278
　　　　　06800

她去上海了

She has gone to Shanghai.

A new semester has begun. As your Chinese level advances, the topics you study in this book will become more interesting.

As you follow Lin Na through this lesson, you will learn how to describe the places you have visited, how to comment on your travel experiences, as well as how to change money at a bank before your departure. You will even learn how to say a sentence in the Shanghai dialect.

一、课文 Text

(一)

在银行换钱
Changing money at the bank

林　娜：力波，你来得[1]真早！

丁力波：刚才银行人少，不用排队。林娜，你今天穿得很漂亮啊。

林　娜：是吗？我来银行换钱，下午我还要去王府井买东西。

丁力波：今天一英镑换多少人民币？

林　娜：一英镑换十一块五毛七分人民币。

明天我要去上海旅行，得用人民币。

[1]: "·" is used to indicate the neutral tone in this book.

丁力波：什么？明天你要去上海吗？你刚从西安回北京。[1] 你真喜欢旅行！在西安玩儿得好不好？

评价动作或行为
Commenting on one's actions or behaviors

林 娜：我玩儿得非常好。

丁力波：吃得怎么样？

林 娜：吃得还可以。[2] 这次住得不太好。

丁力波：你参观兵马俑了没有？

林 娜：我参观兵马俑了。我还买了很多明信片，你到我那儿去看看吧。

丁力波：好啊。我也很想去西安旅行，你给我介绍介绍吧。看，该你了。[3]

* * * *

林 娜：小姐，我想用英镑换人民币。这是五百英镑。

工作人员：好，给您五千七百八十五块人民币。请数一数。

生词 New Words

1. 得	de	StPt	(*a structural particle*) 吃得很好，穿得很漂亮，玩儿得很好
2. 早	zǎo	A	early 来得真早，去得太早，到得很早，睡得不早，你早，都很早
3. 银行	yínháng	N	bank 中国银行
*4. 少	shǎo	A	few, little 人少，银行很少，也很少，不少
5. 排队	páiduì	VO	to form a line, to queue up 不用排队，排队买书，排队挂号，排两个队
排	pái	V	to arrange, to put in order
队	duì	N	a row of people, line
6. 换	huàn	V	to exchange, to change 换钱，换书，换光盘
7. 英镑	yīngbàng	N	pound sterling 换英镑，一英镑，五百英镑
8. 人民币	rénmínbì	N	Renminbi (RMB) 换人民币
人民	rénmín	N	people 中国人民银行，加拿大人民
*9. 得	děi	OpV	to need, must, to have to 得换钱，得排队，得复习语法
10. 用	yòng	V	to use 用钱，用一下电话，用英镑换人民币，得用人民币，用一用
11. 刚	gāng	Adv	just, only a short while ago 刚回北京，刚去银行
12. 从	cóng	Prep	from 从美国回中国，从上海到北京
13. 非常	fēicháng	Adv	very, extremely, highly 非常早，非常漂亮，非常喜欢中国音乐
14. 次	cì	M	(*a measure word for actions*) 这次，那次，一次
15. 参观	cānguān	V	to visit (a place) 参观学院，参观医院，参观公司

16. 兵马俑	bīngmǎyǒng	N	ceremonial clay statues of warriors and horses which are buried with the dead 参观兵马俑
兵	bīng	N	soldier, fighter
17. 明信片	míngxìnpiàn	N	postcard 很多明信片，一张明信片，美术明信片
信	xìn	N	letter 写信，寄信
18. 该	gāi	V	to be sb.'s turn to do sth. 该你了，该我（换钱）了，该他（念）了
19. 工作人员	gōngzuò rényuán		working personnel, staff member 银行工作人员，邮局工作人员，一位工作人员
人员	rényuán	N	personnel, staff
20. 千	qiān	Nu	thousand 两千，五千，八千
21. 数	shǔ	V	to count 数一数，数数，数钱，数人民币
22. 王府井	Wángfǔjǐng	PN	(name of a famous commercial district in Beijing)
23. 西安	Xī'ān	PN	(name of the capital of Shaanxi Province)

注释 Notes

① 你刚从西安回北京。

"You just came back to Beijing from Xi'an."

"从 + N / NP" forms a prepositional phrase that precedes the verb, indicating the starting point of an action.

The object of the preposition "从" is usually a word or a phrase denoting location or time. For example:

我从学院去邮局。

他从英国来中国。

In order to function as the object of "从", a noun or a pronoun that doesn't denote location must be followed by "这儿" or "那儿", thus completing the prepositional phrase which modifies the verb. For example:

他从力波那儿来。

他从谁那儿来？

陈老师从我这儿去银行。

② 吃得还可以。

"The food was passable."

"可以" is used as an adjective here, meaning "good, not bad". "还可以" means "passable, just so-so". For example:

这个电影还可以。

那个留学生汉语说得还可以。

③ 看，该你了。

"Look, it's your turn now."

"该 + N/NP/Pr (+ V) + 了" means "it's somebody's turn (to do something)". For example:

该你念课文了。

2 （二）

马大为：林娜，早！④ 好久不见，你回英国了吗？

林　娜：我没有回英国，我去上海了，昨天刚回北京。

马大为：刚才宋华来了，他也问我，林娜去哪儿了。

林　娜：我给宋华写信了，他怎么不知道？他现在在哪儿？

马大为：他回宿舍了。上海怎么样？听说这两年上海发展得非常快，是不是？

林　娜：是啊，上海很大，也非常漂亮。那儿银行多，商场也多，我很喜欢上海。

马大为：上海东西贵不贵？

林　娜：东西不太贵。上海人做衣服做得真好，我买了很多件。

马大为：上海人喜欢说上海话，他们普通话说得怎么样？

林　娜：他们普通话说得很好，年轻人英语说得也很流利。

马大为：你学没学上海话？

林　娜：学了。我会说"阿拉勿懂"。⑤

马大为：你说什么？我不懂。

林　娜：这就是上海话的"我不懂"。⑥

生词 New Words

1. 好久不见	hǎojiǔ bú jiàn	IE	haven't seen (sb.) for a very long time
好久	hǎojiǔ	A	a very long time
见	jiàn	V	to see, to meet
2. 发展	fāzhǎn	V	to develop
3. 快	kuài	A	fast, quick, rapid 发展得非常快，说得很快，念得不快
4. 话	huà	N	dialect, language 上海话，西安话，中国话
5. 普通话	pǔtōnghuà	N	the common speech (Mandarin) 说普通话，学习普通话
普通	pǔtōng	A	common, general
6. 年轻	niánqīng	A	young 年轻人，非常年轻
轻	qīng	A	light
7. 流利	liúlì	A	fluent 说得很流利，念得非常流利，流利的汉语，流利的英语，流利的普通话
8. 懂	dǒng	V	to understand 懂上海话，不懂英语，懂不懂
9. 就	jiù	Adv	exactly, precisely 就是，就是他，就是这个

补充生词 Supplementary Words

1. 美元	měiyuán	N	U. S. dollar
2. 欧元	ōuyuán	N	Euro
3. 加元	jiāyuán	N	Canadian dollar
4. 元	yuán	M	(*a unit of Chinese currency*)
5. 汇率	huìlǜ	N	exchange rate
6. 现金	xiànjīn	N	cash

7. 信用卡	xìnyòngkǎ	N	credit card
8. 亚洲学系	Yàzhōuxué xì		Department of Asian Studies
9. 城市	chéngshì	N	city
10. 地方	dìfang	N	place
*11. 儿子	érzi	N	son
12. 菜	cài	N	dish

注释 Notes

④ 林娜，早！

"Good morning, Lin Na."

"早！" is an expression commonly employed by Chinese people as a greeting. It is usually used to exchange greetings with someone in the morning. The common reply to it is also "早！" For example:

A：老师早！

B：你们早！

⑤ 我会说"阿拉勿懂"。

"I know how to say 'I don't understand.'"

In Shanghai dialect, the expression "阿拉勿懂" means "I don't understand." In this dialect, "我" can be pronounced "阿拉" ([AʔlA]), whereas "不" is pronounced "勿" ([vəʔ]).

⑥ 这就是上海话的"我不懂"。

"This means 'I don't understand' in Shanghai dialect."

"就" (1) has the function of emphasis. It is used either to confirm a fact, or stress that "this is exactly what the fact is". For example:

这就是北京。

就是这个人。

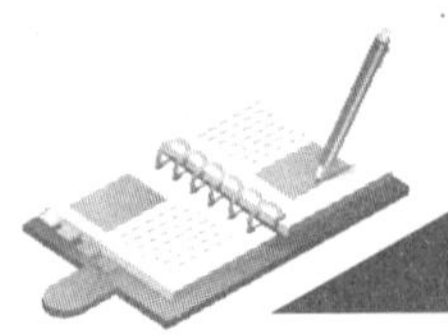

二、练习 Exercises

练习与运用 Drills and Practice

核心句 KEY SENTENCES

1. 你来得真早！
2. 你刚从西安回北京。
3. 今天一英镑换多少人民币？
4. 你到我那儿去看看吧。
5. 林娜，早！好久不见，你回英国了吗？
6. 我没有回英国，我去上海了。
7. 年轻人英语说得也很流利。
8. 这就是上海话的"我不懂"。

1. 熟读下列词组 Read the following phrases until you learn them by heart

（1）学得怎么样　玩儿得怎么样　住得好不好　写得漂亮不漂亮
穿得很好　吃得还可以　念得太快　睡得很晚
起得不早　教得不少　说得不流利　数得不对　买得不多
发展得非常快　休息得不太好
（用）钱用得不多　（问）问题问得很少　（做）练习做得真好

（2）回家了　买东西了　去北京了　学普通话了　参观兵马俑了
喝红葡萄酒了没有　写信了没有　练习口语了没有
送礼物了没有　打扫宿舍了没有　打电话了没有
洗没洗衣服　听没听音乐　参加没参加聚会　复习没复习课文

（3）从学院去医院　从美国到英国　从南方回北京　从他那儿来
从公司租房子

（4）给妈妈写信　给朋友打电话　给弟弟买礼物　给我介绍西安
给他们上语法课

（5）就是他　就是这个人　就是那位教授　就是陈老师的朋友

（6）看看　听听　说说　写写　介绍介绍　参观参观　休息休息
等一等　问一问　数一数　看一看　听一听　写一写　说一说

2. 句型替换 Pattern drills

（1）A：他每天来得早吗？
B：他每天来得很早。
A：你来得早不早？
B：我来得不早。

起　早
睡　晚
吃　多
休息　好

（2）A：你说 汉语 说得很好。
B：哪里，我说 汉语 说得不太好。
A：他汉语 说得怎么样？
B：他汉语 说得还可以。

写　汉字　漂亮
学　语法　好
念　课文　流利
做　练习　快

（3）A：谁教你们语法？
B：梁老师教我们语法。
A：他语法教得怎么样？
B：他教得太快。

口语　很好
汉字　非常快
英语　不太好
文学　还可以

（4）A：昨天你看电影了吗？
B：我没有看电影。
A：你去哪儿了？
B：我去我哥哥那儿了。

上课　医院
参观中学　银行
参加聚会　我朋友那儿
锻炼身体　老师那儿

（5）A：上午你做什么了？

B：我去银行了。

A：你换没换钱？

B：我没换钱。

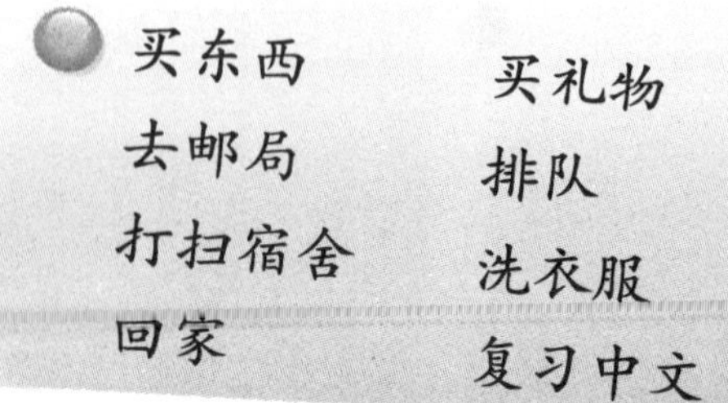

（6）A：明天你要去王府井吗？

B：我要去。

A：你从哪儿去？

B：我从学院去。

A：你跟谁一起去？

B：我跟力波一起去。

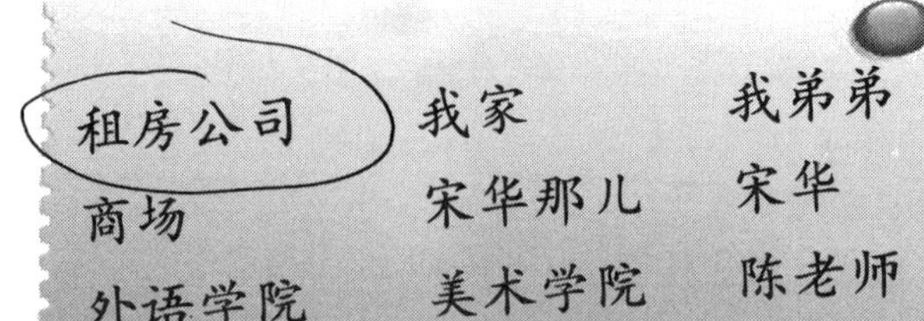

（7）A：请问，现在一英镑换多少人民币？

B：一英镑换十块三毛三分人民币。

A：我想用英镑换人民币，这是300英镑。

美元（měiyuán）	六块八毛一分	500美元
欧元（ōuyuán）	八块九毛四分	200欧元
加元（jiāyuán）	六块六毛八分	700加元

3. 课堂活动 Classroom activity

Ask and answer the following questions with your classmates.

（1）1美元换6.81元（yuán）人民币

A：100美元换多少人民币？　　A：250美元＿＿＿＿＿＿？

B：100美元换681元人民币。　　B：＿＿＿＿＿＿＿＿。

（2）1 欧元换 8.94 元人民币

A：500欧元______________？　　A：620欧元______________？

B：______________________。　　B：______________________。

（3）1 加元换 6.68 元人民币

A：1300加元____________？　　A：1500加元____________？

B：______________________。　　B：______________________。

4. 会话练习　Conversation practice

【在银行换钱　Changing money at the bank】

（1）A：小姐，我想用美元换人民币。

B：您要换多少美元？

A：今天的汇率（huìlǜ）是多少？

B：现在100美元换________________________。

A：我换________________________。

B：好。这是________________________，请您数一数。

（2）A：您好，我想换800元现金（xiànjīn）还信用卡（xìnyòngkǎ）。

B：换人民币还是换美元？

A：________________________。

【评价动作或行为　Commenting on one's actions or behaviors】

（1）A：你知道吗？我去______________________了。

B：你真喜欢旅行！你______________________？

A：玩儿得还可以。

B：这次你吃得怎么样？

A：________________________。

（2）A：你是亚洲学系（Yàzhōuxué xì）的学生吗？

B：是，我学习汉语。

A：你汉语说得很流利。

B：哪里，________________________。

A：谁教你们口语？

B：________________________。

A：老师教得怎么样？

B：________________________。

A：这是你写的汉字吗？写得很漂亮。

B：我写得不快，请多帮助。

（3）A：你看他汉字写得怎么样？

B：________________________。

A：他这个字写得对不对？

B：________________________。

A：应该怎么写？

B：________________________。

【打招呼 Saying hello】

（1）A：早！

B：你早！今天天气很好。

A：是啊，今天天气真好！

（2）A：张师傅早！

B：您早。

A：昨天晚上您睡得好吗？

B：________________________，今天起得很晚。您呢？

A：我休息得很好。

【肯定事情已经发生 Confirming that something has happened】

（1）A：昨天你去哪儿了？我下午到你宿舍找你了，你不在。

B：我去看朋友了，真对不起。

A：____________________。我没有给你打电话，你不知道我要去。

（2）A：好久不见，你去哪儿了？

B：我________________________了。

A：你为什么现在回英国？

B：我妈妈住院了，我回去看她。

【描述去过的地方 Describing a place somebody has visited】

A：听说你刚去______________________了。

B：是啊。________________________得很快。

A：你买东西了吗？那儿的东西好不好？

B：________________________，东西也很多。

A：吃的东西贵不贵？

B：________________________。

A：那儿天气怎么样？

B：________________________。

A：那儿的人说普通话吗？

B：那儿的人普通话说得__________________。你应该去看看。

5. 看图说话 Describe the following pictures

❶ 起得很晚

❷ 做/写得不对

❸ 吃得很多

❹ 来得很早

❺ 买得很多

6. 交际练习 Communication exercises

(1) You went to bank to exchange money, but after talking to the teller, you found that the current exchange rate was not high. Therefore, you decided to change the money later.

(2) After visiting different places, you and your friend are asking about each other's travel experiences.

(3) You are discussing language studies with your Chinese friend. You hope that he/she will make some comments on your study of spoken Chinese, grammar, and Chinese characters.

阅读与复述 Reading Comprehension and Paraphrasing

4 王教授去上海

王教授在北京语言学院工作，他很喜欢旅行。他刚从英国回北京，上海的一个学院请他去上课。这个星期五他去上海了。王教授给那儿的学生上英国文学课，他课上得非常好，学生都很喜欢他的课。

上海是一个大城市（chéngshì），这两年发展得很快。上海的商场很多，商场的东西也非常好。上海人做的衣服很有名。王教授去参观了很多有名的地方（dìfang），他买了不少衣服，还买了很多明信片。他儿子（érzi）在上海工作，是中国银行的工作人员。星期六儿子请他去吃饭，那个餐厅上海菜（cài）做得很好，也不太贵。王教授在上海玩儿得非常好，吃得也很好，住得还可以。一个星期过得真快。

王教授会说西安话，也会说一点儿上海话。可是他上海话说得不太好。他说："现在上海人会说普通话，年轻人普通话和英语都说得很流利，在上海我不用说上海话。"

三、语法　Grammar

1 情态补语(1)　Modal complement (1)

In Chinese, a verb or an adjective is often followed by a complementary or explanatory element, which is known as a complement. There are many kinds of complements, among which the one that describes or evaluates the state of an action or behavior is known as a modal complement. It is usually served by an adjective or an adjectival phrase with the structural particle "得" using between a verb and a modal complement. Its negative form is to use "不" before a modal complement.

V	+ 得	+ Adv	+ A
来	得	很	早
住	得	不	好

The V/A-not-V/A question form is constructed by juxtaposing the affirmative form of the complement with its negative form.

V	+ 得	+ A	+ 不A
玩儿	得	好	不好
发展	得	快	不快

In this kind of sentence, if there is an object following the verb, the verb needs to be reduplicated and followed by “得” and a modal complement. The first verb is often omitted.

(V+) O + V + 得 + Adv + A

Subject	Predicate						
	(V)	O	V	得	Adv	A	Particle
他			来	得	很	早。	
她			住	得		好	吗？
上海			发展	得		快不快？	
他们	（说）	普通话	说	得		怎么样？	
老师	（教）	语法	教	得	不	快。	

Note:

❶ A complement formed by an adjective is usually preceded by “很”. This is similar to the case in which the adjective is used as a predicate. For example: “来得很早”, “说得很快”.

❷ A sentence containing a modal complement focuses on the complement. Therefore, both its question form and the corresponding answer are usually targeted at the complement. Its negative form is made by negating the complement rather than placing “不” before the verb. Hence, it is incorrect to say “他不来得很早”.

❸ In this kind of sentence, an elliptical form can be used to answer a question. For example:

Question	Answer
他汉语说得流利吗？	他汉语说得很流利。
	说得很流利。
	很流利。

2 助词“了”(2)：肯定事情的完成或实现

Particle “了” (2): Confirming the completion or realization of something

In Lesson 13, we learned that the particle “了” (1) (or: “了①”) can follow a verb to denote the completion or realization of an action. In this lesson, the particle “了” (2) (or: “了②”) always appears at the end of a sentence. It emphatically confirms the completion or realization of some event or situation. Please compare the sentences in groups A and B:

A	B
A1: 你去哪儿？ Where are you going?	A2: 你去哪儿了？ Where have you been? *Or*: Where did you go?
B1: 我去商场。 I am going to the shopping mall.	B2: 我去商场了。 I've been to the shopping mall. *Or*: I went to the shopping mall.
A3: 你买什么？ What are you going to buy?	A4: 你买什么了？ What have you bought? *Or*: What did you buy?
B3: 我买衣服。 I am going to buy some clothes.	B4: 我买衣服了。 I've bought some clothes. *Or*: I bought some clothes.

In group A, "去商场" and "买衣服" are not completed actions in the past. In group B, however, these two actions are definitely completed or realized.

To form a V/A-not-V/A question, add "……了没有" to the end of an affirmative sentence or juxtapose the affirmative form of a verb with its negative form "……没……".

V + O + 了

Subject	Predicate			
	Adv	V	O	Pt
我		换	钱	了。
他		去	上海	了。
宋华	没有	回	家	吗？
林娜		去	西安	了没有？
她		参观没参观	兵马俑？	

Note:

❶ The particle "了" (2) always indicates that actions or events have taken place in the past. However, "了" (2) is not always required to indicate past events. To narrate a past event (especially several events taking place consecutively) or describe a scene at a specific moment without confirming the realization of the action, "了" can be left out. For example:

星期六他上午去看电影，下午去参加一个聚会。

❷ If "了" is used after a verb at the end of a sentence, it then performs both function (1) and function (2). For example:

他去了。 我懂了。 刚才宋华来了。	"了" expresses the completion or realization of the action and confirms the completion or realization of some event or situation.

3 动词的重叠 Reduplication of the verb

In Chinese, verbs can be reduplicated. The reduplicative form of a monosyllabic verb is "AA" or "A 一 A", for example, "看看", "说说", "等一等", "用一用", "数一数". The reduplicative form of a disyllabic verb is "AABB", for example, "介绍介绍", "复习复习". A verb is often reduplicated to indicate a short duration of an action or trying to do something, whose function is similar to using "一下" after a verb.

4 100~10,000 的称数法 Numeration for numbers from 100 to 10,000

101 一百〇一	102 一百〇二	……	109 一百〇九	110 一百一十
111 一百一十一	112 一百一十二	……	119 一百一十九	120 一百二十
⋮	⋮		⋮	⋮
191 一百九十一	192 一百九十二	……	199 一百九十九	200 二百
201 二百〇一	202 二百〇二	……	209 二百〇九	210 二百一十
⋮	⋮		⋮	⋮
991 九百九十一	992 九百九十二	……	999 九百九十九	1,000 一千

1,001 一千〇一	1,010 一千〇一十	1,052 一千〇五十二
1,100 一千一百	1,109 一千一百〇九	3,543 三千五百四十三
8,990 八千九百九十	9,999 九千九百九十九	10,000 一万

四、汉字 Chinese Characters

1 汉字的构字法（1） Methods of constructing Chinese characters (1)

When constructing Chinese characters, certain rules are followed in the combination of pronunciation, structure and meaning. Though the forms of modern characters differ vastly from those of the ancient ones, Chinese characters still maintain the characteristics of a logographic writing system. Therefore, understanding the process by which Chinese characters are formed will facilitate the learning of them.

Pictographic method (象形法): This method of construction depicts either the whole image or the partial characteristic of an object. It is the primitive method of forming characters.

a. Depicting the whole image of the object. For example:

人 大 目 口 牙 耳 心 手 足 女 木 水 火 土 丁 刀

日 月 井 田 子 儿 工 弓 衣 车 舟 门 户 虫 马 立

b. Depicting the characteristic of an object. For example:

母 羊 牛 犬 身

c. Depicting both the object and other associated things. For example:

果 天 匕 见

In ancient times, these single-component characters, which we have already learned, were originally pictographic. Nowadays, they are no longer very pictographic but are similar to marks. However, when they are used as the basic components for multi-component characters, the fact that they maintain either their original sounds or meanings certainly helps our understanding of compound characters.

2 认写基本汉字 Learn and write basic Chinese characters

(1) 民 ㇇ ㇕ 尸 𠃜 民
mín the people 5 strokes

(2) 币（幣） 一 丆 𢁾 币
bì currency 4 strokes

(3) 千 丿 二 千
qiān thousand 3 strokes

(4) 久 丿 ク 久
jiǔ long 3 strokes

(5) 奂 丿 ⺈ ⺈ 쇼 五 垂 奂
huàn abundant 7 strokes

(6) 丘 ノ 𠂆 𠂇 斤 丘
qiū mound, hillock 5 strokes

(7) 甬 ㇇ 龴 乛 丙 円 甬 甬
yǒng road, path 7 strokes

(8) 亚(亞) 一 丆 丌 丌 亚 亚
Yà Asia 6 strokes

(9) 车(車) 一 𠂉 左 车
chē vehicle 4 strokes

(10) 重 丿 二 千 亍 盲 盲 重 重 重
zhòng heavy 9 strokes

(11) 尤 一 ナ 九 尤
yóu especially 4 strokes

3 认写课文中的汉字 Learn and write the Chinese characters in the texts

(1) 早 zǎo

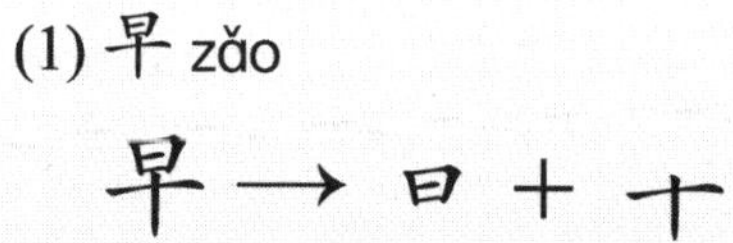

6 strokes

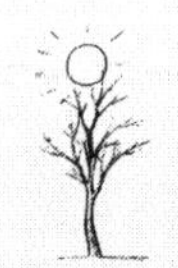

(2) 银行 yínháng（銀行）

银 → 钅 + 艮 11 strokes

(3) 排队 páiduì（排隊）

排 → 扌 + 非 11 strokes

队 → 阝 + 人 4 strokes

(4) 换 huàn

换 → 扌 + 奂 10 strokes

亠 (pángzìtóur, the top of the character "旁(páng)")

6 strokes

(5) 英镑 yīngbàng（英鎊）

镑 → 钅 + 立 + 方 15 strokes

(6) 从 cóng（從）

从 → 人 + 人 4 strokes

(7) 次 cì

次 → 冫 + 欠 6 strokes

(8) 参观 cānguān（參觀）

观 → 又 + 见 6 strokes

(9) 兵马俑 bīngmǎyǒng（兵馬俑）

兵 → 丘 + 八 7 strokes

俑 → 亻 + 甬 9 strokes

(10) 明信片 míngxìnpiàn

信 → 亻 + 言 9 strokes

(11) 工作人员 gōngzuò rényuán（工作人員）

员 → 口 + 贝　　7 strokes

(12) 王府井 Wángfǔjǐng

府 → 广 + 付　　8 strokes

(13) 西安 Xī'ān

安 → 宀 + 女　　6 strokes

(14) 发展 fāzhǎn（發展）

展 → 尸 + 龷 + 𧘇　　10 strokes

(15) 普通话 pǔtōnghuà（普通話）

普 → 丷 + 业 + 日　　12 strokes

通 → 甬 + 辶　　10 strokes

(16) 年轻 niánqīng（年輕）

轻 → 车 + 𢀖　　9 strokes

(On the left side of a character, the fourth stroke of "车" is written as "㇀".)

㐬 (liúzìbiānr, the side of the character "流")

丶 亠 亡 云 产 㐬 㐬　　7 strokes

(17) 流利 liúlì

流 → 氵 + 㐬　　10 strokes

利 → 禾 + 刂　　7 strokes

(18) 懂 dǒng

懂 → 忄 + 艹 + 重　　15 strokes

(19) 就 jiù

就 → 京 + 尤　　12 strokes

文化知识 Cultural Note

洛阳

杭州

Xi'an and the Ancient Chinese Capitals

Xi'an is a renowned ancient Chinese capital and is also one of the four world-famous ancient capitals. Back in the 11th century BC, King Wu of the Western Zhou Dynasty established his capital, named Haojing, where Xi'an is currently located. After that, the Qin Dynasty (221 BC – 206 BC), the Western Han Dynasty (206 BC – 25 AD), the Sui Dynasty (581 AD – 618 AD), and the Tang Dynasty (618 AD – 907 AD), all had their capital cities at Xi'an. Xi'an was the capital city of Chinese civilization for over one thousand years of its five-thousand-year history. In ancient times, Xi'an was called Chang'an. In the year 1369, its name was changed to Xi'an, and has remained the same to the present day. Now the modern city of Xi'an is the capital of Shaanxi Province.

Nanjing is also one of ancient Chinese capitals. The Kingdom of Wu during the Three Kingdoms Period (222 AD – 280 AD) and the Eastern Jin (晋) Dynasty (317 AD – 420 AD) all established their capitals in this city. After the outbreak of the 1911 Revolution, Dr. Sun Yat-sen took office as the provisional president in Nanjing. From 1927 to 1949, Nanjing was the capital of the National Government of China. Now it is the capital of Jiangsu Province.

Beijing was the capital of the Jin (金) , Yuan, Ming, and Qing dynasties for a period of more than eight hundred years. After 1949, it became the capital of the People's Republic of China.

In addition, Luoyang, Kaifeng, and Hangzhou are ranked among the six great ancient Chinese capitals.

北京

西安

南京

开封

我把这事儿忘了

I forgot it.

Filling in a form, getting a library card, going to the library to borrow and return books, paying fines for overdue books: these are some of the things that you are very likely to do in your school life. This lesson will teach you how to express these activities in Chinese. You will also learn two sentence patterns particular to the Chinese language.

我可以从你借钱吗?

一、课文　Text

5 （一）

宋　　华：这是北京图书馆。我们进去吧。

丁 力 波：这个图书馆真大。

宋　　华：办公室在三楼，我们上楼去，先把借书证办了。

丁 力 波：今天就可以借书吗？①

宋　　华：可以，一会儿下来借书……

三楼到了。我看看，是这个办公室。

丁 力 波：先生，我想办借书证。

北京图书馆借书证

姓名：丁力波

性别：男

职业：学生

学校：北京语言学院

工作人员：您带照片来了吗？

丁 力 波：带来了。

工作人员：请先填一张表。

宋　　华：力波，你从那儿拿一张表来，我告诉你怎么填。

丁 力 波：我汉字写得太慢，你来填吧。

宋　　华：不行。现在你在中国生活，应该自己填表。②

丁力波：好吧，我自己写。"姓名"？

宋　华："丁力波"。

丁力波："性别"写什么？

填表
Filling in a form

宋　华：自己看。③

丁力波：自——己——看？啊，性别应该写"男"。"职业"呢？

宋　华：写"学生"。好了。你把这张表和照片交了，一会儿那位先生就给你借书证了。

生词 New Words

1. 把	bǎ	Prep	(*used when the object is the receiver of an action*) 把书看了，把钱换了，把练习做了
2. 忘	wàng	V	to forget 忘了复习课文，把这事儿忘了
3. 图书馆	túshūguǎn	N	library 去图书馆，进图书馆，参观图书馆，一个图书馆
图书	túshū	N	books
馆	guǎn	N	term for certain service establishments or places for cultural activities 饭馆，咖啡馆，美术馆
4. 办公室	bàngōngshì	N	office 经理的办公室，图书馆的办公室，办公室工作人员，一间办公室
办公	bàngōng	VO	to handle official business, to work (usu. in an office) 办公时间

室	shì	N	room 休息室
*5. 上	shàng	V/N	to go up, to get on; last, previous 上来，上去，上楼；上次，上星期，上个月
6. 先	xiān	Adv	first, before 先看电影，先去办公室，先到图书馆
7. 借书证	jièshūzhèng	N	library card 带借书证，办借书证，把借书证办了，一个借书证
借	jiè	V	to borrow, to lend 借钱，借书，借语法书，借图书馆的书
证	zhèng	N	certificate, card 学生证，出生证，工作证
8. 一会儿	yíhuìr	Nu-M	a little while 一会儿就去，一会儿上楼，一会儿去图书馆借书
*9. 下	xià	V/N	to go down, to get off; next 下来，下去，下楼，一会儿下来；下次，下星期，下个月
10. 带	dài	V	to bring 带本子，带照片，带名片，带礼物，带钱，带人民币
11. 填	tián	V	to fill in, to write 怎么填，填什么，填名字，填出生年月日
12. 表	biǎo	N	form, table, list 填表，带表，做一张表
13. 拿	ná	V	to take, to hold, to get 拿去，拿光盘，拿一张表来，拿借书证
14. 慢	màn	A	slow 写得很慢，学得不慢，说得真慢，填得太慢
15. 不行	bùxíng	V	to be no way, to be out of the question
16. 生活	shēnghuó	V/N	to live; life 在中国生活，在北京学习和生活，生活得很好；快乐的生活
17. 自己	zìjǐ	Pr	oneself 你自己，我自己，学生自己，自己看，自己写，自己填
18. 姓名	xìngmíng	N	name 学生的姓名，填姓名

19. 性别	xìngbié	N	sex, gender 填性别
20. 职业	zhíyè	N	occupation, profession 什么职业，教师职业
21. 交	jiāo	V	to hand in, to hand over, to pay (the rent, etc.) 交表，交钱，交照片

注释 Notes

① 今天就可以借书吗？

"Can I start borrowing books today?"

The adverb "就" (2) is often used to suggest the earliness or quickness of an action. It is also used to indicate that an action or event takes place immediately after the previous one. For example:

刚七点，他就来了。

我们现在就去借书。

② 现在你在中国生活，应该自己填表。

"Now that you are living in China, you should fill in the form by yourself."

The pronoun "自己" is frequently used to refer back to the pronoun or noun preceding it for emphasis. e.g. "他自己", "我们自己", "力波自己", "老师自己", "医生自己".

③ 自己看。

Use your own mind.

(二)

宋 华：我们借书证办了多长时间？

丁力波：办了十五分钟，办得真快。

宋 华：今天办证的人不多。力波，听说你们上星期考试了，④

你考得怎么样？

丁 力 波：我口语考得不错，可是翻译考得不太好，语法也有很多问题。我想借新的汉语课本看看。

宋　　华：现在我们就去借书，从这儿出去。我得先把上次借的书还了。

还书
Returning books

丁 力 波：这儿的书可以借多长时间？⑤

宋　　华：可以借一个月。先生，我还书。

工作人员：好。……您的书过期了，您得交罚款。

宋　　华：真对不起，这个月太忙，我把这事儿忘了。罚多少钱？

工作人员：一本书过期一天罚两毛，⑥ 您借了四本书，过了十天，应该交八块钱。

宋　　华：给您八块。请问，汉语课本在哪儿？

工作人员：那儿有电脑，您可以先查查。

借书
Borrowing books

丁 力 波：有外国人学汉语的课本吗？

工作人员：有。您找一找《新实用汉语课本》。

生词 New Words

1. 长	cháng	A	long 时间很长，借多长时间，办了很长时间
2. 考试	kǎoshì	V/N	to give or take an examination; examination, test 今天考试；口语考试，语法考试，汉字考试
考	kǎo	V	to give or take an examination, to test 考口语，考生词，考美术，考文化
3. 不错	búcuò	A	not bad 考得不错，填得不错，生活得不错，很不错
4. 翻译	fānyì	V	to translate, to interpret 翻译英语书，翻译课文，做翻译练习，考翻译
5. 新	xīn	A	new 新书，新借书证，新问题，新朋友
6. 课本	kèběn	N	textbook 新的汉语课本，借英语课本，他买的课本
7. 出	chū	V	to go or come out 出来，出去，从这儿出去
8. 还	huán	V	to give back, to return 还书，还课本，还钱
9. 过期	guòqī	VO	to be overdue 过期了，没有过期，什么时候过期

	过	guò	V	to pass
	期	qī	N	a period of time
10.	罚款	fákuǎn	VO/N	to impose a fine or forfeit; fine 过期罚款；交罚款
	罚	fá	V	to punish, to penalize 罚钱，罚多少钱，罚十块钱
	款	kuǎn	N	a sum of money
11.	电脑	diànnǎo	N	computer 图书馆的电脑，买电脑，用电脑
	脑	nǎo	N	brain
12.	查	chá	V	to check, to look up 查课本，查生词，查语法，用电脑查
13.	《新实用汉语课本》	Xīn Shíyòng Hànyǔ Kèběn	PN	*New Practical Chinese Reader*
	实用	shíyòng	A	practical 实用的课本，很实用

补充生词 Supplementary Words

1.	阅览室	yuèlǎnshì	N	reading room
2.	杂志	zázhì	N	magazine
3.	问答	wèndá	V/N	to ask and answer questions; questions and answers
4.	预订	yùdìng	V	to reserve, to book
5.	房间	fángjiān	N	room
6.	国籍	guójí	N	nationality
7.	护照	hùzhào	N	passport
8.	钥匙	yàoshi	N	key
9.	目录	mùlù	N	catalog, list
10.	续借	xùjiè	V	to renew

11. 年龄	niánlíng	N	age
12. 广东	Guǎngdōng	PN	Guangdong Province
13. 茶楼	chálóu	N	tearoom, tea house
14. 老人	lǎorén	N	the elderly, the aged, old man or woman
15. 开始	kāishǐ	V	to start, to begin
*16. 孩子	háizi	N	child
17. 热闹	rènao	A	lively, bustling with noise and excitement
18. 新闻	xīnwén	N	news

注释 Notes

④ 听说你们上星期考试了。

"I heard that you had an exam last week."

Both "上" and "下" are used with reference to the order of things or to time sequence, with "上" meaning "last" or "previous", and "下" meaning "next" or "the following".

last / previous		this		next / the following	
上次	last time	这次	this time	下次	next time
上星期五	last Friday	(这个)星期五	this Friday	下星期五	next Friday
上个月	last month	这个月	this month	下个月	next month

⑤ 这儿的书可以借多长时间?

"How long is the loan period for a book here?"

⑥ 一本书过期一天罚两毛。

"The fine for an overdue book is two *mao* per day."

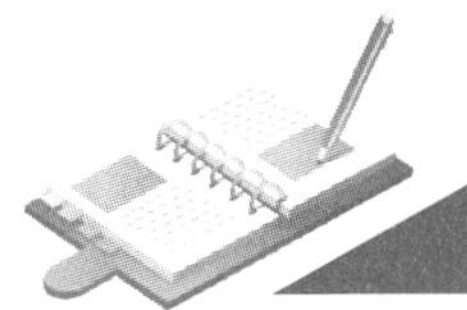

二、练习 Exercises

练习与运用 Drills and Practice

核心句 KEY SENTENCES

1. 我们进去吧。
2. 我们上楼去，先把借书证办了。
3. 您带照片来了吗？
4. 现在你在中国生活，应该自己填表。
5. 一会儿那位先生就给你借书证了。
6. 这儿的书可以借多长时间？
7. 您的书过期了，您得交罚款。
8. 真对不起，这个月太忙，我把这事儿忘了。

1. 熟读下列词组 Read the following phrases until you learn them by heart

（1）现在就去　今天就来　星期六就去看电影　下午就去图书馆借书
一会儿就来　一会儿就回家　一会儿就复习汉语语法　一会儿就写汉字

（2）自己写　自己念　自己拿　自己带　自己复习　自己锻炼　自己旅行
她们自己去借书　她自己去买东西　他自己洗衣服　他们自己翻译课文
马大为自己租房子　我自己打扫宿舍　我们自己练习口语

（3）上来　上去　下来　下去　进来　进去　出来　出去　上楼去　下楼来
寄钱去　寄明信片来　回宿舍去　回家来　到西安去　到北京来
带照片来　带英镑去　拿一本书来

（4）把这本书看了　把钱换了　把礼物拿了　把饭吃了　把咖啡喝了
把衣服洗了　把这张表交了　把借书证办了　把图书馆的书还了
把那本书借了　把这事儿忘了

（5）借一个月　等一会儿　看一个星期　住两年　复习三天　睡二十分钟
来了五分钟　等了两小时　用了一个月　参观了三天　学习了一年

2. 句型替换 Pattern drills

（1）A：现在几点？
B：现在10点。
A：他从王府井回来了没有？
B：没有。他一会儿就回来。

8:45	办公室	出来
7:15	八楼	下来
11:30	一楼	上来

（2）A：张小姐在吗？
B：不在，她上课去了。
A：她带语法书去了吗？
B：她没有带语法书去。

下楼	今天的报纸
回家	练习本
到阅览室(yuèlǎnshì)	借书证

（3）A：他给你拿什么来了？
B：他给我拿《新实用汉语课本》来了。

《 = quotation mark

寄	明信片
送	电脑
买	普通话光盘

（4）A：那张表呢？
B：他把那张表交了。

他的药	吃
他的咖啡	喝
他写的信	寄
图书馆的杂志(zázhì)	还

（5）A：我们出去散步，好吗？
B：对不起，现在不行。
A：你有事儿吗？
B：我得把今天的练习做了。

课文	复习
生词	翻译
汉字	写

（6）A：上星期六，你跟力波一起去银行换钱了吗？
B：没有，我自己去了。
A：你等了多长时间？
B：我等了一会儿。

邮局	寄东西	10分钟
医院	看病	半小时
图书馆	还书	5分钟

（7）A：下个月我就回美国去了。
B：是吗？这次你在美国要住多长时间？
A：要住一年。

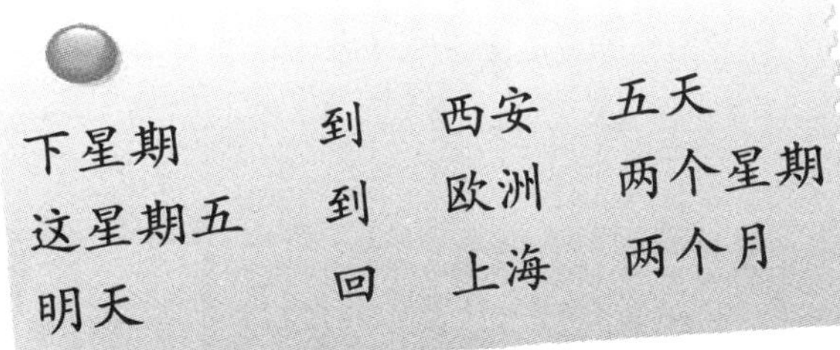

（8）A：你外语考了多长时间？
B：我考了两个小时。
A：你考得怎么样？
B：我口语考得不错，可是翻译考得不太好。

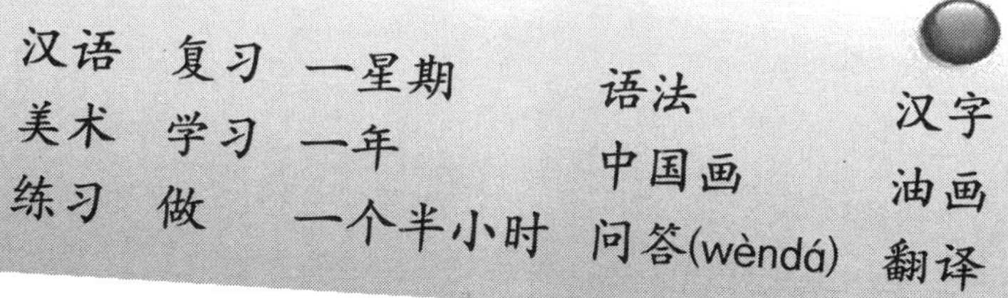

3. 课堂活动 Classroom activity

Ask three of your classmates in Chinese, how much time they spend each day on the following activities, and then report your findings to the whole class:

念课文　　练习口语　　做语法练习　　写汉字

4. 会话练习 Conversation practice

【填表 Filling in a form】

（1）A：先生，我预订（yùdìng）了一个房间（fángjiān）。我姓____________，叫____________。

B：我查一下。对，请先填一下这张表。

A：请问，怎么填？

B：这儿填您的姓名、性别和国籍（guójí），这儿填您的护照（hùzhào）号。

A：您看看，我填得对吗？

B：对。这是钥匙（yàoshi）。您的房间是668号。

【借书 Borrowing books】

（1）A：请问，有新的____________？

B：您可以查一查目录（mùlù）。

A：在哪儿查？

B：那儿有电脑，您自己____________。

（2）A：先生，我想借这五本书。

B：好。您带借书证来了吗？

A：____________。请问您这儿的书可以借____________？

B：____________。

【还书 Returning books】

A：先生，我还上次借的书。

B：好的。您上次借了五本书，这儿是四本。

A：是吗？真对不起，我把那本书的名字忘了，您能帮我查一查吗？

B：可以。您上次借的书是____________。

A：谢谢，我可以续借（xùjiè）这本书吗？

B：您可以续借一个月。

【认识新朋友　Meeting a new friend】

（1）A：您好，您要出去啊？

B：您好！您也住这儿？

A：我住九楼。这是我的名片。

B：谢谢。__________________，我没有带名片。我姓王，住三楼。

A：王先生，认识您很高兴。有时间上来坐坐。

B：好的。

（2）B：__________________？

A：啊，是王先生，快进来吧。请坐，请喝茶。

B：谢谢。

*　*　*　*　*　*

B：不早了，我该回去了。

A：有时间常来玩儿。

B：谢谢。您不要出来了。

A：好，慢走。

【暂时离开　Leaving a place temporarily】

（1）A：张先生，您的电话。

B：好，我就来。

(to C, D) 对不起，我__________________，一会儿就回来。

（2）A：张先生在吗？

B：在，我就是。有事儿吗？

A：经理请你去一下。

B：好，我一会儿就去。

(to C, D) 你们先喝咖啡，我一会儿______________。

5. 看图说话 Describe the following pictures

❶ 等一下　❷ 快下来　❸ 从哪儿出____？　❹ 快出来

6. 交际练习 Communication exercises

(1) You go to the university library to borrow books about the Chinese language. First, you ask the librarian where the grammar books are located, and how to find them. Then you ask whether there are any new or good textbooks for spoken Chinese. The librarian will answer all of your questions.

(2) Last time, you borrowed five Chinese books on grammar, spoken Chinese, translation, and Chinese characters. You have kept these books for over a month. Today when you go to the library to return them, you realize that they are overdue and you have to pay fines.

(3) You want to get a library card of your university. Please fill in the following form:

姓名		性别	
年龄 (niánlíng)		系	
国籍		专业	

阅读与复述 Reading Comprehension and Paraphrasing

8 广东（Guǎngdōng）的茶楼（chálóu）

不少广东老人（lǎorén）的每一天都从茶楼开始（kāishǐ）。他们都起得很早，五点半就出来散步、锻炼身体，六点钟就到了茶楼。那儿老人很多，他们跟认识的人问好，跟朋友说说昨天的事儿。王先

dai (bring)

生每天都带报纸来，他喜欢自己看看报纸，喝喝茶，等女儿和小孙女儿来。他等了一会儿，她们都来了。这时候，很多家的爸爸、妈妈、外婆、奶奶，还有孩子（háizi）们，也都来了，一家人在一起吃饭、喝茶、休息。孩子们不想吃，也不想喝，他们喜欢在一起玩儿，真热闹（rènao）啊！很多年轻人也都在这儿看报纸，他们要知道今天的新闻（xīnwén）。广东人常说，他们来喝茶，喝的是茶楼里的热闹，喝的是一家人一起吃饭的快乐。把茶喝了，把东西吃了，报纸也看完了，年轻人就去工作了。老人们新的一天也开始了。

三、语法　Grammar

1 简单趋向补语　The simple directional complement

“来” and “去” are often placed after certain verbs to act as their complements, showing the direction of their actions. Such complements are called simple directional complements. If the action moves towards the speaker or proceeds towards the object(s) under discussion, “来” is used; and if the action moves away from the speaker or proceeds away from the object(s) under discussion, “去” is used. For example:

A：请进来。
(The speaker is standing inside.)

D、E：她上来了。
(The speakers are standing upstairs.)

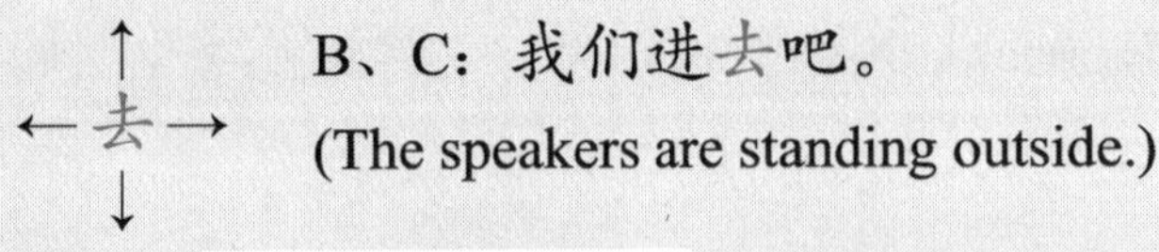

B、C：我们进去吧。

(The speakers are standing outside.)

D、E：她上去了。

(The speakers are standing downstairs.)

If a verb with a simple directional complement has an object, it should be placed between the verb and its complement. To negate the completion of an action, the negative adverb "没(有)" is used. To form the V/A-not-V/A question with this construction, use the affirmative and negative forms of the predicative verb.

V + O + 来 / 去

Subject	Predicate				
	Adverbial	V	O	来/去	Pt
我们	先	进		去	吧。
她们		出		来	了。
他们		上	楼	去	了。
你	没（有）	回	家	去	吗？
你	明天	拿不拿	明信片	来？	
他		带没带	照片	来？	

Note: The verb in this type of sentence cannot be modified by the particle "了" (1), but the particle "了" (2) can be used at the end of the sentence to show that something has already happened. Thus, "你回了家去吗？" is not correct.

2 "把" 字句 (1) The "把" sentence (1)

The "把" sentence is a kind of sentence with a verbal predicate. It is frequently used in Chinese to show how the action in the sentence disposes of an object and how this disposal affects the object, i.e. whether the object has been transposed, or its state has been changed. For example:

General statement	vs.	Emphasis on disposal
A：你去做什么了？		A：你的书呢？怎么不在这儿了？
B：我去还书了。		B：我把书还了。(so you can't find it here now)
A：她的生日是几号？		A：昨天你为什么不参加她的生日聚会？
B：我忘了(她的生日)。		B：真对不起，我把她的生日忘了。(so I've made a mistake)

In the "把" sentence, the preposition "把" and its object — the thing(s) to be disposed of — must function together as an adverbial and be placed after the subject and before the verb.

S + 把 + O + V + Other elements

Subject	Predicate					
	OpV	Adverbial	把	O (disposed of)	V	Other elements
我			把	这事儿	忘	了。
你			把	那张表和照片	交	了吗？
我	得	先	把	上次借的书	还	了。
你			把	借书证	办	了没有？

Note:

❶ The main verb in the "把" sentence must be a transitive one, and it often has the meaning of "dispose of" or "manipulate". Verbs such as "有", "在", "是", "来", "去", "回", "喜欢", "觉得" and "知道" do not have the meaning of "dispose of" or "manipulate", so they cannot be used in the "把" sentence.

❷ The object in the "把" sentence is usually definite in the speaker's mind. Therefore, "我先把一本书还了" is incorrect, while "我先把那本书还了" or "我先把上次借的书还了" can be used instead.

❸ The verb in the "把" sentence must take some other element(s) after it. The "把" sentences discussed in this lesson all have the particle "了" at the end (and we will introduce the other "把" sentences with different element(s) later). "我把这事儿忘" is incorrect, while "我把这事儿忘了" can be used instead.

❹ An optative verb or adverb (functioning as an adverbial) must be put before "把". For example: "我得先把上次借的书还了。"

3 时量补语（1） The complement of duration (1)

The complement of duration is used after a verb to indicate the duration of an action or state. When the verb is followed by an object, it is reduplicated after the object and then followed by a complement of duration. The first verb is usually omitted in this construction, and "多长时间" is often used in its interrogative form.

(V+) O + V + Complement of duration

Subject	Predicate				
	(V)	O	V	Pt	Complement of duration
你			等		一会儿。
丁力波			学习	了	半年。
我们	（办）	借书证	办	了	多长时间？
我	（考）	外语	考	了	两个小时。

Note: Only a time phrase indicating a period of time such as "一分钟", "两小时", "三天", "四个月", "五年" and "一会儿", can be used as the complement of duration. Time phrases indicating a point of time on the time scale, such as "三点钟", "一月一号", "2010 年", cannot be used as the complements of duration, since they do not express a duration of time. For example, "我等了一点半" is incorrect.

To create its negative form, a negative adverb is usually placed before the predicative verb of the sentence with a complement of duration. For example:

丁力波没有学习半年，他学习了三个月。

A：你外语考了两个小时吗？

B：我外语没有考两个小时。

四、汉字 Chinese Characters

1 汉字的构字法（2） Methods of constructing Chinese characters (2)

Ideographic method (指事法): This is a method in which new characters are created by adding signs to conventional symbols and pictographs. There is only a small number of characters that fall under this category, and they are basically of two types:

a. Those created on the basis of the conventional symbols established in primitive society. For example: 一，二，三，四，五，六，七.

b. Those created by adding indicative signs to pictographs. For example: 刃，本，早，上，中，下.

2 认写基本汉字　Learn and write basic Chinese characters

(1) 表　一 = 丰 主 夫 表 表 表
biǎo　form　8 strokes

(2) 卅　丿 川 川 卅
sà　thirty　4 strokes

(3) 官　丶 丷 宀 宁 宁 官 官 官
guān　official　8 strokes

(4) 正　一 丅 下 正 正
zhèng　right　5 strokes

(5) 式　一 = 亍 王 式 式
shì　style　6 strokes

3 认写课文中的汉字　Learn and write the Chinese characters in the texts

(1) 把 bǎ

把 → 扌 + 巴　7 strokes

(2) 忘 wàng

忘 → 亡 + 心　7 strokes

(3) 图书馆 túshūguǎn（圖書館）

图 → 囗 + 冬　8 strokes

馆 → 饣 + 官 11 strokes

(4) 办公室 bàngōngshì（辦公室）

室 → 宀 + 至 9 strokes

(5) 借书证 jièshūzhèng（借書證）

借 → 亻 + 昔 + 日 10 strokes

证 → 讠 + 正 7 strokes

(6) 带 dài (帶)

带 → 卅 + 冖 + 巾 9 strokes

(7) 填 tián

填 → 土 + 真 13 strokes

(8) 慢 màn

慢 → 忄 + 日 + 罒 + 又 14 strokes

(9) 生活 shēnghuó

活 → 氵 + 舌 9 strokes

(10) 性别 xìngbié

性 → 忄 + 生 8 strokes

别 → 口 + 力 + 刂 7 strokes

(11) 职业 zhíyè（職業）

职 → 耳 + 只 11 strokes

(12) 交 jiāo

交 → 亠 + 父 6 strokes

(13) 考试 kǎoshì（考試）

考 → 耂 + 丂　　6 strokes

试 → 讠 + 式　　8 strokes

(14) 不错 búcuò

错 → 钅 + 昔　　13 strokes

釆 (fānzìtóur, the top of the character “翻”)　　7 strokes

丿 ノ 丷 立 平 乎 釆

(15) 翻译 fānyì（翻譯）

翻 → 釆 + 田 + 羽 + 羽　　18 strokes

译 → 讠 + 又 + 丰　　7 strokes

(16) 新 xīn

新 → 立 + 木 + 斤　　13 strokes

(17) 罚款 fákuǎn (罰款)

罚 → 罒 + 讠 + 刂　　9 strokes

款 → 士 + 示 + 欠　　12 strokes

(18) 电脑 diànnǎo（電腦）

脑 → 月 + 亠 + 凶　　10 strokes

(19) 查 chá

查 → 木 + 日 + 一　　9 strokes

(20) 实用 shíyòng（實用）

实 → 宀 + 头　　8 strokes

文化知识 Cultural Note

The Educational System of China

The educational system of China consists of primary and secondary education, secondary and higher vocational education and higher education.

Chinese children usually start their schooling at the age of six or seven. They spend six years in an elementary school. After that, they enter a junior middle school to study for three more years. These nine years of schooling are generally referred to as "nine-year compulsory education", and are popularized in most parts of China.

After graduating from a junior middle school, many students enter a senior middle school, whereas some choose to go to a specialized secondary school or a vocational secondary school (generally called "vocational senior middle school"). The period of study for both types of school is three years. After graduating, students may seek employment or continue their studies at the higher education level.

In higher education, the study period for a university education is usually four years, but some programmes (medicine, for instance) require five years of study. At the time of graduation, if a student meets all the academic requirements, a bachelor's degree is then conferred upon him or her by the university authorized by the state. After graduating from a university, one may opt for further studies toward master's and doctoral degrees. Each degree usually takes three years to obtain. Some master's programmes are two years in length, while the study period for some PhD's programmes take four years. Like most universities in the world, Chinese universities offer three academic degrees, i.e., the bachelor's, the master's, and the doctorate.

这件旗袍比那件漂亮

This cheongsam is more beautiful than that one.

Have you ever worn Chinese-style clothes before? Do you know what a Chinese cheongsam is? When shopping for clothes, do you usually compare color, price, size and style? In this lesson you will learn how to choose clothes and make comparisons in Chinese.

一、课文 Text

9 （一）

丁力波：小云，哪儿卖中式衣服？

王小云：你不知道吗？你来北京多长时间了？①

丁力波：我来北京半年了。可是你在北京已经二十年了，你是北京人，当然比我知道得多。

王小云：你说得对。现在北京的商店和商场多极了，② 大商场的东西比小商店的东西贵，可是小商店的东西不一定比大商场的差。你为什么现在想买中式衣服？

丁力波：从下星期开始，我要学太极拳，我得穿一套中式衣服。

王小云：好极了！③ 你穿中式衣服一定很帅。你喜欢什么颜色的？黑的还是红的？

丁力波：我喜欢白的。

描述人或事物
Describing somebody or something

王小云：我也喜欢白的，白的漂亮。你想买好的还是买便宜的？

丁力波：我不要太贵的，也不要太便宜的。你说该去哪儿买？

王小云：去王府井吧。那儿东西多，可能贵一点儿。

丁力波：贵一点儿没关系。我们下午就去吧，我还想去公园走走。

生词 New Words

1.	旗袍	qípáo	N	cheongsam, a long close-fitting dress with a high neck and slit skirt 一件旗袍，这件旗袍，中国的旗袍
2.	比	bǐ	Prep	than (*indicating comparison*) 比那件漂亮，比他好，比今天冷，比这件贵一点儿
3.	卖	mài	V	to sell 卖衣服，卖光盘，卖苹果，卖中药，卖东西
4.	中式	zhōngshì	A	Chinese style 中式衣服，中式房子
	式	shì	Suf	(*used as a suffix to indicate sth. or sb. belongs to some type or style*)
5.	已经	yǐjīng	Adv	already 已经二十年了，已经来了，已经买旗袍了
6.	商店	shāngdiàn	N	shop, store 小商店，北京的商店，去商店买东西，一个商店
	*商	shāng	N	commerce, business
	店	diàn	N	shop, store
7.	极了	jí le		extremely 多极了，慢极了，漂亮极了，流利极了

8. 一定	yídìng	Adv	must, surely 一定很新，一定很脏，一定知道，不一定早，不一定懂
9. 差	chà	A	not up to standard, poor, bad 很差，差极了，不一定差，不一定比大商场的东西差
10. 开始	kāishǐ	V	to start, to begin 从下星期开始，从现在开始，从八点开始考试，开始学中文，开始工作
11. 太极拳	tàijíquán	N	*tai chi* 学太极拳，打太极拳
*12. 套	tào	M	set, suit, suite 一套中式衣服，一套大房子，一套新课本
13. 帅	shuài	A	handsome 很帅，帅极了，比他帅，一定很帅
14. 颜色	yánsè	N	color 什么颜色，漂亮的颜色，旗袍的颜色，衣服的颜色
15. 黑	hēi	A	black 黑的，黑颜色，黑衣服
*16. 红	hóng	A	red 红的，红颜色，红苹果
17. 白	bái	A	white 白的，白颜色，白旗袍
18. 便宜	piányi	A	cheap 便宜的，一套便宜的衣服，一定很便宜
*19. 没关系	méi guānxi	IE	never mind, it doesn't matter 贵一点儿没关系，慢一点儿没关系，少一点儿没关系
20. 公园	gōngyuán	N	park 去公园玩儿，去公园打太极拳，到公园去，一个公园
21. 走	zǒu	V	to walk, to go 去公园走走，走了一个小时，走得快

注释 Notes

① 你来北京多长时间了？

"How long have you been in Beijing?"

Some actions, such as "来，去，到", do not endure over time, so a time-measure complement must be used to indicate a period of time from the occurance of this kind of actions until the time of speaking. When the verb is followed by an object, the time-measure complement must be placed after the object. For example:

我来中国已经一年了。

他去图书馆已经两个小时了。

② 现在北京的商店和商场多极了。

"Now there are plenty of stores and shopping malls in Beijing."

In spoken language, "极了" or "多了" is often placed after an adjective as a complement to indicate an extent or degree. "极了" denotes the highest degree, while "多了" indicates a great extent of difference. For example:

	A +	极了 / 多了
这件旗袍	漂亮	极了。
他	高兴	极了。
那本书比这本书	贵	多了。
他哥哥比他	年轻	多了。

③ 好极了!

"That's wonderful!"

In spoken language, this is an expression indicating absolute agreement or satisfaction. It is more emphatic than "太好了".

Note the range of expressions used to describe the qualities of things:

好极了，太好了（marvelous, excellent）

↓

非常好，很好（very good），好（good）

↓

不错（not bad），还可以，马马虎虎（passable, just so-so）

↓

不太好（not very good）

↓

不好，差，坏（bad）

10（二）

宋　华：两个小时过去了，你要的衣服还没买。

林　娜：谁说我没有买？我已经买了衬衫了。④

宋　华：你要的旗袍呢？

林　娜：刚才看的旗袍都不错，我真想都买了。

宋　华：我们还有时间，可以再多看看。这件绿的怎么样？

林　娜：啊，这件漂亮极了，颜色、样子都比刚才看的旗袍好。

售货员：您可以试一试。

买衣服
Buying clothes

林　娜：好。我觉得这件大点儿，是不是？

售货员：我给您换一件小的。这件是三十八号，比那件小两号。您再拿去试试吧。

林　娜：这件比那件合适，宋华，你看怎么样？

宋　华：我觉得这件太短了。

售货员：对，您比我高，得穿长点儿的，我再给您找找。有了，这件红的比那件绿的长两公分。您再试一试这件。

林　娜：小姐，太麻烦您了，真不好意思。⑤这件很合适。

宋　华：这件红旗袍比那件绿的漂亮。

林　娜：可是也贵多了。

宋　华：比那件贵多少？

林　娜：贵九十块钱。

宋　华：丝绸的当然贵一点儿。

林　娜：好吧，我就买这件。⑥宋华，现在该去买你的了。你穿多大号的？想不想试试那套西服？

宋　华：好，我看看。

生词 New Words

1. 小时	xiǎoshí	N	hour 两个小时，几个小时，多少小时
2. 过去	guòqu	V	to pass 两个小时过去了，三天过去了
3. 衬衫	chènshān	N	shirt 一件衬衫，白衬衫，中式衬衫，买了衬衫了
4. 绿	lǜ	A	green 绿的，绿颜色，绿衬衫，绿苹果
5. 样子	yàngzi	N	shape, style, model, pattern 样子好，衬衫的样子，旗袍的样子
6. 售货员	shòuhuòyuán	N	shop assistant, salesclerk
售	shòu	V	to sell 售书
货	huò	N	goods 进货，送货
7. 试	shì	V	to try on, to have a try 试试，试一试，试试这件，试一试那件衣服
8. 觉得	juéde	V	to feel, to think 觉得太长，觉得很合适，觉得这件大点儿，觉得非常帅，觉得便宜极了
9. 合适	héshì	A	suitable, appropriate, right 很合适，合适极了，这件绿的比那件合适
10. 短	duǎn	A	short 短旗袍，短衬衫，短极了，短一点儿，觉得太短了
11. 高	gāo	A	high, tall 比我高，高一点儿，房租高
12. 公分	gōngfēn	N	centimetre 两公分，短一公分，比那套长两公分
13. 麻烦	máfan	V/A	to bother sb., to trouble sb.; troublesome 麻烦您，太麻烦您了；很麻烦，不麻烦
14. 丝绸	sīchóu	N	silk 丝绸的，丝绸衬衫，中国丝绸
15. 西服	xīfú	N	Western-style clothes, suit 一套西服，穿西服，西服的样子，合适的西服

补充生词 Supplementary Words

1. 双	shuāng	M	pair
2. 鞋	xié	N	shoes
3. 头发	tóufa	N	hair
4. 打折	dǎzhé	VO	to sell at a discount, to give a discount　打九折 (to sell at ten percent discount)
5. 条	tiáo	M	*(a measure word for long, narrow objects, such as trousers, skirts, snakes, etc.)*
6. 裤子	kùzi	N	trousers, pants
7. 相声	xiàngsheng	N	comic dialogue, crosstalk
8. 了不起	liǎobuqǐ	IE	amazing, terrific, extraordinary
9. 薄	báo	A	thin
10. 页	yè	M	page
11. 料子	liàozi	N	material for making clothes
12. 布	bù	N	cloth, fabric
13. 总是	zǒngshì	Adv	always
*14. 表	biǎo	N	watch

注释　Notes

④我已经买了衬衫了。

"I have already bought the shirt."

A verb plus the particle "了" (1) is a perfective construction. If the object does not have a numeral classifier compound or an attributive, it requires the particle "了" (2) to complete the sentence. These two particles are used together to indicate the completion or realization of the action expressed by the verb. They also emphasize that the event or situation has already occurred. For example:

我买了衬衫了。

我吃了饭了。

⑤ 小姐，太麻烦您了，真不好意思。

"Miss, I'm really sorry to have troubled you so much."

This expression conveys apology as well as heartfelt thanks.

⑥ 好吧，我就买这件。

"All right, I'll buy this one."

This is a common expression used in shopping. The word "就" shows emphasis.

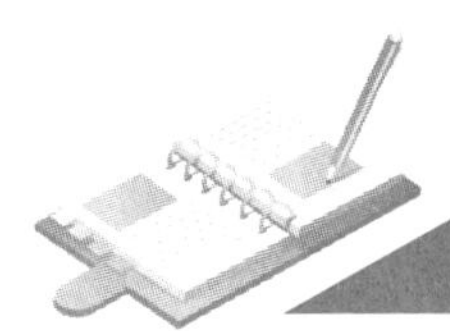

二、练习 Exercises

练习与运用 Drills and Practice

核心句 KEY SENTENCES

1. 你来北京多长时间了？
2. 你当然比我知道得多。
3. 现在北京的商店和商场多极了。
4. 你喜欢什么颜色的？黑的还是红的？
5. 我已经买了衬衫了。
6. 这件红的比那件绿的长两公分。
7. 这件红旗袍比那件绿的漂亮。
8. 可是也贵多了。

1. 熟读下列词组 Read the following phrases until you learn them by heart

（1）黑的 红的 白的 绿的 早的 晚的 快的 慢的 合适的 有名的
这间大的 那间小的 这个长的 那个短的 这瓶多的 那瓶少的

这套中式的 那套漂亮的 这件贵的 那件便宜的
中国的 外国的 中文的 外语的 语法的 口语的
老师的 医生的 外婆的 女儿的 司机的 工作人员的
学院的 办公室的 图书馆的 商店的

（2）比他好 比我忙 比西安大 比这件贵 比今天冷 比我的宿舍脏
比我来得早 比他说得流利 比他朋友写得好 比你休息得晚
比我们生活得快乐 比这儿发展得快

（3）贵三十块钱 便宜六百块 长两公分 短五公分 多一个少四十张
比她大一岁 比他早七个小时 比我晚一个星期 比小云快十分钟
比大为慢一点儿 比林娜高两公分

（4）多极了 疼极了 对极了 好极了 可爱极了 容易极了 便宜极了
贵多了 新多了 早多了 长多了 多多了 差多了 短多了
流利多了 舒服多了 年轻多了 漂亮多了 合适多了

（5）来北京半年了 去欧洲一年了 去西安十天了
到银行已经半个小时了 去公园已经一个半小时了

（6）写了50个汉字了 问了两个问题了 看了一本汉语书了
复习了十个生词了 试了三件旗袍了

2. 句型替换 Pattern drills

（1）A：他来中国已经多长时间了？
B：他来中国半年了。

去	上海	两个月
来	语言学院	一年
去	商店	20分钟
来	公园	一个小时

（2）A：这件旗袍怎么样？
B：这件旗袍比那件旗袍漂亮，
这件漂亮极了。

个	电影	有意思
个	医院	大
瓶	红葡萄酒	贵
位	售货员	好

（3）A：今天比昨天冷吗？
B：我觉得今天不比昨天冷。

上午	下午	忙
小商店的东西	大商场的东西	便宜
这个课本	那个课本	合适
他	他哥哥	帅

（4）A：这件衬衫大还是那件衬衫大？
B：这件衬衫大。
A：这件衬衫比那件衬衫大多少？
B：这件衬衫比那件衬衫大两公分。

套	西服	贵	200块钱
双(shuāng)	鞋(xié)	小	1号
件	旗袍	长	一点儿
个	楼	高	多了

（5）A：他比他朋友来得早吗？
B：不，他朋友比他来得早。

走	快
睡	晚
吃	多
介绍	好

（6）A：你课文翻译得真好！
B：哪里，我翻译得不好。
她翻译课文比我翻译得好。

太极拳	学	快
汉语	说	流利
汉字	写	漂亮
口语	考	好

3. 课堂活动 Classroom activity

Complete the following comparisons.

（1）汉语书：23块；英语书：37块

⟶ 汉语书比英语书便宜，汉语书比英语书便宜多少？

汉语书比英语书便宜__________块。

（2）汉字课本：18.50元；口语课本：26.90元

→ 口语课本比汉字课本______，口语课本比汉字课本______多少？

口语课本比汉字课本______块。

（3）我们系：350人；你们系：240人

→ 我们系的人比你们系的人______，我们系的人比你们系的人______多少？

我们系的人比______人。

（4）王老师：43岁；陈老师：30岁

→ 王老师比陈老师______，王老师比陈老师______多少？

王老师比______岁。

（5）这件旗袍：120公分；那件旗袍：117公分

→ 这件旗袍比那件旗袍______，这件旗袍比那件旗袍______多少？

这件旗袍比______公分。

4. 会话练习　Conversation exercises

【比较　Making comparisons】

（1）A：小云，你是北京人，给我们介绍介绍北京吧。你应该比______。

B：好。北京这几年发展得很快，现在大商场和银行多______。

A：听说上海的商场也非常多。

B：你说得对，上海的商场可能比______。

（2）A：力波，你来北京多长时间了？

B：______。

A：我觉得你汉语比我说得______。

B：哪里，你的语法和汉字______多了。

【描述人或事物 Describing somebody or something】

（1）A：请问，________________？

B：哪位张老师？

A：对不起，我不知道他的名字，他在________________工作。

B：男的还是女的？

A：男的。他比您高，岁数也比您大一点儿，头发（tóufa）有点儿白。

B：我知道了，他叫张大生，在二楼209办公室。

A：谢谢。

（2）A：好久不见。你今天穿得真漂亮！

B：谢谢。这是我刚在________________买的新衣服。

A：颜色好极了，样子也很新，我喜欢中式的。

B：是啊，中式的比西服________________。

【买衣服 Buying clothes】

（1）A：小姐，我想买双鞋。

B：________________？

A：我穿42号的。

B：您看看这双。

A：可以试一下吗？

B：可以。合适吗？

A：我觉得小了点儿。

B：________________。这双比那双大半号。

A：这双真合适。＿＿＿＿＿＿＿＿＿？

B：580块。

A：能打折（dǎzhé）吗？便宜点儿吧。

B：好吧，给您打九折。

（2）A：你觉得这条（tiáo）裤子（kùzi）怎么样？

B：比刚才那条好。小姐，＿＿＿＿＿＿＿＿＿？

C：350块。

A：有便宜点儿的吗？

C：有。＿＿＿＿＿＿＿＿＿？

A：我穿75公分的。

C：这条合适。

A：多少钱？

C：199块。

A：＿＿＿＿＿＿＿＿＿。

C：您给多少？

A：100块。

C：100块太少了。

B：那我们走吧。

C：等一等。150块给您。

A：还是太贵了，不要了。

C：好吧，做个朋友，120块怎么样？

5. 看图会话 Describe the following pictures

❶ 这儿的苹果比那儿的苹果________。
那儿的苹果比________________。
这儿的苹果比那儿的苹果______多了。
那儿的苹果比______________多了。

❷ 你看，哥哥比______________。
弟弟比________________。
哥哥______________多了。
弟弟______________多了。

❸ 这件衣服比那件衣服__________，
那件衣服________________。
这件衣服________________，
那件衣服________________。
你说，哪件衣服好？
________________________。

❹ 这个宿舍______________，那个宿舍______________。
这个宿舍比______________，那个宿舍比______________。
你喜欢哪个宿舍？

6. 交际练习 Communication exercises

(1) You have just returned from Beijing. Describe to your relatives the difference between China and your own country, or compare Beijing to a city in your country.

(2) What does your best friend like? What does he/she like to do on the weekend? Call and talk to your friend now.

(3) You went shopping in a mall. At first you wanted to buy a suit, but it was too expensive, so you didn't buy it. Then you wanted to buy some shirts, but they were either too big or too small, or too long or too short. You didn't find the suitable color or style, so you didn't buy any shirts. Finally, you bought a Chinese-style dress that appealed to you.

阅读与复述 Reading Comprehension and Paraphrasing

12 高一点儿（相声 xiàngsheng）

A：王先生，听说你也开始写相声了？

B：我写得很少，今年写了五个很短的相声，您呢？

A：我工作很忙，也写得不多。今年写了十五个不太短的相声。

B：比我多十个！您真了不起（liǎobuqǐ）。

A：不客气。你写相声有问题，可以来问我。你还翻译了一本书，对不对？

B：对，书很薄（báo），两百页（yè）。

A：我也翻译了一本很薄的书。

B：多少页？

A：五百页。

B：比我的多三百页！您真了不起。

A：不客气。你翻译有问题，可以来问我。你的衬衫是什么料子（liàozi）的？

B：是布（bù）的。

A：我穿的衬衫是丝绸的。

B：您的比我的好多了。

A：不客气。你今年多大？

B：我今年三十，您呢？

A：我今年三十一。

B：您比我大一岁。

A：不客气。你多高？

B：一百七十二公分，您呢？

A：我现在一百七十三公分，比你高一点儿。

B：是啊，您总是（zǒngshì）比我高一点儿。

A：不客气。你的表（biǎo）现在几点？

B：九点。

A：我的现在十点。

B：您的表也比我的快一个小时。

A：不客气。

B：——啊？

三、语法 Grammar

1 “的”字短语（1） The “的” phrase (1)

The “的” phrase is constructed by placing “的” after a noun, a pronoun, an adjective, a verb, a noun or a verbal phrase. It is equivalent to a noun and expresses some distinction.

Pr / N / A +	的
我	的 (mine)
老师	的 (the teacher's)
丝绸	的 (the silk one)
大	的 (the big one)

The “的” phrase can be used as a subject or an object in a sentence. For example:

丝绸的很贵，我没有丝绸的。

我喜欢绿的，他喜欢红的。

2 用介词“比”表示比较（1）

Making comparisons by using the preposition “比” (1)

The preposition “比” may be used to compare the qualities and characteristics of two things. “比” and its object form a prepositional phrase and are often placed before the adjective in a sentence with an adjectival predicate.

S ＋ 比 ＋ N / Pr ＋ A

Subject	Predicate		
	比	N / Pr	A
这件旗袍	比	那件旗袍	漂亮。
大商场的东西	比	小商店的	多。
这件衬衫	比	那件衬衫	合适。
小云	比	他	忙。

The preposition “比” with its object may be placed before a verb to express comparison in a sentence with a verbal predicate.

S ＋ 比 ＋ N/Pr ＋ VP

Subject	Predicate			
	N	比	N / Pr	VP
你		比	我	知道　得　多。
田小姐		比	我	翻译　得　好。
他们	汉语	比	我们	说　得　流利。

The adverb "不" is placed before "比" to form a negative comparative sentence. "x不比y + 形容词" means "x is antonym of A (comparative form) + than y" or "x is as + A / antonym of A + as y". For example:

他不比我高。（meaning "I am taller than him" or "he is as tall as me"）

小商店的东西不比大商场的东西差。（meaning "things in small stores are better than those in big shopping malls" or " things in small stores are as good as those in big shopping malls"）

Note:

❶ The auxiliary verbs and adverbs must be placed before "比". For example:

你应该比我知道得多。
他可能比我忙。
这件衣服当然比那件衣服好。

❷ The adverbs "很", "真" or "非常" cannot be used before the adjective in a "比" sentence with an adjectival predicate. For example, "他比我很忙" is incorrect.

3 数量补语 The complement of quantity

In a "比" sentence with an adjectival predicate, the complement of quantity (a numeral-measure word phrase) can be used after the main element of the predicate to express specific differences between two things or persons.

比 + N / Pr + A + Numeral-measure word phrase

Subject	Predicate			
	比	N / Pr (the object of comparison)	A (the aspect of comparison)	Numeral-measure word phrase (the result of comparison)
这件衣服	比	那件衣服	大	一号。
这本书	比	那本书	贵	20块钱。
这件	比	那件	长	两公分。
我们系	比	他们系	多	90个学生。

The word "一点儿" is used to indicate a slight difference between two things or persons, while "多了" is used to indicate that the difference is great. For example:

这件衣服比那件贵一点儿。

这个电脑比那个新多了。

The question form for this type of sentence is "A + 多少". For example:

你们系比他们系多多少人?

这件衣服比那件贵多少（钱）?

四、汉字　Chinese Characters

1 汉字的构字法(3)　Methods of constructing Chinese characters (3)

Associative method (会意法): This method of construction combines two or more characters to create a new character with a new meaning, which is derived from the association of the original meanings of all the individual components. For example, "从" is constructed by placing one "person" after another, meaning "to follow". We have learned the following characters in this category:

林，比，北，明，信，友，孙，多，步，出，看，拿，坐，休，分，品

2 认写基本汉字　Learn and write basic Chinese characters

(1) 比　　一 ㇀ 比 比
bǐ　　to compare　　4 strokes

(2) 已　　㇆ ㇆ 已
yǐ　　already　　3 strokes

(3) 及　　丿 乃 及
jí　　and　　3 strokes

(4) 产　　丶 亠 亠 产 产 产
chǎn　　to produce, to give birth to　　6 strokes

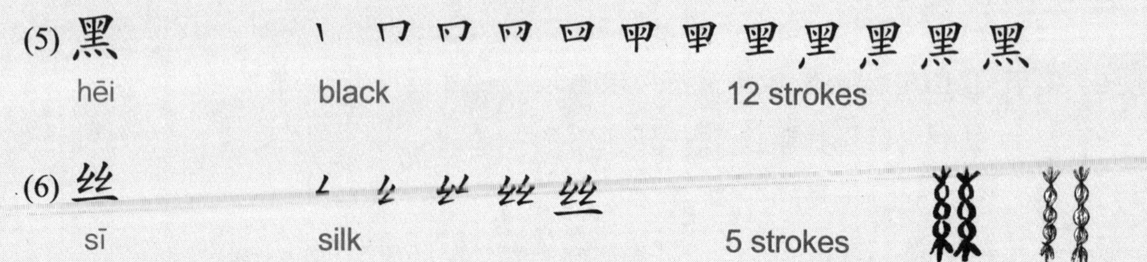

(5) 黑 hēi black 12 strokes

(6) 丝 sī silk 5 strokes

3 认写课文中的汉字 Learn and write the Chinese characters in the texts

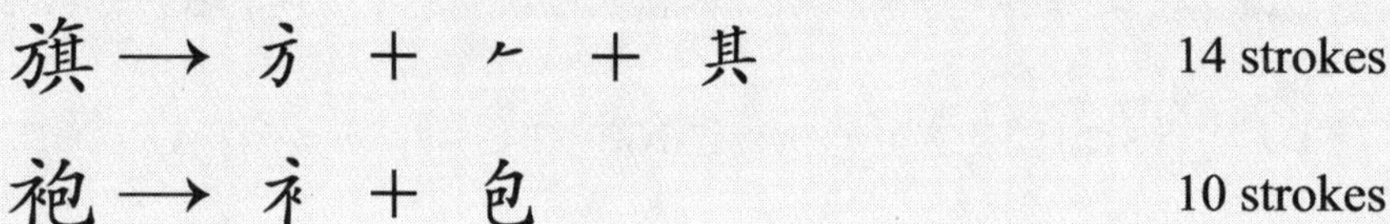

衤 (yīzìpángr, the side of cloth) 5 strokes

("衣" is written as "衤" on the left side of a character.)

(1) 旗袍 qípáo

旗 → 方 + 𠂉 + 其 14 strokes

袍 → 衤 + 包 10 strokes

(2) 卖 mài (賣)

卖 → 十 + 买 8 strokes

(3) 商店 shāngdiàn

店 → 广 + 占 8 strokes

(4) 极 jí (極)

极 → 木 + 及 7 strokes

(5) 一定 yídìng

定 → 宀 + 疋 8 strokes

(6) 开始 kāishǐ (開始)

始 → 女 + 厶 + 口 8 strokes

龹 (juànzìtóur, the top of the character "卷" (juàn))

丶 丷 䒑 䒑 兰 龹 6 strokes

(7) 太极拳 tàijíquán（太極拳）

拳 → 龹 + 手 10 strokes

(8) 套 tào

套 → 大 + 镸 10 strokes

(9) 帅 shuài（帥）

帅 → 刂 + 巾 5 strokes

⺈ (dāozìtóur, the "knife" top) ノ ⺈ 2 strokes

("刀" is written as "⺈" on the top of a character.)

(10) 颜色 yánsè（顏色）

颜 → 产 + 彡 + 页 15 strokes

色 → ⺈ + 巴 6 strokes

(11) 便宜 piányi

便 → 亻 + 更 9 strokes

宜 (yí) → 宀 + 且 8 strokes

(12) 没关系 méi guānxi（沒關係）

关 → 丷 + 天 6 strokes

(13) 公园 gōngyuán （公園）

园 → 囗 + 元 7 strokes

(14) 衬衫 chènshān（襯衫）

衬 → 衤 + 寸　　8 strokes

衫 → 衤 + 彡　　8 strokes

(15) 绿 lǜ（綠）

绿 → 纟 + 录　　11 strokes

(16) 售货员 shòuhuòyuán（售貨員）

售 → 隹 + 口　　11 strokes

货 → 化 + 贝　　8 strokes

(17) 合适 héshì（合適）

适 → 舌 + 辶　　9 strokes

(18) 短 duǎn

短 → 矢 + 豆　　12 strokes

(19) 麻烦 máfan（麻煩）

麻 → 广 + 林　　11 strokes

烦（fán）→ 火 + 页　　10 strokes

(20) 丝绸 sīchóu（絲綢）

绸 → 纟 + 冂 + 土 + 口　　11 strokes

文化知识 Cultural Note

Traditional Chinese Garment

China has always been reputed as the "Kingdom of Dresses". Dating back to thousands of years, Chinese silk had become world-famous along with the "Silk Road". Traditional Chinese garment is best represented by *Hanfu* and cheongsam.

Hanfu is the traditional Chinese garment, whose origin can be traced back from the legendary antiquity to the Ming Dynasty. It is mainly characterized by a cross collar, a right-tilted front garment and a girded waist belted by a sash and a belt hook, thus creating a carefree impression. Nevertheless, each style has its own popularity in different dynasties, among which the Han, Tang and Ming were especially distinctive.

Among *Hanfu*, the most conspicuous one is Tang Attire. The Tang Dynasty saw a remarkable development of Chinese politics and economy, a prosperous culture and art, and a frequent communication with European and Asian ethnic groups. Therefore, Tang Attire is rich in diversity, distinctive in styles and magnificent in tendency. Its patterns are delicate and beautiful. With silk as its main material, it is renowned for its softness and gentleness. The style of women's clothes is becoming increasingly loose with the neck and shoulders exposed in some designs. Tang Attire also influences the clothes of the neighboring countries, from which Japanese kimono and Korean dresses have learned a lot in terms of color and form.

Cheongsam was originated from the ancient Manchu garment. It gained popularity across China since the Qing Dynasty and almost becomes the most common clothes for Chinese women. Through continuous innovation, it is developed into many different varieties in which particular attention is paid to the color, decoration and the beauty of human figure. Cheongsam presents a strong Chinese flavor and reflects the beauty of traditional Chinese garment. It has not only become the representative of Chinese clothes, but also been widely acknowledged as the symbol of traditional clothes of oriental women.

In addition, other Chinese ethnic groups' garments are also beautiful with their own distinctive characteristics. They are not only important components of the ethnic groups' splendid history and culture, but also the most remarkable symbols of each ethnic group.

我听懂了，可是记错了

I understood what I was told, but remembered it wrongly.

Urban transportation in China currently depends mainly on buses, subways and taxis. Beijing enjoys a very advanced public transit system. The bus routes are so numerous that it is possible to take the wrong bus. Our friend, Ma Dawei, took the wrong bus this time because he didn't remember the place name of his destination correctly.

一、课文　Text

13（一）

在邮局 At the post office

马大为：小姐，我要寄这个包裹。

工作人员：好，我看一下。

马大为：这些书都是新的。① 这四本书是中文的，那两本书是英文的。这本大词典是旧的……

描述事物 Describing something

工作人员：好了，② 请包好。

马大为：对不起，这是我刚学的课文，我想练习练习。

工作人员：您汉语说得很流利。您要往哪儿寄？③

马大为：美国。

工作人员：您寄航空还是海运？

马 大 为：寄航空比海运贵，可是比海运快多了。寄航空吧。

工作人员：邮费是106块。请在这儿写上您的名字。

马 大 为：小姐，我还要取一个包裹。

工作人员：请把包裹通知单给我。对不起，您的包裹不在我们邮局取，您得去海关取。④

提醒
Reminding

马 大 为：请问，海关在哪儿？

工作人员：在建国门。别忘了把您的护照带去。⑤

马 大 为：谢谢。

工作人员：不客气。

生词 New Words

1. 记	jì	V	to remember, to bear in mind 记生词，记汉字，记得快，记得慢
2. 错	cuò	A	wrong, erroneous 记错，听错，写错，说错，做错，坐错
3. 包裹	bāoguǒ	N	parcel, package 寄包裹，一个包裹，寄这个包裹
4. 些	xiē	M	some 一些，这些，那些，这些书，那些学生
5. 英文	Yīngwén	N	English 英文书，这些英文书，那些英文课本

6. 词典	cídiǎn	N	dictionary 英文词典，中文词典，一本大词典，查词典
7. 旧	jiù	A	old, used 旧词典，旧书，旧衣服，旧衬衫
8. 包	bāo	V	to wrap 包书，包好
9. 往	wǎng	Prep	to, toward 往美国，往西安，往欧洲寄，往哪儿走
10. 航空	hángkōng	N	aviation 寄航空，航空公司，航空小姐
空	kōng	N	sky, air 空中
11. 海运	hǎiyùn	N	sea transportation, ocean shipping 寄海运，海运公司
海	hǎi	N	sea, big lake 海边，海上，海里
12. 邮费	yóufèi	N	postage 交邮费，多少邮费
费	fèi	N	fee, expense, charge 车费，书费，学费，水电费
13. 取	qǔ	V	to take, to get, to fetch 到银行取钱，到邮局取包裹，取照片，取东西
14. 通知单	tōngzhīdān	N	letter of notice 包裹通知单，取通知单
通知	tōngzhī	V/N	to notify, to inform; notification 通知你；写通知
单	dān	N	sheet, list 收费单，床单
15. 海关	hǎiguān	N	customhouse, customs 去海关，海关工作人员
16. 别	bié	Adv	don't 别忘了，别过期了，别写错了
17. 护照	hùzhào	N	passport 带护照，办护照，取护照，看护照
18. 客气	kèqi	A	polite, courteous 不客气，不要客气，别客气，太客气
19. 建国门	Jiànguó Mén	PN	Jianguo Men (a place in Beijing)
门	mén	N	door, gate, entrance 开门，关门

注释 Notes

① 这些书都是新的。

"All these books are new."

"些" represents an uncertain quantity, commonly used with "这", "那" or "哪", to modify a noun. For example:

这些书 (these books)　　那些老师 (those teachers)　　哪些电影 (which movies)

It is also commonly used with "一". For example:

一些书 (some books)　　一些人 (some people)

② 好了……

"All right..."

"好了" is used to express the wish to discontinue an action, meaning "don't say it any more". For example:

好了，不要再说了。

③ 您要往哪儿寄？

"Where do you want to mail it to?"

The preposition "往" and the noun that indicates place or direction are used together to make up the preposition-object phrase. "Prep 往 + PW" represents the direction of the action. For example:

往学院去　　往里走　　往欧洲寄

Compare: "Prep 在 + PW" represents the place of the action. For example:

在这儿写　　在北京学习

④ 对不起，您的包裹不在我们邮局取，您得去海关取。

"Sorry, your package is to be picked up at customs, not at our post office."

Foreign packages sent to China are usually picked up at the local post office. Sometimes it is necessary to go to the customs office to collect them.

⑤ 别忘了把您的护照带去。

"Don't forget to take your passport with you."

"别忘了" indicates reminding.

14（二）

丁力波：大为，现在该去海关办你的事儿了。从这儿怎么去海关？

马大为：海关在……我想想，叫什么门。

丁力波：看，这儿有803路公共汽车，经过前门。

不能确定
Being uncertain

马大为：对，好像是前门吧。车来了，咱们先上去。⑥

*　*　*　*

售票员：请大家往里走。⑦下一站，前门。下车的乘客请拿好自己的东西；刚上车的乘客请刷卡，没卡的请买票。⑧

坐公共汽车
Taking the bus

马大为：小姐，请问海关是不是在前门？

售票员：海关是在建国门，不是在前门。

丁力波：我们坐错车了。

售票员：没关系，您可以在前门下车，在那儿换地铁到建国门。

北京巴士股份有限公司(五)专线票
A17　票价：2元　066790
报销凭证
投放巴士广告
支持公交事业

马大为：没有坐错？好极了！买两张到前门的。

售票员：一块一张。您这是五块，找您三块。请拿好票。⑨

丁力波：大为，你说昨天邮局的工作人员告诉你了，你听懂了没有？

马大为：我听懂了，可是记错了。

丁力波：我得查一查：你把护照带来了吗？

马大为：当然带来了，你放心吧！

丁力波：包裹通知单呢？

马大为：糟糕，我把包裹通知单忘了。

生词 New Words

1. 路	lù	N	route 803路，323路，331路
2. 公共汽车	gōnggòng qìchē		bus 810路公共汽车，坐公共汽车
公共	gōnggòng	A	public, common, communal 公共厕所
汽车	qìchē	N	automobile, motor vehicle, car
车	chē	N	vehicle 开车，买车，坐车
3. 经过	jīngguò	V	to pass, to go through, to go by 经过王府井，经过建国门，经过家美租房公司，经过美国
4. 好像	hǎoxiàng	Adv	seem, like 好像是前门，好像是陈老师，好像是《新实用汉语课本》
像	xiàng	Adv	seem, appear
5. 咱们	zánmen	Pr	we, us 咱们认识一下，咱们一起去
6. 售票员	shòupiàoyuán	N	ticket seller, conductor
票	piào	N	ticket 车票，公共汽车票，电影票

7.	大家	dàjiā	Pr	all, everybody　大家好，请大家进来，请大家多帮助
8.	里（边）	lǐ(bian)	N	in, inside, within　往里走
9.	站	zhàn	N	station, stop　两站，下一站，汽车站，公共汽车站
10.	乘客	chéngkè	N	passenger　下车的乘客，刚上车的乘客，到王府井的乘客
	乘	chéng	V	to ride　乘车，乘汽车，乘公共汽车
	客	kè	N	visitor, guest　请客，送客
11.	刷卡	shuākǎ	VO	to swipe a card
	刷	shuā	V	to swipe　刷卡，刷牙
	卡	kǎ	N	card　电话卡，公交卡
12.	地铁	dìtiě	N	underground railway, subway　乘地铁，换地铁，坐地铁
13.	放心	fàngxīn	VO	to set one's mind at rest, to be at ease, to feel relieved　请放心，放心吧，不放心
14.	糟糕	zāogāo	A	in a wretched state, in a mess, too bad　太糟糕，真糟糕
15.	前门	Qiánmén	PN	Qianmen (a place in Beijing)

补充生词 Supplementary Words

1.	公斤	gōngjīn	M	kilogram (kg.)
2.	邮票	yóupiào	N	stamp
3.	纪念	jìniàn	N	commemoration
4.	然后	ránhòu	Conj	then
5.	准备	zhǔnbèi	V / N	to prepare, to get ready; preparation
6.	聪明	cōngming	A	clever, bright

7. 封	fēng	M	(*a measure word for letters*)
8. 信封	xìnfēng	N	envelope
9. 贴	tiē	V	to stick, to paste
10. 孙子	sūnzi	N	grandson

注释 Notes

⑥ 车来了，咱们先上去。

"Here is the bus; let's get on first."

The meaning of "咱们" is equivalent to "我们", and is commonly used in spoken Chinese. However, "咱们" includes the listener; "我们" usually does not include the listener. For example:

A and B go to the library to borrow books; A says to the librarian: 先生，我们来借书。(Sir, we want to borrow books.)

Then, A says to B: 咱们借几本书？(How many books are we going to borrow?)

⑦ 请大家往里走。

"Please move to the middle of the bus."

The pronoun "大家" indicates everyone in a certain area or group. For example:

大家好。

请大家进来。

大家都来了。

我告诉大家一件事儿。

"大家" is often used after "你们", "我们", "咱们" for emphatic purposes. For example:

明天我们大家都去上海。

你们大家都想学汉语吗？

In China, there is a ticket seller on most buses. The number of self-service ticketing buses is increasing. Meanwhile, public transportation IC cards enjoy growing popularity.

⑧ 没卡的请买票。

"Passengers without cards need to buy tickets, please."

"没卡的" is a form of the "的" phrase, which means "没卡的乘客"。"(没/不 +)V + 的" or "VP + 的" can also form the "的" phrases. For example:

这本书是借的，不是买的。（是借的书，不是买的书：The book is borrowed, not purchased.）

买两张到前门的。（到前门的票：tickets to Qianmen）

⑨ 您这是五块，找您三块。请拿好票。

"You gave me five *kuai*; three *kuai* is your change. Please hold onto your ticket."

These are daily expressions used by bus ticket sellers. In some Chinese cities, the ticket is checked when passengers get off the bus; thus the ticket sellers say, "Please hold onto your ticket."

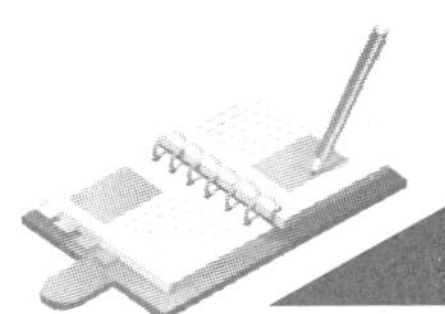

二、练习 Exercises

练习与运用 Drills and Practice

核心句 KEY SENTENCES

1. 这些书都是新的。
2. 这四本书是中文的，那两本书是英文的。
3. 请把包裹通知单给我。
4. 别忘了把您的护照带去。
5. 买两张到前门的。
6. 请大家往里走。
7. 下车的乘客请拿好自己的东西。
8. 我听懂了，可是记错了。

1. 熟读下列词组 Read the following phrases until you learn them by heart

（1）一些书　一些咖啡　这些词典　那些包裹　这些专业　那些医院
看一些课本　买一些衣服　吃这些中药　记那些生词

（2）往里走　往这儿看　往哪儿去　往美国寄　往33楼来　往宿舍走
往宋华家去　往加拿大打电话

（3）咱们先上车　咱们去锻炼身体　咱们一起去商场　咱们来念课文
咱们去海关取包裹

（4）大家好　大家都很高兴　祝大家快乐
请大家参观　请大家喝咖啡　请大家吃烤鸭　请大家看电影
请大家放心　请大家进来　请大家帮助我　请大家参加生日聚会
你们大家都来玩儿吧　我们大家都说汉语　咱们大家一起去公园

（5）是新的　是旧的　是贵的　是便宜的　是对的　是错的　是容易的
是我的　是咱们的　是你们大家的　是文学的　是美术的　是丝绸的
是买的　是租的　是借的　是寄的　是送的　是喝的　是吃的
是看病的　是来参观的

（6）写上名字　带上护照　包好包裹　拿好车票　看懂英文　听懂上海话
记错名字　做错练习　写错汉字　拿错包裹　坐错公共汽车
穿错衣服

（7）把通知单给我　把礼物送他　把课本还你　把中文词典给他
把名片拿来　把护照带去　把教授请来　把借书证带去
把新课本借来

2. 句型替换 Pattern drills

（1）A：你听懂他的话了吗？
B：我听懂了一些，还有一些没有听懂。

听	老师讲的语法
看	这个电影
看	今天的课文
看	这张通知单

（2）A：她写对你的名字了没有？
B：没有，她写错了。

做对	练习	错
听错	他的话	对
记错	你的电话号	对
坐错	公共汽车	对
念对	这些生词	错
打错	电话	对

（3）A：她说什么了？
B：她说请大家拿好自己的东西。

排	队
写	汉字
练习	口语
复习	这一课课文
带	护照和通知单

（4）A：你把钱给司机了没有？
B：我把钱给他了。

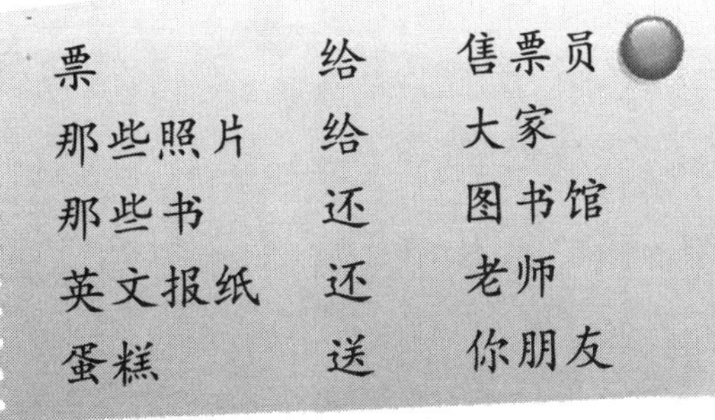

票	给	售票员
那些照片	给	大家
那些书	还	图书馆
英文报纸	还	老师
蛋糕	送	你朋友

（5）A：他想把什么寄去？
B：他想把那本新书寄去。

寄	来	兵马俑的明信片
带	来	他家的小狗
带	去	那张光盘
拿	来	刚买的苹果
拿	去	这个包裹

（6）A：那本词典是你的吗？

B：哪本词典？

A：那本英文的。

B：那不是我的，是图书馆的。

间	房子	大	我姐姐
件	衬衫	丝绸	我朋友
套	西服	新	我哥哥
个	电脑	白	办公室
张	明信片	兵马俑	林娜

（7）A：这张票是不是你买的？

B：这张票不是我买的，我买的是下星期二的。

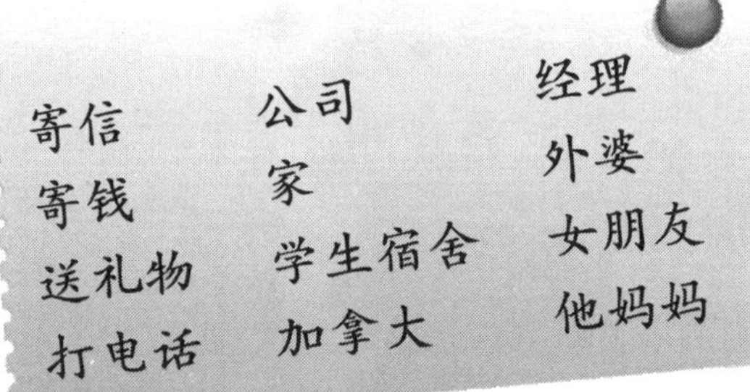

（8）A：他往哪儿寄包裹？

B：他往西安寄包裹。

A：他给谁寄包裹？

B：他给他弟弟寄包裹。

寄信	公司	经理
寄钱	家	外婆
送礼物	学生宿舍	女朋友
打电话	加拿大	他妈妈

3. 课堂活动 Classroom activity

Complete the following question-and-answer exercises (A asks the first question, B answers it; B asks the second question, C answers it; ...)

（1）马大为要寄什么东西？

（2）他要往哪儿寄包裹？

（3）寄航空贵还是寄海运贵？航空比海运快吗？

（4）邮局的工作人员让马大为去哪儿取包裹？

（5）邮局的工作人员让马大为把什么带去？

（6）海关是不是在前门？

（7）马大为买了几张票？

（8）马大为买的票是到哪儿的？

（9）他们为什么要在那儿下车？

（10）马大为听懂邮局工作人员的话了吗？

（11）马大为把什么忘了？

4. 会话练习　Conversation exercises

【在邮局　At the post office】

（1）A：先生，我要寄这个包裹。

B：我看一下。

A：这些都是________________。

B：好了，请包好。您要往哪儿寄？

A：________________________。

B：您想寄航空还是海运？

A：我要寄__________________。邮费多少钱？

B：你的包裹一共五公斤（gōngjīn），邮费是____________________。

A：请问这个包裹几天能到？

B：要一星期。

（2）A：小姐，您好。我来取一个包裹。

B：请把包裹通知单__________。

A：给您。

B：我要看一看您的护照。好，请写上您的姓名。

A：在这儿吗？

B：对。这是您的包裹，请拿好。

（3）A：我要买邮票（yóupiào）：十张一块二的，十张八毛的。

B：一共20块。

A：我还要买纪念（jìniàn）邮票。

B：您要什么样儿的？

A：我要买兵马俑的。

B：______________________________？

A：五套。

【描述事物 Describing something】

（1）A：我的本子在哪儿？

B：______________________________吗？

A：那不是我的，我的本子是新的。

B：你的本子是什么颜色的？

A：______________________________。

B：这儿有红的、白的、黑的……，这是不是你的？

A：对，这是我的。

【提醒 Reminding】

（1）A：力波，下午没有课，咱们一起去图书馆吧。

B：______________________________。

A：我下午等你，别忘了把要还的书带去。

B：______________________________。

（2）A：我明天去邮局。

B：______________________________？

A：我要取一个包裹，是朋友从美国寄来的。

B：别忘了______________________________。

【不能确定　Being uncertain】

（1）A：你知道那位先生是谁吗？

B：他是……，我想想，__________是王什么中。

A：对，是王华中。

（2）A："休息"的"休"字怎么写？

B：先写"亻"，然后（ránhòu）……，写什么？__________是"本"。

A：不对，是"木"。

【坐公共汽车　Taking the bus】

（1）　A：____________路公共汽车来了，咱们上去吧。

B：好。往里走，我来买票。买两张票，到____________。

售票员：一张____________。您这是____________，找您____________。请拿好票。

B：谢谢。

售票员：下一站，王府井。下车的乘客请准备（zhǔnbèi）好。王府井到了，下车的乘客请拿好自己的东西。

（2）乘　客：小姐，请问去王府井是不是坐这路车？

售票员：________________。

乘　客：糟糕，我坐错车了。

售票员：________________。您可以在前门下车，换810路公共汽车到王府井。

乘　客：谢谢，到站请告诉我们一下，好吗？

售票员：没问题，还有三站。

5. 看图说话 Describe the following pictures

❶ 这件西服是_______________的，
那件西服是_______________的。

❷ 这本书是_______________的，
它是_______________的。
那本书是_______________的，
它是_______________的。

❸ 学　　生：小姐，我来办借书证。
工作人员：请把您的_______________给我。
学　　生：好。
工作人员：请给我两张_______________。
学　　生：给您。
工作人员：请把_______________给我，再给我十块钱。
学　　生：给。
工作人员：好了，您的借书证办好了。

6. 交际练习 Communication exercises

(1) You go to the post office to mail a parcel to a friend back home. There are many things in the parcel and you show them to the clerk one by one. Initially you want to send it by air, since that is faster, but you change your mind after you find out that the postage is very costly because you have so many things to mail.

(2) Describe one of your experiences of going to the post office to pick up a package or withdraw money.

(3) You get on a bus. While you are buying your ticket, you find out that you are on the wrong bus. The ticket seller tells you how to change buses to reach your destination.

阅读与复述 Reading Comprehension and Paraphrasing

16

聪明（cōngming）的儿子

1.寄信

爸爸写了两封（fēng）信，一封信的信封（xìnfēng）是大的，一封是小的。他让儿子去邮局寄。过了一会儿，儿子回家了。爸爸问："你把信寄了吗？"儿子说："寄了。爸爸，您把邮票贴（tiē）错了。往西安寄的信是小的，您贴了十块钱邮票；往加拿大寄的信是大的，您贴了一块二毛钱邮票。"爸爸问儿子："你把邮票换了吗？"儿子说："您已经贴好邮票了，我不能换邮票，我把里边的信换了。"

2.把我寄去

爸爸买来一套音乐光盘，说："把这套光盘给奶奶，她喜欢听音乐。"他包好光盘，贴上邮票，和儿子一起到邮局把光盘寄了。过了两个星期，奶奶来信了，她说："下个月让我的小孙子（sūnzi）到上海来玩儿吧，我很想他。"爸爸想了一会儿，对儿子说："下个月我和你妈妈都很忙，谁送你去啊？"儿子说："没关系，爸爸，您在我身上贴上邮票，把我寄去！"

3. 爸爸没有帮我

儿子每天的练习都做得不对，可是昨天的练习都做对了。老师很高兴，问他："每天你练习都做得不好，为什么昨天做得很好？你爸爸昨天一定帮助你了。"儿子说："没有。老师，我爸爸昨天晚上没有回家，我想我应该自己做了。"

三、语法 Grammar

1 结果补语 The resultative complement

The resultative complement explains the result of an action. It usually consists of a verb or an adjective.

V	+ V / A	
听	懂	to listen and understand
写	上	to write down
包	好	to wrap (the parcel) well
拿	好	to hold onto
记	错	to remember incorrectly
坐	错	to take the wrong (bus)

Resultative complements are closely bound to verbs. There cannot be other words in between. The particle "了" or any objects must be placed behind the resultative complement.

Subject	Predicate				
	V	V / A(complement)	Pt "了"	O	Pt "了"
我	听	懂			了。
马大为	包	好	了	那个包裹。	
下车的乘客	拿	好		自己的东西。	
我们	坐	错		车	了。

If expressed by a verb with a resultative complement, the action is usually completed. Thus, "没（有）" is commonly used in negation, and "……了没有" is used for a V/A-not-V/A question. For example:

A：你听懂了没有？

B：我没听懂。

A：马大为包好包裹了没有？

B：他没有包好包裹。

The adjective "好" in this lesson is used as a resultative complement, indicating that an action is completed to satisfaction. For example:

我们一定要学好汉语。

请大家坐好，现在上课。

2 "把"字句（2）　The "把" sentence（2）

There are two types of "把" sentence in this lesson:

A. "把" sentence with the predicative verb "给"

This type of "把" sentence commonly indicates giving something to somebody.

S ＋ 把 ＋ O (sth.) ＋ V (to give) ＋ O (sb.)

Subject	Predicate					
	Adv	把	O (sth.)	V (to give)	O (sb.)	Pt "了"
你		把	你的护照	给	我。	
你		把	护照	给	我。	
我	没(有)	把	包裹	给	她。	
他		把	礼物	送	我	了。

B. "把" sentence with a simple directional complement

The basic form of the "把" sentence with a simple directional complement is:

S + 把 + O + V + 来/去 (+了)

Subject	Predicate					
	Adverbial	把	O	V	来/去	(Pt "了")
你		把	你的护照	带	去。	
我	今天	把	护照	带	来	了。
马大为	昨天	把	那本书	拿	去	了。
我		把	借图书馆的书	拿	来	了。
我	也	把	林娜	请	来	了。

3 "是"字句 (2) The "是" sentence (2)

We have already learned the "是" sentence, for example "我是马大为". Its subject and object are nouns or pronouns. The function of the "的" phrase is equivalent to that of a noun; thus it can also serve as the subject and the object of a "是" sentence.

S + 是 + N / A / Pr / VP + 的

Subject	Predicate		
	Adv	是	"的" phrase
这张包裹通知单		是	你的。
这本大词典		是	旧的。
这四本书		是	中文的。
这本书	不	是	英文的。
英文的	不	是	马大为的。
中文的		是	买的。

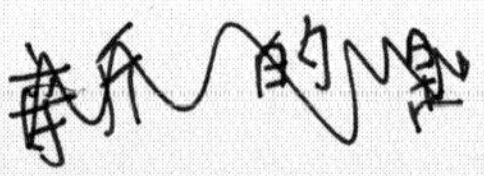

四、汉字 Chinese Characters

1 汉字的构字法(4) Methods of constructing Chinese characters (4)

Phonetic loan method (假借法): This method uses the shape and sound of a readily available character to represent another word that has the same sound. For example, the original meaning of "斤" was "axe"; it is now borrowed as a measure word to represent "a unit of weight", which has the same sound. "我" was originally used to represent a type of weapon; now it is used as the first person pronoun. "来" originally meant "wheat"; it is now borrowed to mean "come", because the sounds were the same in ancient times.

2 认写基本汉字 Learn and write basic Chinese characters

(1) 巳 sì — the sixth of the twelve Earthly Branches — 3 strokes

(2) 弗 fú — not — 5 strokes

(3) 象 xiàng — elephant — 11 strokes

(4) 聿 yù — originally meant "writing brush" — 6 strokes

(5) 乘 chéng — to ride — 10 strokes

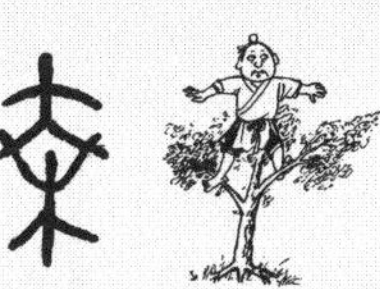

(6) 失 shī — to lose — 5 strokes

3 认写课文中的汉字 Learn and write the Chinese characters in the texts

(1) 记 jì（記）

记 → 讠 + 己 5 strokes

(2) 包裹 bāoguǒ

包 → 勹 + 巳 5 strokes

裹 → 亠 + 果 + 𧘇 14 strokes

(3) 些 xiē

些 → 止 + 匕 + 二 8 strokes

(4) 词典 cídiǎn（詞典）

典 → 曲 + 八 8 strokes

(5) 旧 jiù（舊）

旧 → 丨 + 日 5 strokes

(6) 往 wǎng

往 → 彳 + 主 8 strokes

(7) 航空 hángkōng

航 → 舟 + 亠 + 几 10 strokes

空 → 穴 + 工 8 strokes

(8) 海运 hǎiyùn（海運）

运 → 云 + 辶 7 strokes

(9) 邮费 yóufèi（郵費）

费 → 弗 + 贝 9 strokes

(10) 取 qǔ

取 → 耳 + 又 8 strokes

(11) 通知单 tōngzhīdān（通知單）

单 → 丷 + 甲 + 一 8 strokes

(12) 护照 hùzhào（護照）

护 → 扌 + 户 7 strokes

(13) 客气 kèqi（客氣）

客 → 宀 + 夂 + 口 9 strokes

(14) 建国门 Jiànguó Mén（建國門）

建 → 聿 + 廴 8 strokes

(15) 路 lù

路 → 𧾷 + 夂 + 口 13 strokes

(16) 汽车 qìchē（汽車）

汽 → 氵 + 气 7 strokes

(17) 好像 hǎoxiàng

像 → 亻 + 象 13 strokes

(18) 咱们 zánmen（咱們）

咱 → 口 + 自　　9 strokes

(19) 售票员 shòupiàoyuán（售票員）

票 → 西 + 示　　11 strokes

(20) 里边 lǐbian（裏邊）

边 → 力 + 辶　　5 strokes

(21) 站 zhàn

站 → 立 + 占　　10 strokes

(22) 地铁 dìtiě（地鐵）

地 → 土 + 也　　6 strokes

铁 → 钅 + 失　　10 strokes

(23) 放心 fàngxīn

放 → 方 + 攵　　8 strokes

(24) 糟糕 zāogāo

糟 → 米 + 一 + 曲 + 日　　17 strokes

(25) 前门 Qiánmén（前門）

前 → 丷 + 一 + 月 + 刂　　9 strokes

文化知识 Cultural Note

Chinese Transportation

Since the reform and opening-up, Chinese transportation industry enjoys a rapid development.

In terms of railway, the operating mileage of China's railway has reached 86,000 kilometres, ranking the second place in the world by the end of 2009. The railway network has covered all the provinces, regions and cities, including Tibet.

In terms of road, by the end of 2008, the total length of roads has hit 3,730,200 kilometres, which has increased by 45 times compared with that of the early years after the founding of P.R.C. The roads have reached to all the cities and counties in China, accessible to 99% townships and 81% villages. China began its expressway construction in the middle of 1980s. Now, the total mileage of expressways has reached 60,300 kilometres, ranking the second place in the world only after USA.

In terms of aviation, by the end of 2008, there were nearly 1,400 routes of Chinese civil aviation to over 150 Chinese cities, more than 90 cities in over 40 countries and regions.

中国画跟油画不一样

Traditional Chinese paintings differ from oil paintings.

Have you ever seen a traditional Chinese painting? Our friend Ding Libo not only appreciates it, but also knows how to paint traditional Chinese paintings. He is going to tell us the differences between traditional Chinese paintings and oil paintings. In this lesson, you will learn a new way to make comparisons.

中国画跟油画不一样

也很喜欢中国画，从我十岁开始，

奶奶教我

一、课文　Text

17（一）

丁力波：咱们来早了，美术馆还没有开门呢。①

林　娜：来早了比来晚了好。今天我一定要参观一个上午。

丁力波：你真喜欢中国画！

表达持续的时间
Expressing duration of time

林　娜：是啊，我非常喜欢徐悲鸿画的马。

丁力波：我跟你一样，也很喜欢中国画。从我十岁开始，妈妈就教我画中国画。你说说，我中国画画了多少年了？

林　娜：啊，已经画了十一年了！我真不知道您还是一位"老画家"。

丁力波：不敢当。② 我爸爸跟我妈妈一样喜欢中国画，可是他自己不会画。我爸爸也有很多爱好，他喜欢唱中国京剧。现在他在家还常常唱京剧。

谈爱好
Talking about hobbies

林 娜：他唱得怎么样？

丁力波：他唱京剧跟我画中国画一样，马马虎虎。

林 娜：我想买一幅中国画。大画家画的一定很贵，是不是？

丁力波：徐悲鸿画的马当然贵极了。我认识一位“老画家”，他画的马不贵。

林 娜：这位老画家是谁？

丁力波：是丁力波啊！我可以把我画好的马送你。③

生词 New Words

1.	中国画	zhōngguóhuà	N	traditional Chinese painting 看中国画，喜欢中国画，买中国画，介绍中国画
	画儿	huàr	N	painting
2.	油画	yóuhuà	N	oil painting 画油画，买油画，卖油画，看油画
	油	yóu	N	oil
3.	一样	yíyàng	A	same, alike 一样快，一样美，和……一样帅，一样糟糕，一样不一样
4.	美术馆	měishùguǎn	N	art gallery 参观美术馆，到美术馆去
5.	开门	kāimén	VO	to open a door, to begin a day's business 商店开门，邮局九点开门，银行不开门，还没有开门呢

6. 画	huà	V	to paint 画画儿，画马，画中国画，画油画
7. 老	lǎo	A	old, senior 老人，老师傅，老先生，老教授
8. 画家	huàjiā	N	painter, artist 老画家，年轻的画家，有名的画家
*家	jiā	Suf	(*used as a suffix to indicde sb. is a specialist*) 旅行家，文学家，美术家
9. 不敢当	bù gǎndāng	IE	I really don't deserve this.
10. 爱好	àihào	N/V	hobby; to like 有很多爱好，有什么爱好，爱好画画儿
11. 唱	chàng	V	to sing
*12. 京剧	jīngjù	N	Beijing opera 唱京剧
13. 马马虎虎	mǎmǎhūhū	A	so-so, passable 唱得马马虎虎，写得马马虎虎，翻译得马马虎虎，考得马马虎虎
马虎	mǎhu	A	careless
14. 幅	fú	M	(*a measure word for paintings, cloth, etc.*) 一幅画儿，一幅油画，两幅中国画
15. 徐悲鸿	Xú Bēihóng	PN	(name of a well-known Chinese painter)

注释　Notes

① 咱们来早了，美术馆还没有开门呢。

"We came too early. The art gallery is not open yet."

The structure "还没（有）＋ V ＋ 呢" indicates that an event or a situation has not happened or occured yet, but it will happen or occur. Compare the following:

他回家了没有？

他没有回家。（He didn't go home.）

他还没有回家呢。（He hasn't gone home yet.）

② 不敢当。

"I really don't deserve this."

This phrase is used as a reply to someone's compliment. For example:

A：您给了我很多帮助，您真是我的老师。

B：不敢当。您也常常帮助我，我非常感谢。

Lin Na calls Libo an "experienced painter" in fun. Libo's answer is also meant to be a joke.

③ 我可以把我画好的马送你。

"I can give you the horse I drew."

When used as a resultative complement, the word "好" can also convey the meaning of completion. For example: 画好，做好.

18（二）

丁力波：咱们已经看了一个半小时的画儿了，二楼的还没有看呢。现在是不是坐电梯上楼去？④

林　娜：好吧。力波，你觉得中国画跟油画一样不一样？

丁力波：当然一样，都是画儿啊。

比较
Making comparisons

林　娜：别开玩笑。

丁力波：我没有开玩笑，我是说中国画跟油画一样美。

林　娜：你说说哪儿不一样？

丁力波：你找对人了，我来告诉你吧。⑤中国画和油画用的材料不一样。

林　娜：怎么不一样？

丁力波：中国画用纸，油画常常用布；中国画主要用墨和水画，油画一定要用油彩画。

林　娜：对，还有别的吗？

丁力波：油画没有空白，中国画常常有空白。你看这幅徐悲鸿的画儿，画家只画了一匹马，没有画别的。

林　娜：可是我们觉得还有别的东西。让我们来想象一下：那匹马往咱们这儿跑来了，我觉得它跑得非常快，好像还有风。

丁力波：对了。这就跟齐白石画的虾一样，它们游来游去，真可爱！⑥你看，画家画水了吗？

林　娜：没画，可是我觉得有水。

丁力波：中国画是不是跟油画很不一样？

林　娜：谢谢你的介绍。可是我还想看看“老画家”画的马怎么样。

生词 New Words

1. 电梯	diàntī	N	elevator 坐电梯上楼，等电梯
2. 开玩笑	kāi wánxiào	VO	to crack a joke, to make fun of 别开玩笑，开我的玩笑
3. 材料	cáiliào	N	material 用的材料，画画儿的材料，做衣服的材料
4. 纸	zhǐ	N	paper 用纸，买纸，一张纸
5. 布	bù	N	cloth 布料，布衣服，用布做衣服
6. 主要	zhǔyào	A	main 主要是，主要有，主要的语法，主要的问题
7. 墨	mò	N	Chinese ink 用墨画，用墨写
8. 油彩	yóucǎi	N	greasepaint 用油彩画
9. 别的	biéde	Pr	other 别的画儿，别的画家，别的乘客，别的时间，别的颜色，别的样子
10. 空白	kòngbái	N	blank space 有空白，空白的表
11. 只	zhǐ	Adv	only 只有，只说，只觉得，只画马，只唱京剧，只考课文，只记汉字
12. 匹	pǐ	M	(*a measure word for horses*) 一匹马
13. 想象	xiǎngxiàng	V	to imagine 想象一下，喜欢想象
14. 跑	pǎo	V	to run 跑来，跑去，跑得很快，往宿舍跑
15. 它	tā	Pr	it
16. 风	fēng	N	wind 有风，没有风，大风
17. 虾	xiā	N	shrimp 画虾，吃虾
18. 它们	tāmen	Pr	they (*referring to things or animals*)
19. 游	yóu	V	to swim 游得很快，游了一个小时，游来游去
20. 齐白石	Qí Báishí	PN	(name of a well-known Chinese painter)

补充生词 Supplementary Words

1. 骑	qí	V	to ride, to sit on the back of
2. 自行车	zìxíngchē	N	bike, bicycle
3. 远	yuǎn	A	far
4. 跑步	pǎobù	VO	to run, to jog
5. 书法	shūfǎ	N	handwriting, calligraphy
6. 业余	yèyú	A	amateur
7. 节目	jiémù	N	programme
8. 以前	yǐqián	N	before, formerly, previously
9. 瘦	shòu	A	thin
10. 减肥	jiǎnféi	VO	to lose weight
11. 管	guǎn	V	to discipline
12. 生气	shēngqì	VO	to get angry, to take offense
13. 钢琴	gāngqín	N	piano
*14. 书店	shūdiàn	N	bookstore, bookshop
*15. 教育	jiàoyù	V	to teach, to educate
16. 营业员	yíngyèyuán	N	staff of a shop, post office and a bank, etc.
17. 观点	guāndiǎn	N	point of view

注释 Notes

④ 现在是不是坐电梯上楼去？

"Should we take the elevator upstairs now?"

We have already learned the interrogative sentence "……，是不是？" in Lesson 10. The structure "是不是" can be placed not only at the end of a sentence, but also at the beginning or in the middle of a sentence. The meanings are basically the same. For example:

他是不是已经来了？ （ = 他已经来了，是不是？）

是不是林娜真去上海了？ （ = 林娜真去上海了，是不是？）

The affirmative answer to this kind of sentence can be "是啊". The negative answer, however, needs to negate the part about which the question asks. For example, the negative answers of the above example sentences can respectively be:

——他没有来。

——（不是，）林娜没有去上海。

⑤ 我来告诉你吧。

"Let me tell you."

The structure "来 + V / VP" is commonly used in spoken Chinese. Here, the word "来" does not express a concrete action, but rather the meaning of "will do something". The structure with "来" has the same meaning as that without "来". For example:

我来介绍一下。（= 我介绍一下。）

你来试试。（= 你试试。）

⑥ 它们游来游去。

"They swim back and forth."

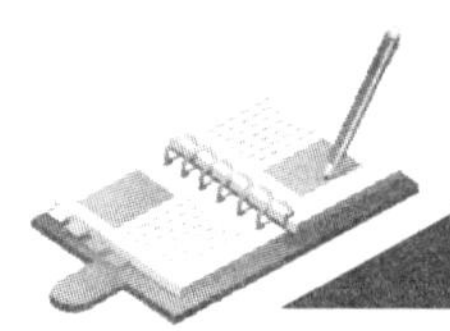

二、练习 Exercises

练习与运用 Drills and Practice

核心句 KEY SENTENCES

1. 美术馆还没有开门呢。
2. 你说说，我中国画画了多少年了？
3. 我爸爸跟我妈妈一样喜欢中国画。
4. 咱们已经看了一个半小时的画儿了。
5. 现在（咱们）是不是坐电梯上楼去？
6. 中国画跟油画一样不一样？
7. 中国画跟油画一样美。
8. 中国画主要用墨和水画。

1. 熟读下列词组 Read the following phrases until you learn them by heart

（1）跟那个问题一样　跟油画不一样　跟那个公司一样不一样
跟他哥哥一样帅　跟中国人一样流利　跟那个学院一样有名
跟她一样想去旅行　跟他一样喜欢音乐　跟我一样会唱京剧

（2）参观了一个上午了　锻炼了四十分钟了　在北京生活了一年了
汉语学习了半年了　英语教了十年了　课文念了二十分钟了
做了一个小时的练习　打了十分钟的电话　睡了八个小时的觉
排了一刻钟的队　散了一会儿步

（3）我来查一查　我来说说　我来画　我来告诉你　我来打扫房间
我来帮助你

（4）坐电梯上楼　坐公共汽车去美术馆　坐地铁去王府井　用墨画
用油彩画　用纸做练习　用丝绸做旗袍

（5）还没有呢　还没有开门呢　还没有写好呢　还没有办好呢
还没有走呢　还没有吃饭呢　还没有复习呢　还没有取呢
还没有懂呢　还没有开始呢

2. 句型替换 Pattern drills

（1）A: 这本词典跟那本（词典）一样吗？
B: 这本词典跟那本不一样。
这本比那本新。

你的电脑	他的	新
这儿的房租	那儿的	便宜
北京的天气	你们那儿(的)	冷

（2）A: 这件旗袍跟那件一样长吗？
B: 这件旗袍跟那件不一样长。
这件比那件短一点儿。

这个公园	那个	大	小一点儿
这位画家	那位	年轻	老一点儿
那个电梯	这个	快	慢多了
北京美术馆	上海美术馆	新	旧多了

（3）A：你有什么爱好？
B：我喜欢画 中国画。
A：我跟你一样喜欢画 中国画。

打	太极拳
唱	京剧
看	电影

（4）A：昨天你锻炼了多长时间？
B：昨天我只锻炼了半个小时。
A：今天你锻炼了多长时间了？
B：今天我锻炼了一个小时了。

跑	一个小时
游	45分钟
走	1.5小时
参观	两个小时

（5）A：你做好练习了没有？
B：还没有做好呢。
A：你已经做了多长时间的练习了？
B：我已经做了50分钟的练习了。

画	画儿
翻译	课文
写	生词
填	表
查	词典

（6）A：你（排队）排了多长时间了？
B：我排了一刻钟了。
A：是不是工作人员太慢了？

换	钱	十分钟	人	多
寄	包裹	二十分钟	工作人员	少
办	证	十天	工作人员	忙
坐	车	一个半小时	车	慢
买	衣服	两小时	漂亮衣服	多

（7）A：他用什么写课文？

B：他用电脑写课文。

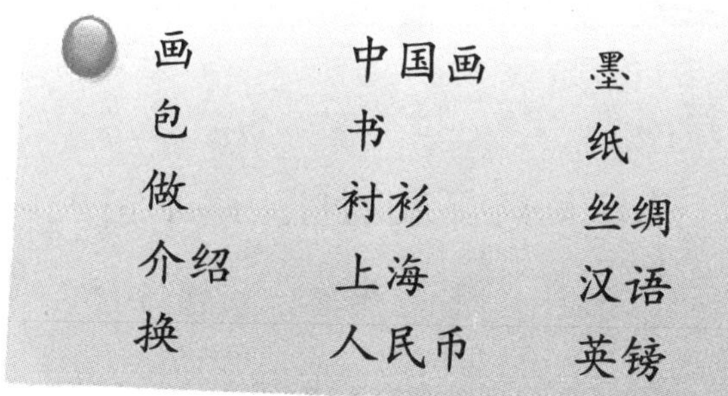

（8）A：你每天怎么回家？

B：我每天坐公共汽车回家。

来学院　坐375路车
到公司　坐地铁
回家　走
去办公室　骑(qí)自行车(zìxíngchē)

3. 课堂活动　Classroom activity

(1) Divide the class into two groups (A and B). Group A chooses two items or things to ask Group B, "x 跟 y 一样不一样？" Group B replies quickly and then chooses two other items or things to ask Group A. The two groups practice like this in turn.

(2) Ask your partner to identify the similarities and differences between the two characters in each of the following groups (the key words: 左边 left side, 右边 right side, 意思 meaning, 读音 dúyīn pronunciation).

A 妈　吗　B 爸　吧　C 音乐　快乐　D 他　她　E 法　汉

(3) Say a sentence in turn with the following pattern: "我 + V + Complement of duration (+的) + O".

Example: 我锻炼了半个小时。

我写了一个小时（的）汉字。

4. 会话练习 Conversation exercises

【表达持续的时间 Expressing duration of time】

（1）A：你汉语说得很流利，跟中国人一样。

B：不敢当，还差得远（yuǎn）呢。

A：你学了几年的中文了？

B：______________________。

A：你要在中国学习几年？

B：______________________，还有一年的时间。

（2）A：你（教书）教了多少年了？

B：我教了十年了。

A：啊，您是老教师了。

B：______________________。

（3）A：咱们跑步（pǎobù）跑了多长时间了？

B：______________________。

A：还跑不跑了？

B：再跑一会儿吧。

【谈爱好 Talking about hobbies】

（1）A：你有什么爱好？

B：我喜欢中国的书法（shūfǎ）。

A：______________________？

B：我学了两年了。

A：______________________？

B：马马虎虎。

（2）A：业余（yèyú）时间你常常做什么？

B：我常常看电视。

A：你喜欢什么节目（jiémù）？

B：＿＿＿＿＿＿＿＿。你呢？

A：我喜欢看京剧。

【寒暄　Exchanging greetings】

（1）A：好久不见了，你还跟以前（yǐqián）＿＿＿＿年轻。

B：哪里，我老多了。你＿＿＿＿以前瘦（shòu）一点儿。

A：是啊，我减肥（jiǎnféi）了。

（2）A：您来中国＿＿＿＿＿＿＿了？

B：我来了一年了。

A：生活过得＿＿＿＿＿＿＿？

B：我过得很好，跟在英国一样。

A：你觉得这儿的天气怎么样？

B：这儿的天气跟我们那儿＿＿＿＿＿＿＿，比我们那儿冷。

【告别　Saying good-bye】

A：您忙吧，我该回去了。

B：还早呢，再坐一会儿吧。

A：我还有点儿事，我得回学院去。

B：在这儿吃饭吧。

A：不用了，＿＿＿＿＿＿＿＿。

B：＿＿＿＿＿＿＿＿，在这儿就跟在自己家一样。

5. 看图说话 Describe the following pictures

❶ 他爱好……
他跑了……

❷ 她爱好……
她唱了……

❸ 他喜欢……
他打了……

❹ 他喜欢……
他画了……

6. 交际练习 Communication exercises

(1) Talk about your hobbies with your friends to find out if you have anything in common.

(2) Talk about your study or work experiences with your friends.

(3) Discuss a picture or a movie with your friends and talk about your opinions.

阅读与复述 Reading Comprehension and Paraphrasing

20 管（guǎn）孩子还是不管孩子

我女儿今年10岁，她已经开始不听我们的话了，常常让我和她爸爸生气（shēngqì）。我们让她学画画儿，每个星期天我都不休息，跟她一起坐公共汽车到老师家去。可是刚学了两个月，她说画画儿不容易，不想学了。我们让她学钢琴（gāngqín），把钢琴也买来了。现在刚学了一个月，她说学钢琴跟学画儿一样没意思。我们不知道该怎么办，是不是别的孩子都跟我的女儿一样？

昨天我到书店（shūdiàn）去，想找一本怎么教育（jiàoyù）孩子的书。营业员（yíngyèyuán）给我找出了三本书：一本是《别管孩子》，一本是《孩子不能不管》，还有一本是《管还是不管孩子》。我把三本书都买来了，也都看了，可是三本书的观点（guāndiǎn）一本跟一本不一样。

我常常想，应该怎样教育孩子，外国人的观点跟中国人不一样，大人的观点跟孩子不一样，孩子跟孩子也不一样。大人让孩子学钢琴，可是这个孩子可能听到钢琴就头疼；大人想让孩子学画儿，可是孩子喜欢唱京剧。听说外国的孩子下课就可以做自己喜欢的事情，中国的孩子晚上9点还要做练习。我朋友的孩子不用她爸爸妈妈管，可是我女儿……

管孩子还是不管孩子，真是一个大问题啊！

三、语法 Grammar

1 "跟……（不）一样"表示比较
Using "跟……（不）一样" to make comparisons

The comparative structure "跟……一样" indicates that two things are the same or similar. If they are different, the structure "跟……不一样" is used. In a V/A-not-V/A question, the structure "一样不一样" is used.

跟 + NP (+ 不) + 一样 (+ A / V O)

Subject	Predicate			
	跟	NP	（不）一样	A / V O
这张表	跟	那张（表）	一样。	
上海话	跟	普通话	不一样。	
中国画	跟	油画	一样不一样？	
这个中学	跟	那个（中学）	一样	有名。
这件西服	跟	那件（西服）	不一样	长。
我爸爸	跟	我妈妈	一样	喜欢 中国画。

If the two central words indicating the two items being compared are the same, the second central word may be omitted.

2 时量补语（2） The complement of duration (2)

In a sentence with a complement of duration, if the particle "了" is used after the verb at the end of the sentence, it means that the action is still going on. Compare the following:

（我）已经画了11年了。（I have been practising drawing for 11 years.）
（The practice of drawing is still going on.）
（我）已经画了11年。（I have drawn for 11 years.）

（This does not indicate whether or not the practice of drawing is going on at present.）

If the verb taking an object in a sentence with a complement of duration, it can also be placed between the verb and the object. The particle "的" can be inserted between the complement of duration and the object.

V	+	Complement of duration	(+的)	+ O	
你要	听	多长时间	（的）	音乐？	
我要	听	半小时	（的）	音乐。	
你	学 了	多长时间	（的）	汉语？	
我	学 了	两年	（的）	汉语。	
你	看 了	多长时间	（的）	画儿	了？
我	看 了	一个半小时	（的）	画儿	了。

Note: If the object is a personal pronoun, it cannot be placed after the complement of duration. We cannot say: “我等了一个小时的他。”

3 连动句（2）：表示工具或方式

Sentences with serial verb phrases (2): indicating means or manner

In the sentences with serial verb phrases in this lesson, the first verb usually expresses the means or manner that the action indicated by the second verb is performed. For example:

我们坐电梯上楼去。

他每天坐公共汽车回家。

画家用墨和水画中国画。

林娜用汉语介绍西安。

四、汉字　Chinese Characters

1 汉字的构字法（5）　Methods of constructing Chinese characters (5)

The pictophonetic method (形声法) (1)

The majority of Chinese characters are “pictophonetic”. A semantic component and a phonetic component are combined to make up a new character. Pictophonetic characters fall into the following categories:

In its basic form, a pictophonetic character is constructed by placing the semantic component on the left and the phonetic component on the right. For example: 饭，姑，妈，吗，吧，锻，机，快，块，理，们，哪，娜，请，情，物，泳，钟，洲，住，俑，懂，把，馆，证，慢，职，极，样，幅，像，虾，衬，护，试.

2 认写基本汉字 Learn and write basic Chinese characters

(1) 夭 ノ 二 チ 夭
yāo to die young 4 strokes

(2) 斗 丶 丷 二 斗
dǒu (an object shaped like a cup or dipper) 4 strokes

(3) 石 一 ア ズ 石 石
shí stone 5 strokes

(4) 氏 ノ 𠂆 𠂇 氏
shì family name, surname 4 strokes

3 认写课文中的汉字 Learn and write the Chinese characters in the texts

(1) 油画 yóuhuà（油畫）

油 → 氵 + 由 8 strokes

画 → 一 + 田 + 凵 8 strokes

(2) 不敢当 bù gǎndāng（不敢當）

敢 → 耳 + 攵 11 strokes

(3) 唱 chàng

唱 → 口 + 日 + 曰 11 strokes

虍 (hǔzìtóur, the top of the character "虎")

丨 ⺊ ⺊ 广 卢 虍　6 strokes

(4) 马马虎虎 mǎmǎhūhū（馬馬虎虎）

虎（hǔ）→ 虍 ＋ 几　8 strokes

(5) 幅 fú

幅 → 巾 ＋ 畐　12 strokes

(6) 徐悲鸿 Xú Bēihóng（徐悲鴻）

徐 → 彳 ＋ 人 ＋ 一 ＋ 朩　10 strokes

悲 → 非 ＋ 心　12 strokes

鸿 → 氵 ＋ 工 ＋ 鸟　11 strokes

(7) 电梯 diàntī（電梯）

梯 → 木 ＋ 弟　11 strokes

(8) 开玩笑 kāi wánxiào（開玩笑）

笑 → ⺮ ＋ 夭　10 strokes

(9) 材料 cáiliào

材 → 木 ＋ 才　7 strokes

料 → 米 ＋ 斗　10 strokes

(10) 纸 zhǐ（紙）

纸 → 纟 ＋ 氏　7 strokes

(11) 布 bù

布 → 𠂇 ＋ 巾　5 strokes

(12) 墨 mò

墨 → 黑 + 土 15 strokes

(13) 油彩 yóucǎi

彩 → 爫 + 木 + 彡 11 strokes

(14) 匹 pǐ

匹 → 匚 + 儿 4 strokes

(15) 跑 pǎo

跑 → 𧾷 + 包 12 strokes

(16) 它 tā

它 → 宀 + 匕 5 strokes

(17) 风 fēng（風）

风 → 几 + 㐅 4 strokes

(18) 虾 xiā（蝦）

虾 → 虫 + 下 9 strokes

(19) 游 yóu

游 → 氵 + 方 + 𠂉 + 子 12 strokes

(20) 齐白石 Qí Báishí（齊白石）

齐 → 文 + 丿丨 6 strokes

文化知识 Cultural Note

Traditional Chinese Painting

A traditional Chinese painting is created using a special Chinese writing brush, ink, and paper, with traditional Chinese painting techniques. It is very different from the Western oil painting. Based on the tools and materials employed, the traditional Chinese painting could be called water-and-ink painting (水墨画 shuǐmòhuà) or color-and-ink painting (彩墨画 cǎimòhuà), which enjoys equal popularity as oil painting, watercolor painting, and gouache. In terms of the subject, the traditional Chinese painting can be classified into three categories: figure painting, landscape painting, and flower-and-bird painting, while in terms of the painting method, the traditional Chinese painting can be classified as "fine brush work paintings" (工笔 gōngbǐ) and "freehand brushwork painting" (写意 xiěyì).

Traditional Chinese paintings often express painters' feelings through mountains, rivers, flowers, and birds. Another striking feature of the traditional Chinese painting is that it emphasizes "likeness in essence" (神似 shénsì) but not "strict resemblance in appearance" (形似 xíngsì). The composition of a picture should rather be "between likeness and unlikeness." Because the images and the composition of the traditional Chinese painting have to be subordinated to the expression of the meanings and feelings, painters usually exaggerate or stress things that they want to represent and abandon or omit things that they do not. In this way, the traditional Chinese painting has developed into a style that sticks to the reality while not attending to every detail.

宣纸 xuānzhǐ

文房四宝 wénfáng sìbǎo

复习 Review

过 新 年

Celebrating the New Year

Lin Na and Ding Libo are going to Song Hua's place to have chafing dishes. In the evening, they will go to a concert of traditional Chinese music. This is the way in which they will celebrate the New Year in China. In this review lesson, we will summarize the grammar points in the previous five lessons.

一、课文 Text

王小云：中午咱们都去宋华家吃火锅，他爸爸、妈妈要我们跟他们一起过新年。

林　娜：在北京过新年一定很有意思。小云，为什么北京很多饭馆都有火锅？是不是因为现在天气冷，所以北京人常吃火锅？①

问原因
Asking for reasons

王小云：不是。北京人就爱吃火锅，主要是涮羊肉，天气热的时候也吃。② 北京的涮羊肉跟北京烤鸭一样有名。

林　娜：过新年的时候北京人都吃涮羊肉吗？

王小云：不一定。

林 娜：你说说北京人怎么过新年。

王小云：跟西方人一样，很多人去旅行。也可能开车去郊区玩儿，或者去锻炼身体。③

林 娜：晚上常常做些什么？

催促
Urging somebody

王小云：晚上看京剧、听音乐会或者跟朋友聚会。我说林娜，快点儿吧！④你化妆化了半个小时了。咱们得早点儿走。

林 娜：一会儿就好。今天晚上咱们还要去听音乐会，所以得正式一点儿。

王小云：你知道吗？今天晚上听中国民乐，它跟西方音乐很不一样。

林 娜：我知道，中国民乐主要是用民族乐器演奏的中国音乐。刚来的时候我不太习惯听民乐，可是现在我很爱听。

王小云：你喜欢《春江花月夜》吗？

林 娜：啊，《春江花月夜》美极了。⑤我已经买了这个乐曲的光盘，今天还要再买一些，给我朋友寄去。咱们怎么去宋华家？坐出租车还是坐公共汽车？

王小云：今天路上的车一定很多。出租车比公共汽车快多了，坐出租车吧。

林　娜：咱们还没有买礼物呢。送花儿是西方人的习惯，我们参加聚会的时候也可以带吃的、喝的。中国人去朋友家的时候送什么？

王小云：过去常送一些吃的、喝的或者用的，现在的年轻人跟西方人一样，也常送花儿。

林　娜：咱们买些花儿，再带些吃的吧。

王小云：好。别忘了把照相机带去。

林　娜：我的照相机呢？⑥

王小云：在电话旁边。

林　娜：大为和力波怎么不给咱们打个电话？

王小云：我不知道大为能不能去，因为他要跟女朋友一起去旅行。

力波一定去，他说要从这儿出发。

林 娜：再等一等他吧。

王小云：好。咱们把陆雨平也叫去，让他写一篇文章，介绍留学生在中国怎么过新年。

* * *

丁力波：小云，林娜，新年好！恭喜恭喜！⑦

林 娜：恭喜你！大为呢？

新年祝愿
New Year's wishes

丁力波：大为昨天晚上就坐火车去南方了。

王小云：你又来晚了。⑧

丁力波：真不好意思。二位小姐别着急，出租车已经来了。

王小云：你把出租车叫来了，太好了。⑨ 咱们快走。

林 娜：你给宋华带什么礼物去？

丁力波：今年是马年，我又画了一匹马。你们看，画得怎么样？

生词 New Words

No.	Word	Pinyin	POS	Meaning / Examples
1.	新年	xīnnián	N	new year 新年好，过新年，祝贺新年
2.	火锅	huǒguō	N	[illegible], hotpot 吃火锅，在饭馆吃火锅
	火	huǒ	N	fire, heat
	锅	guō	N	pot, pan
3.	饭馆	fànguǎn(r)	N	restaurant 有名的饭馆，去饭馆吃饭
4.	因为	yīnwèi	Conj	because
5.	所以	suǒyǐ	Conj	so
6.	爱	ài	V	to love 爱妈妈，爱音乐，爱唱，爱画，爱开玩笑，爱吃火锅
7.	涮羊肉	shuàn yángròu		thin slices of mutton boiled in water 吃涮羊肉，爱吃涮羊肉，主要是涮羊肉
	涮	shuàn	V	to cook thin slices of meat in boiling water
	羊	yáng	N	sheep
	肉	ròu	N	meat
8.	热	rè	A	hot 天气很热，天热
9.	开车	kāichē	VO	to drive a car 开车去饭馆，开车到王府井，开车回学院
	开	kāi	V	to drive, to operate 开汽车，开公共汽车，开电梯
10.	郊区	jiāoqū	N	suburb, outskirts 上海郊区，在郊区，去郊区玩儿，开车去郊区
11.	或者	huòzhě	Conj	or 你或者他，今天或者明天，寄航空或者海运，去郊区玩儿或者锻炼身体
12.	音乐会	yīnyuèhuì	N	concert 听音乐会，参加音乐会，买音乐会的票

13. 化妆	huàzhuāng	VO	to make up 爱化妆，得化妆，不用化妆，化妆化了半个小时
化	huà	V	to change
妆	zhuāng	N	make-up
14. 正式	zhèngshì	A	formal 正式学习，正式上课，正式参加，穿得正式一点儿
15. 民乐	mínyuè	N	folk music played with traditional instruments 中国民乐，民乐光盘，听民乐，爱民乐
16. 西方	xīfāng	N	the West 西方人，西方音乐，西方美术，西方文学，西方电影
西	xī	N	west
17. 民族	mínzú	N	ethnic group, nation, nationality 每个民族，中国的民族，民族音乐，民族音乐会
18. 乐器	yuèqì	N	musical instrument 民族乐器，西方乐器，主要乐器
器	qì	N	utensil
19. 演奏	yǎnzòu	V	to play a musical instrument in a performance 演奏了一个小时，正式演奏，用民族乐器演奏
演	yǎn	V	to perform, to play
奏	zòu	V	to play a musical instrument
20. 习惯	xíguàn	V/ N	to be accustomed to; habit 很习惯，不太习惯，习惯这儿的生活，习惯听民乐；西方人的习惯，好习惯

21.	乐曲	yuèqǔ	N	musical composition 民族乐曲，西方乐曲，有名的乐曲
	曲	qǔ	N	tune, melody
22.	出租车	chūzūchē	N	taxi, cab 叫出租车，坐出租车，开出租车，出租车站，出租车司机
	出租	chūzū	V	to hire, to rent
23.	路上	lùshang	N	on the road, on the way 路上的车，路上的人，路上要多长时间
24.	花儿	huār	N	flower 买花儿，卖花儿，送花儿，画花儿
*25.	过去	guòqù	N	past 过去的事情，过去的习惯，过去的生活
26.	照相机	zhàoxiàngjī	N	camera 用一下照相机，带照相机
	照相	zhàoxiàng	VO	to take a picture, to photograph
	机	jī	N	machine, engine
27.	旁边	pángbiān	N	side 旁边的画儿，旁边的厕所，商店旁边，邮局旁边，在电话旁边
28.	出发	chūfā	V	to set out, to start off 从学院出发，从这儿出发，九点出发
29.	篇	piān	M	(*a measure word for essays and articles*) 一篇课文，两篇文章
30.	文章	wénzhāng	N	essay, article 写一篇文章，看文章，长文章
31.	恭喜	gōngxǐ	V	to congratulate 恭喜你，恭喜恭喜
32.	火车	huǒchē	N	train 坐火车去南方，火车票，火车站
33.	又	yòu	Adv	again 又来晚了，又去上海，又买光盘，又画了一匹马
34.	着急	zháojí	A	worried 不用着急，很着急，非常着急

35. 春江花月夜	Chūn Jiāng Huā Yuè Yè	PN	*Moonlit Night on the Flowery Spring Riverside* (a famous, traditional Chinese music composition)
春	chūn	N	spring
江	jiāng	N	river
月	yuè	N	moon
夜	yè	N	night

补充生词 Supplementary Words

1. 小学	xiǎoxué	N	primary school
2. 辆	liàng	M	(*a measure word for vehicles*)
3. 音乐厅	yīnyuètīng	N	concert hall
4. 幸福	xìngfú	A	happy
5. 万事如意	wànshì rúyì	IE	May all your wishes come true.
6. 画蛇添足	huà shé tiān zú	IE	to draw a snake and add feet to it, meaning to ruin the effect by adding something superfluous
7. 最	zuì	Adv	most, least, best, to the highest or lowest alegree
8. 脚	jiǎo	N	foot
9. 完	wán	V	to finish
10. 多余	duōyú	A	superfluous, uncalled for, redundant

注释 Notes

① 是不是因为现在天气冷，所以北京人常吃火锅？

"Is it because the weather is becoming colder that people in Beijing often have chafing dishes?"

"因为……所以……" is used to connect two clauses in a compound cause-effect sentence. The clause in which "因为" is used usually comes first to indicate the reason. It is followed by a clause in which "所以" is used to indicate the result. One may also use only one of the two conjunctions in a sentence. For example:

因为大为感冒了，所以他没有来上课。

（因为）他们要去听音乐会，所以得穿得正式一点儿。

因为今天银行排队的人多，（所以）他想明天再去换钱。

② 北京人就爱吃火锅，主要是涮羊肉，天气热的时候也吃。

"The people in Beijing like having chafing dishes, mostly boiled mutton slices, and they eat it even when the weather is hot."

The construction "……的时候" is often used in the sentence as an adverbial of time (similar to "when" and "while" in English), indicating the period of time when an action or event takes place. "时候" can be preceded by a verb, a verbal phrase, or a subject-predicate phrase. For example:

上课的时候，老师让我们多说汉语。

去图书馆的时候，别忘了带你的借书证。

天气热的时候，要多喝水。

中国人去朋友家的时候，常送吃的、喝的或者用的。

③ 也可能开车去郊区玩儿，或者去锻炼身体。

"(They) might also drive to the suburbs for fun, or go out to do exercises."

Both the conjunctions "或者" and "还是" can be used to connect two possibilities "还是" is used in an interrogative sentence, and "或者" is normally used in a declarative sentence. For example:

明天你去找我还是我来找你？

明天我去找你，或者你到我那儿去。

④ 我说林娜，快点儿吧！

"Hey, Lin Na. You'd better hurry."

The expression "我说" is used to interrupt or start a new topic.

⑤ 啊，《春江花月夜》美极了。

"Oh, *Moonlit Night on the Flowery Spring Riverside* is extremely beautiful."

Moonlit Night on the Flowery Spring Riverside is a famous ancient Chinese musical composition which depicts the beautiful scenery by the riverside on a moonlit night in spring, when all the flowers are in full bloom.

⑥ 我的照相机呢？

"Where is my camera?"

In Lesson Seven, we learned how to form an elliptical interrogative sentence with "呢", and we know that what is asked in this type of question is made clear by the context. Students are taught in this lesson that if no context is available, "NP + 呢" is often used to ask the location, i.e. "Where is NP?". In this case, "NP + 呢?" is equivalent to "NP在哪儿?" For example:

你的文章呢？（= 你的文章在哪儿？）

大为呢？（= 大为在哪儿？）

⑦ 恭喜恭喜！

"Congratulations!"

This is an idiomatic expression frequently used for congratulating people on happy events, for example, "恭喜你！" or "恭喜你买了新房子！" Here, the usage of "恭喜" is the same as "祝贺", except that "祝贺" is more formal. In the Spring Festival or on New Year's Day, we often say, "恭喜恭喜！" to extend our New Year's greetings (the word "祝贺" is not used this way).

⑧ 你又来晚了。

"You are late again."

Both the adverbs "又" (1) and "再" (1) express the recurrence of an action or a state. "再" (1) is used in a situation where the action or state has not recurred yet, whereas "又" (1) is normally used in a situation where the action or state has already occurred again. For example:

他上午来了，他说下午再来。

(The action has not happened again yet, so we cannot say "他说下午又来".)

他上午来了，下午又来了。

(The action has already happened again, so we cannot say "下午再来了".)

⑨ 你把出租车叫来了，太好了。

"You have hailed a taxi. That's great."

"叫出租车" means "to hail a taxi".

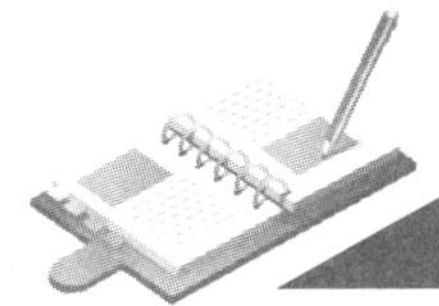

二、练习 Exercises

练习与运用 Drills and Practice

核心句 KEY SENTENCES

1. 是不是因为现在天气冷，所以北京人常吃火锅？
2. 刚来的时候我不太习惯听民乐。
3. 过去常送一些吃的、喝的或者用的。
4. 我的照相机呢？
5. 他说要从这儿出发。
6. 新年好！恭喜恭喜！
7. 你又来晚了。

1. 熟读下列词组 Read the following phrases until you learn them by heart

（1）开学的时候　锻炼的时候　休息的时候　感冒的时候　旅行的时候
演奏的时候　打扫的时候　上课的时候　排队的时候　打工的时候
考试的时候　挂号的时候　发烧的时候　睡觉的时候
过新年的时候　在北京的时候　取包裹的时候　画画儿的时候
坐公共汽车的时候　买衣服的时候
邮局开门的时候　银行休息的时候　天气热的时候　他住院的时候
我们去朋友家的时候

（2）演奏中国乐曲　演奏民乐　演奏了《梁祝》　演奏了《春江花月夜》
用民族乐器演奏　演奏了两个小时　演奏得好极了　演奏得马马虎虎

（3）开车去郊区玩儿　（开）车开得不快　（开）车开了一个上午
开了四个小时的车　把车开来

（4）又来晚了 又去早了 又感冒了 又过期了
又学了一百个汉字 又买了一件旗袍

2. 句型替换 Pattern drills

（1）A：这个星期天你想去哪儿？
B：我想去美术馆或者去图书馆。
A：上午去还是下午去？
B：上午去。

商场 商店
银行 邮局
公司 朋友家
王府井 前门
美术学院 音乐学院

（2）A：过新年的时候，你做什么了？
B：过新年的时候，我跟朋友去饭馆吃饭了。

过圣诞节 给爸爸妈妈打电话
过生日 跟朋友一起吃蛋糕
参观美术馆 买画儿
上语法课 问老师问题
办借书证 填表

（3）A：天气热的时候，他也吃火锅吗？
B：天气热的时候，他也吃火锅。

天气非常冷 散步
学习忙 去公园玩儿
路上的车多 自己开车
嗓子发炎 上课

（4）A：昨天你是不是去办公室了？
B：是啊，今天上午我又去了。
A：你什么时候再去？
B：明天下午再去。

听 中国民乐
用 这个电脑
送 她花儿
练习 那个乐曲

（5）A：你习惯吃 涮羊肉吗？
B：我已经习惯了。
他还有点儿不习惯。

吃	中国菜
喝	咖啡
听	中国民乐
用	这儿的电脑
坐	公共汽车

（6）A：他为什么没有来参加聚会？
B：因为他不爱吃火锅。
（所以没有来参加聚会。）

上课	病了
回家	公司有事儿
去公园玩儿	要写一篇文章
听音乐会	没有票
开车来	身体不太舒服

3. 课堂活动 Classroom activity

This game is to be played by two groups of students. The students in Group A use “为什么” to ask ten questions regarding the previous five lessons, and the students in Group B use “因为……所以……” to answer these questions. The scoring method is as follows: Group B will get one point whenever they make a correct answer; if they give an incorrect answer, Group A will get the point. After all the ten questions have been asked, the two groups reverse roles, so that Group B asks a new set of ten questions. The group with the higher score wins.

4. 会话练习 Conversation exercises

【问原因 Asking for reasons】

（1）A：老师，咱们为什么八点上课？

B：这是我们这儿的习惯，中学、小学（xiǎoxué）也都是八点上课。

A：这儿的商店或商场每天几点开门？

B：______________。银行、邮局、海关或者公司也是九点开始办公。

（2）A：今天你怎么没有把照相机带来？

B：因为我起（床）晚了，出来的时候我把照相机忘了。

C：没关系，我带照相机来了，你们________________。

【催促 Urging somebody】

（1）A：大为，你的电话。

B：等一下。

A：快，是你女朋友！

B：是吗？我就____________。

（2）A：快点儿，该出发了。

B：咱们说好几点出发？

A：________________________。

B：现在五点二十五，还有五分钟呢，别着急。

A：别忘了，咱们得先到图书馆，从那儿出发！

（3）A：咱们坐几路车？

B：应该坐__________________。

A：看，307来了，快跑！

B：（To the bus driver）师傅，请等一下！

（4）A：喂，是出租汽车公司吗？

B：是啊。您哪里？

A：我是语言学院留学生宿舍楼，我要一辆（liàng）出租车。

B：________________________________？

A：我去北京音乐厅（yīnyuètīng）。能不能快点儿？

B：没问题，车一会儿就到。

【新年祝愿 New Year's wishes】

（1）A：新年好！

B：________________________！

（2）A：祝你新年快乐！

B：祝你全家幸福（xìngfú）！

（3）A：____________________！

B：谢谢！也祝你新的一年万事如意（wànshì rúyì）！

5. 看图说话 Describe the following pictures

❶ 不一样

❷ 习惯

❸ 送礼物，或者

❹ 坐出租车

6. 交际练习 Communication exercises

(1) Tell your friend what people eat and do to celebrate the New Year in your hometown.

(2) You are waiting for your friend to get ready to go to the park. What would you say to hurry him / her up?

(3) You are in a hurry to get to the concert hall. How do you tell this to the taxi driver?

阅读与复述 Reading Comprehension and Paraphrasing

23 画蛇添足 (huà shé tiān zú)

一天，几个朋友在一起喝酒。他们人很多，可是酒太少，只有一瓶。应该把这瓶酒给谁呢？一个年轻人说："我们每人都画一条蛇，画得最 (zuì) 快的人喝这瓶酒，好吗？"大家都说："好！"

他们开始画蛇。那个年轻人比别的人画得快，他非常高兴，说："你们画得太慢了！我比你们画得快多了！看，现在我还有时间，我再给蛇添上脚 (jiǎo) 吧。"他就开始画蛇的脚了。

一会儿，他旁边的一个人说："我画完 (wán) 了，这瓶酒应该给我。"年轻人听了很着急，说："不对！你画得比我慢，我早就画完了。你看，我还给蛇添了脚呢。这瓶酒是我的。"旁边的那个人说："大家都知道蛇没有脚，你画了脚，所以你画的不是蛇。最早画完蛇的是我，不是你。"

大家说："他说得对。我们应该把这瓶酒给他。"

所以，一个人做了多余 (duōyú) 的事儿，就叫"画蛇添足"。

三、语法复习 Grammar Review

1 汉语句子的六种基本成分
The six basic functional components of a Chinese sentence

The basic functional components of a Chinese sentence are the subject, the predicate, the object, the attributive, the adverbial, and the complement.

We have already learned that a noun, a pronoun, or a noun phrase can all function as the subject. In addition, a verbal phrase, an adjectival phrase, and a subject-predicate phrase may also serve as the subject. Usually a verb, an adjective, a verbal phrase, or an adjectival phrase can function as the predicate. A subject-predicate phrase or a nominal phrase can also serve as the predicate. The subject usually precedes the predicate. For example:

这些书都是新的。
他 来北京了。
马大为 头疼。
白的 漂亮。
现在 七点四十。
寄航空比海运贵。
贵一点儿 没关系。
我们去打球，好吗？

When the context is clear, the subject is often omitted. Sometimes the predicate can also be omitted. For example:

A：你带照片来了吗？
B：（我）带来了。

A：谁有词典？
B：我（有词典）。

As a part of the predicate, the object is usually placed after the verb. We have learned that usually a noun, a pronoun, a nominal phrase, a verbal phrase, or a subject-predicate phrase can function as the object. For example:

他有哥哥。

我不认识他。

买两张到前门的。

他喜欢吃烤鸭。

我觉得这件太长了。

Some verbs may be followed by two objects. For example:

谁教你 汉语?

我问老师一个问题。

The attributive is mainly used to modify a noun and must be placed before the element it modifies. We have learned that an adjective, an adjectival phrase, a noun, or a pronoun often functions as the attributive. In addition, a verb, a verbal phrase, or a subject-predicate phrase can also serve as the attributive (please refer to Lesson 14 in the Workbook of Volume I).

The adverbial is used to modify a verb or an adjective. We have already learned that adverbs are often used as adverbials. In addition, time nouns, prepositional phrases, and adjectives can also be used as adverbials. For example:

他们也都看了这个京剧。

力波一定去。

你今天穿得很漂亮啊!

你从那儿拿一张表来。

咱们快走。

The complement is a sentence component placed after a verb or an adjective to give additional information about the verb or adjective. For example:

他来得很早。 (modal complement)

这个年轻人(说)英语说得很流利。

我们进去吧。 (directional complement)

你带照片来了吗?

这儿的书可以借一个月。 (complement of duration)

他(画)中国画已经画了十一年了。

这件红的比那件绿的短两公分。 (complement of quantity)

我觉得这件小一点儿。

这件漂亮极了。 (complement of degree)

这件比那件贵多了。

我听懂了，可是记错了。 (resultative complement)

2 动词谓语句（1） The sentence with a verbal predicate (1)

The following is a summary of the kinds of sentences in which the verb is a major element of the predicate:

（1）Sentences with "是"

她是英国留学生。

这四本书是中文的。

（2）Sentences with "有"

我们系有三十五位老师。

他没有女朋友。

（3）Sentences without an object

我在北京生活。

（4）Sentences with a single object

他每天锻炼身体。

（5）Sentences with double objects

她送他一瓶酒。

我告诉你一件事儿。

（6）Sentences with a verb or a verbal phrase as the object

现在开始工作。

北京人爱吃火锅。

我会说一点儿汉语。

（7）Sentences with a subject-predicate phrase as the object

我不知道他是经理。

听说上海发展得非常快。

(8) Sentences with serial verb phrases

他去商场买东西。

现在是不是坐电梯上楼去?

(9) Pivotal sentences

他请我吃饭。

妈妈不让她喝咖啡。

(10) The "把" sentence

我把这事儿忘了。

请把通知单给我。

他把护照拿来了。

四、汉字 Chinese Characters

1 汉字的构字法(6) Methods of constructing Chinese characters (6)

The pictophonetic method (形声法) (2)

In this method, a character is formed by placing the phonetic component on the left and the semantic component on the right. For example: 放，翻，刚，故，和，剧，鸭，瓶，颜，邮.

2 认写基本汉字 Learn and write basic Chinese characters

(1) 丸 丿 九 丸
wán pill 3 strokes

(2) 曲 丨 冂 冃 冇 曲 曲
qǔ melody 6 strokes

3 认写课文中的汉字 Learn and write the Chinese characters in the texts

(1) 火锅 huǒguō（火鍋）

锅 → 钅 + 口 + 内 12 strokes

(2) 因为 yīnwèi（因爲）

因 → 囗 + 大 6 strokes

(3) 涮羊肉 shuàn yángròu

涮 → 氵 + 尸 + 巾 + 刂 11 strokes

肉 → 冂 + 人 + 人 6 strokes

(4) 热 rè（熱）

热 → 扌 + 丸 + 灬 10 strokes

(5) 郊区 jiāoqū（郊區）

郊 → 交 + 阝 8 strokes

区 → 匚 + 乂 4 strokes

(6) 或者 huòzhě

或 → 戈 + 口 + 一 8 strokes

（一 𠂇 丆 可 豆 式 或 或）

(7) 化妆 huàzhuāng（化妝）

化 → 亻 + 匕 4 strokes

妆 → 丬 + 女 6 strokes

(8) 民族 mínzú

族 → 方 + ⺈ + 矢　　11 strokes

(9) 乐器 yuèqì（樂器）

器 → 口 + 口 + 犬 + 口 + 口　　16 strokes

𡗗 (chūnzìtóur, the top of the character "春(chūn)")

一 二 三 丰 𡗗　　5 strokes

(10) 演奏 yǎnzòu

演 → 氵 + 宀 + 一 + 由 + 八　　14 strokes

奏 → 𡗗 + 天　　9 strokes

毌 guàn　ㄴ 口 毌 毌　　4 strokes

(Note: Pay attention to the differences between "毌" and "母".)

(11) 习惯 xíguàn（習慣）

惯 → 忄 + 毌 + 贝　　11 strokes

(12) 花儿 huār（花兒）

花 → 艹 + 化　　7 strokes

(13) 照相机 zhàoxiàngjī（照相機）

相 → 木 + 目　　9 strokes

(14) 旁边 pángbiān（旁邊）

旁 → 亠 + 方　　10 strokes

冊 (biǎnzìxīnr, the inside part of the character "扁 (biǎn)")

丨 冂 冂 冊 冊 5 strokes

(15) 篇 piān

篇 → ⺮ + 户 + 冊 15 strokes

(16) 文章 wénzhāng

章 → 立 + 早 11 strokes

⺗ (gōngzìdǐr, the bottom part of the character "恭")

亅 小 小 ⺗ 4 strokes

(17) 恭喜 gōngxǐ

恭 → 共 + ⺗ 10 strokes

(18) 着急 zháojí（著急）

着 → 羊 + 目 11 strokes

急 → ⺈ + ⺕ + 心 9 strokes

夊 (yèxiàjiǎor, part at the lower-right corner of the character "夜")

丿 ク 夕 夊 4 strokes

(19) 春江花月夜 Chūn Jiāng Huā Yuè Yè

春 → 夫 + 日 9 strokes

江 → 氵 + 工 6 strokes

夜 → 亠 + 亻 + 夊 8 strokes

学唱中文歌

Sing a song

24 茉莉花

Mòlì Huā

Jasmine Flower

文化知识 Cultural Note

Festivals and Customs in China

Besides National Day (October 1st) and International Labour Day (May 1st), which are the two major official holidays celebrated all over the country, there are many other traditional holidays and festivals in China.

The Spring Festival (Chinese New Year's Day) falls on the first day of the first month on the Chinese lunar calendar (usually in January or February of the solar calendar), and the day before it is Chinese New Year's Eve. The Han people and many ethnic minorities in China all celebrate the Spring Festival, with activities such as setting off firecrackers, pasting *chunlian* (couplets matching each other in sound and meaning, written on red paper) on the door, extending New Year's greetings to each other, and performing the *yangge* (literally, "rice seedling song") dance and the lion dance.

The fifteenth day of the first lunar month is the *Yuanxiao* Festival, also known as the Lantern Festival or *Shangyuan* Festival. The major activities for *Yuanxiao* Festival is making and enjoying festive lanterns. The special food for this festive day is called *yuanxiao*, a ball-shaped dumpling made of glutinous rice flour with sweet sesame or meat stuffing.

Qingming (Clear and Bright) Festival is on the fourth or fifth day of April. This is the time of year when people go out to the tombs and memorials to pay tribute to the dearly departed and national heroes.

Duanwu or the Dragon Boat Festival is celebrated on the fifth day of the fifth lunar month (June of the solar calendar). This festival commemorates the great poet-stateman Qu Yuan in ancient China who drowned himself for being denied a chance to serve his state. The special food for this festival is called *zongzi* made of glutinous rice wrapped in bamboo leaves. People would also hold the dragon boat race on this day, every year.

The Mid-Autumn Festival, which falls on the fifteenth day of the eighth lunar month (September of the solar calendar), is a time when the whole family enjoys getting together to look at the full moon, and to eat moon cakes.

我们的队员是从不同国家来的

Our team members are from different countries.

Lu Yuping, the reporter, is carrying out an interview to find out how the International Students' Soccer Team won the Chinese College Students' Soccer Team. In this lesson, we will learn how to emphasize the time and location of a past event, and the manner in which it has occurred, as well as also how to talk about direction and location.

一、课文　Text

25（一）

陆雨平：听说上星期你们留学生队赢了一场足球比赛。我想写一篇文章，介绍一下留学生足球队的事儿。

丁力波：太好了。你是怎么知道的？

陆雨平：我是听你的同学说的。① 别忘了我是记者，我今天是来问你们问题的。你们留学生队是跟谁比赛的？

丁力波：我们队是跟中国大学生队比赛的。

陆雨平：你们是在哪儿比赛的？

王小云：是在我们学校比赛的。

强调过去的时间、地点
Emphasizing the time and location of a past event

陆雨平：中国大学生队的水平比你们高吧？②

丁力波：他们的水平比我们高多了。

王小云：宋华说，大学生队的教练是从国家队来的。

陆雨平：他是什么时候从国家队下来的？

王小云：他是去年从国家队下来的。这位教练来了以后，大学生队的水平提高得很快。③

丁力波：大学生队的10号踢得很好。左边的5号、右边的12号跑得都很快。

陆雨平：你们留学生队呢？

丁力波：我们的队员是从不同国家来的，我们不常练习。

陆雨平：你们是怎么赢的？

丁力波：上半场0比0。下半场他们帮助我们进了一个球，是1比0赢的。④

谈体育比赛
Talking about an athletic contest

生词 New Words

1. 队员	duìyuán	N	team member 我们的队员，有名的队员，年轻的队员，很多队员，老队员，新队员，一个队员
*队	duì	N	team 你们队，我们队，中国队，留学生队，语言学院队
2. 不同	bùtóng	A	different 不同的人，不同的学生，不同时间，不同语言，不同岁数
3. 国家	guójiā	N	country 国家队，不同国家，我们国家，一个国家，哪个国家
4. 赢	yíng	V	to win 我赢，他赢，赢他们，赢了没有
5. 场	chǎng	M	(*a measure word for sports, films, performances*) 一场电影，上半场，下半场
6. 足球	zúqiú	N	soccer 足球队，足球队员，看足球，一场足球
足	zú	N	foot
球	qiú	N	ball 打球，看球，进了一个球
7. 比赛	bǐsài	N/V	match; to compete, to have a match 一场比赛，一场足球比赛，赢了一场比赛；比赛足球，跟留学生队比赛
赛	sài	N/V	race, match; to compete, to race 足球赛，看了一场足球赛；赛跑
8. 同学	tóngxué	N	classmate, schoolmate 你的同学，女同学，男同学，新同学，老同学，同学们
*9. 记者	jìzhě	N	reporter 一个/位记者，别的记者，外国记者
10. 大学生	dàxuéshēng	N	university student, college student 大学生队，一个大学生，中国大学生
11. 学校	xuéxiào	N	school 我们学校，这个学校，有名的学校，学校办公室

12. 水平	shuǐpíng	N	level 大学生队的水平，普通话水平，汉语水平高，专业水平不高
13. 教练	jiàoliàn	N	coach 大学生队的教练，足球队的教练，那位教练
14. 去年	qùnián	N	last year 去年三月，去年圣诞节，去年开始，去年认识
15. 以后	yǐhòu	N	after, afterwards 来了以后，走了以后，开学以后
16. 提高	tígāo	V	to improve, to increase 提高得很快，提高水平，提高房租
提	tí	V	to lift
17. 踢	tī	V	to play (literally "to kick") 踢足球，踢球，踢得很好
18. 左边	zuǒbian	N	the left (side) 左边的队员，左边的房子，队员左边，书的左边，在学校左边
左	zuǒ	N	left
19. 右边	yòubian	N	the right (side) 右边的队员，右边的房子，我右边，在饭馆右边
右	yòu	N	right

注释 Notes

① 我是听你的同学说的。

"I heard it from your classmates."

Students in the same class or school call each other "同学"; for example: "他是我同学", "这是宋华同学". Teachers or other people can also call a student "同学"; for example: "同学们".

② 中国大学生队的水平比你们高吧？

"Doesn't the Chinese College Students' Team play better than yours?"

In addition to softening the tone in sentences expressing persuasion, a request, or an order, the modal particle "吧" can also be used in interrogative sentences to denote a tone of estimation or uncertainty.

For example:

我是马大为，您是家美租房公司的经理吧？

今天是十九号吧？

你喜欢听音乐会吧？

③ 这位教练来了以后，大学生队的水平提高得很快。

"Ever since this coach arrived, the College Students' Team has improved rapidly."

The word "以后" refers to a time later than the present time or a specific moment. It functions as an adverbial modifier in sentences. Besides being used by itself, "以后" (as well as "以前", which will be studied in the next lesson) can also be used together with a noun, a verb phrase, or a subject-predicate phrase, etc., to form a phrase. For example: "新年以后, 五年以后, 开学以后". It can not only describe things in the past, but also things in the future. For example:

我认识你以后，汉语口语水平提高得很快。

以后我要跟你一起练习普通话。

④ 上半场0比0。下半场他们帮助我们进了一个球，是1比0赢的。

"The score was 0 to 0 in the first half of the game. In the second half, they 'helped' us score a goal. Then it was 1 to 0, and we won."

The word "比" here indicates the score of the two competing sides or teams. One may use "几比几" to ask about the score.

26（二）

陆雨平：我还要问问你们：你们去看大为租的房子了没有？房子在哪儿？

王小云：去了，房子在学校东边，⑤ 离学校不太远。⑥ 那儿叫花园小区，大为住八号楼。

陆雨平：你们是怎么去的？

丁力波：我们是坐公共汽车去的。车站就在小区前边。下车以后先往右拐，再往前走三分钟，就到八号楼了。⑦

陆雨平：那儿怎么样？

丁力波：很好。八号楼下边是一个小花园，左边有一个商店，商店旁边是书店。右边是银行和邮局。大为的房子在八号楼九层，上边还有六层。

谈方位
Talking about direction and location

陆雨平：房子不大吧？

王小云：那套房子一共有56平方米。

丁力波：进门以后，左边是卫生间，右边是客厅。

陆雨平：厨房在哪儿？

王小云：厨房在客厅北边，卧室在客厅东边。卧室外边有一个大阳台。

丁力波：记者先生，你问了很多问题，你也要写一篇文章介绍马大为租的房子吧？

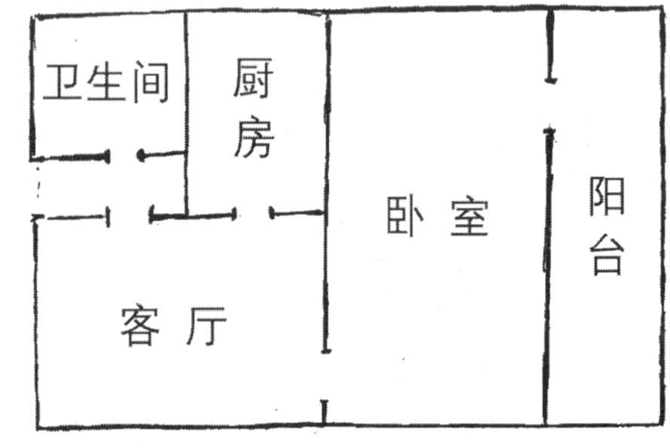

陆雨平：问问题是记者的职业习惯啊。

生词 New Words

1. 东边	dōngbian	N	the east (side) 东边的商场，学校东边，美术馆东边，在中国银行东边
东	dōng	N	east 往东走
2. 离	lí	Prep	away, off, from 离学校，离这儿，离那儿，离商店
3. 远	yuǎn	A	far 不远，很远，非常远，太远，离学院不太远
4. 车站	chēzhàn	N	bus stop
5. 前边	qiánbian	N	front 前边的公园，前边的人，花园小区前边，图书馆前边，在宿舍前边
前	qián	N	front, forward 往前走
6. 拐	guǎi	V	to turn 往右拐，往左拐，往东拐，先往右拐
7. 下边	xiàbian	N	below 楼下边，床下边，在书下边，下边的生词，下边的纸
* 下	xià	N	below, down
8. 书店	shūdiàn	N	bookstore 外文书店，新华书店
9. 上边	shàngbian	N	above 上边的衣服，上边的报纸，九层上边，邮局上边，在本子上边
* 上	shàng	N	upper, up 往上走
10. 平方米	píngfāngmǐ	M	square meter 56平方米，多少平方米，有100平方米
平方	píngfāng	N/M	square; abbreviation for "square meter" 2的平方；有十几个平方
平米	píngmǐ	M	abbreviation for "square meter" 56平米，多少平米
11. 卫生间	wèishēngjiān	N	washroom, restroom 一个卫生间，一间卫生间，一间小卫生间

	卫生	wèishēng	N	hygiene, sanitation 公共卫生
*12.	客厅	kètīng	N	living room 一个客厅，一间客厅，一间大客厅
13.	北边	běibian	N	the north (side) 北边的房子，卫生间北边，客厅北边，在花园小区北边
	北	běi	N	north 北楼，往北走，往北拐
*14.	卧室	wòshì	N	bedroom 一个卧室，一间卧室，小卧室
	卧	wò	V	to lie down
15.	外边	wàibian	N	outside 去外边玩儿，去外边看看，到外边走走
16.	阳台	yángtái	N	balcony 一个阳台，一个大阳台
17.	花园小区	Huāyuán Xiǎoqū	PN	Garden District 叫花园小区，住花园小区
	花园	huāyuán	N	garden 花园东边，花园里边，花园左边，大花园，一个漂亮的花园
	区	qū	N	district, section, area 学院区，宿舍区

补充生词 Supplementary Words

1.	电影院	diànyǐngyuàn	N	cinema
2.	咖啡馆	kāfēiguǎn	N	coffee bar
3.	南边	nánbian	N	the south (side)
4.	足球场	zúqiúchǎng	N	soccer field
5.	出差	chūchāi	VO	to go on a business trip
6.	后边	hòubian	N	back, behind
7.	输	shū	V	to lose
8.	天堂	tiāntáng	N	heaven, paradise

9. 苏杭	Sū Háng	PN	Suzhou and Hangzhou
苏州	Sūzhōu	PN	Suzhou (a city in Jiangsu Province)
杭州	Hángzhōu	PN	Hangzhou (capital of Zhejiang Province)
10. 山水	shānshuǐ	N	mountains and rivers, scenery with hills and waters
山	shān	N	hill, mountain
11. 园林	yuánlín	N	garden, park
12. 修建	xiūjiàn	V	to build, to construct
13. 美丽	měilì	A	beautiful, pretty
14. 古典	gǔdiǎn	A	classical
15. 诗人	shīrén	N	poet
16. 设计	shèjì	V	to design
17. 建筑师	jiànzhùshī	N	architect

注释 Notes

⑤ 房子在学校东边。

"The house is to the east of the school."

Chinese people are accustomed to using "东", "西", "南", "北" to denote direction and location. For example: "学院东边", "厨房西边", "在医院北边". In addition, "前", "后", "左", "右" can also be used to denote direction and location. For example: "客厅前边, 卧室左边, 卫生间右边".

⑥ 离学校不太远。

"It's not too far away from the school."

The preposition "离" often forms a prepositional phrase with a noun of place: "离 + PW". Placed before a verb, it indicates distance. For example:

语言学院离王府井很远。

北京图书馆离中国银行不太远。

We have learned that: "在 + PW" denotes the place where an action happens; "从 + PW" denotes the starting point of an action; "往 + PW" denotes the direction towards which an action moves.

⑦ 下车以后先往右拐，再往前走三分钟，就到八号楼了。

"After getting off the bus, turn right first, and walk straight ahead for three minutes, then you will see Building 8."

The adverb "再"(2) may indicate that an action starts after another action ends (The adverb "先" is often inserted before the first verb to form the construction "先……再……"), or after a certain situation or time. For example:

我们上课以后先翻译生词，再复习课文。

看完电影再走吧。

现在太早了，我们十点钟再去。

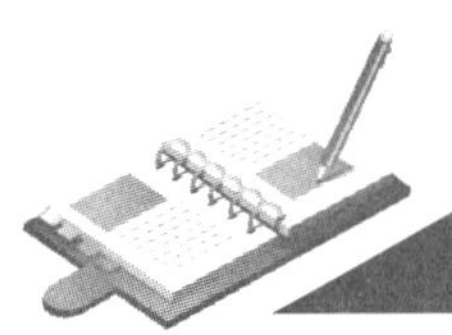

二、练习 Exercises

练习与运用 Drills and Practice

核心句 KEY SENTENCES

1. 你们是在哪儿比赛的？
2. 他是去年从国家队下来的。
3. 我们的队员是从不同国家来的。
4. 房子离学校不太远。
5. 我们是坐公共汽车去的。
6. 下车以后先往右拐，再往前走三分钟，就到八号楼了。
7. 八号楼下边是一个小花园，左边有一个商店。
8. 房子不大吧？
9. 卧室在客厅东边。卧室外边有一个大阳台。

1. 熟读下列词组 Read the following phrases until you learn them by heart

（1）十分钟以后　半小时以后　三天以后　一星期以后　两个月以后

看了以后　写了以后　听了以后　懂了以后

复习以后　考试以后　上课以后　认识他以后　回答问题以后

练习汉字以后　取了包裹以后　提高了水平以后

（2）离商场　离医院　离宿舍　离公司　离邮局　离北楼　离南方

离广州很远　离王府井不远　离北京图书馆不太远

离中国美术馆非常远

（3）九点钟再来　明天再交　复习了课文再睡觉　打了电话再去

翻译了句子再休息

先办证，再借书　先买票，再参观　先锻炼，再休息

先介绍汉字，再学习生词

（4）是去年认识的　是新年寄的　是星期五晚上走的

是1990年10月25号出生的　是在海关取的　是在加拿大买的

是在家里写的　是在图书馆查的　是坐公共汽车去的

是用墨画的　是用民族乐器演奏的　是用英文说的

（5）前边有一个公园　左边有一个公司　右边有一个商场　上边还有两层

里边是厨房　外边是阳台　东边是宿舍　北边是邮局

下边就是大为的新房子　客厅在卧室北边　卫生间在阳台东边

花园小区在语言学院东边

（6）中式衣服不便宜吧　他们队的水平不太高吧

您就是留学生队的教练吧

2. 句型替换 Pattern drills

（1）A：她去西安了没有？

B：她去西安了。

A：她是什么时候去西安的？

B：她是昨天去西安的。

她先去西安，再去上海。

上海	上星期五	美国
美术馆	上午	王府井
学校	下午3点	银行
医院	上午9点	公司

（2）A：他是从哪儿来的？
B：他是从国家队来的。
A：他是跟谁一起来的？
B：他是跟教练一起来的。

美国	他同学
加拿大	他弟弟
英国	一位记者
欧洲	一位画家

（3）A：他去办公室了没有？
B：他去办公室了。
A：他是怎么去的？
B：他是坐公共汽车去的。

南方	坐火车
王府井	坐出租车
花园小区	开车
宿舍楼	走路

（4）A：他们是来工作的吧？
B：他们不是来工作的，
他们是来旅行的。

学习	参观
玩儿	比赛
找你	找宋华
学汉语	学音乐
借书	还书

（5）A：卫生间在里边吗？
B：卫生间不在里边，在外边。

阳台	东边	北边
饭馆	上边	下边
客厅	前边	那儿
卧室	左边	右边

（6）A：宿舍楼前边有什么？
B：宿舍楼前边有一个花园。
A：这个花园大不大？
B：这个花园不太大。

银行旁边	邮局
商店左边	书店
商场东边	医院
图书馆北边	饭馆

（7）A：请问学校里边有邮局吗？

B：有一个邮局。

A：邮局在哪儿？

B：邮局在宿舍楼东边。

A：离这儿远不远？

B：不太远。

银行	商店旁边
图书馆	办公楼左边
饭馆	花园北边
医院	汉语系前边

（8）A：学校东边是什么地方？

B：学校东边是美术馆。

前边	电影院（diànyǐngyuàn）
北边	咖啡馆（kāfēiguǎn）
南边（nánbian）	足球场（zúqiúchǎng）

3. 课堂活动　Classroom activity

Interview your classmate or teacher as a reporter about something that has happened in the past, using the construction “是……的”. For example, Ms. Chen’s mother was sick, so she went to Xi’an to visit her mother. Three days later, she returned to Beijing by train with her friend.

4. 会话练习　Conversation exercises

【强调过去的时间和地点　Emphasizing the time and location of a past event】

（1）A：您的孩子今年几岁了？

B：他今年________。

A：他是________年出生的吧？

B：对，他是________的。

A：他是在哪儿出生的？

B：他是________的。

（2）A：你是什么时候到北京的？怎么不先给我打个电话？

B：我打电话了，你不在。我是__________到这儿的。

A：你是怎么来的？

B：我是__________来的。

A：你是来旅行的吧？

B：不是，我这次是来出差（chūchāi）的，只在这儿住三天。

A：太短了！晚上有时间吗？到我家去玩儿，好吗？

B：一定去。我是跟一位教授一起来的，我先打电话告诉他一下儿。

【谈体育比赛 Talking about an athletic contest】

A：昨天你去看足球赛了吗？

B：__________。谁跟谁比赛？

A：咱们系足球队跟外语系足球队比赛。

B：咱们队__________了吗？

A：输（shū）了！0比2。他们的两个球都是下半场进的。

B：咱们系的队怎么踢得这么糟糕？

【谈方位 Talking about direction and location】

（1）A：您是租房公司吗？我想租一套50平方米的房子，有吗？

B：我查一下。有，白石小区有一套55平方米的，在建国门北边。

A：那很好，离我们公司不远。那儿__________？

B：那儿很好：小区东边有一个大公园，前边不远就有一个大商场。小区旁边就是公共汽车站。

A：那儿__________________？

B：有，医院在后边（hòubian）。医院旁边还有银行和邮局。

A：__________________？

B：每月两千五。

A：房租有点儿贵。我想想，再给您打电话。

（2）B：这是六号楼十五层，上边还有三层。

A：我想看看房子。

B：请进。

A：__________在哪儿？

B：厨房在右边，左边是客厅，客厅有26平方米。

A：__________呢？

B：有两个卧室，都在客厅南边。大卧室外边还有一个阳台。

A：这儿是卫生间吗？卫生间有点儿小。

B：这个卫生间是5平方米。

A：好吧，我们再到别的楼看看。

【问路　Asking for directions】

（1）A：请问，新邮局在哪儿？

B：对不起，我不住这儿，我也__________。

*　　　*　　　*　　　*

A：麻烦您，问一下，这儿有一个新邮局吗？

C：有，在前边。中国银行的北边就是__________。

A：谢谢您。

C：不客气。

（2）A：请问，____________________？

B：从这儿坐945路公共汽车，到花园路下车。下车以后先往前走，再往左拐，走10分钟就到了。

A：谢谢。

5. 看图说话 Describe the following pictures

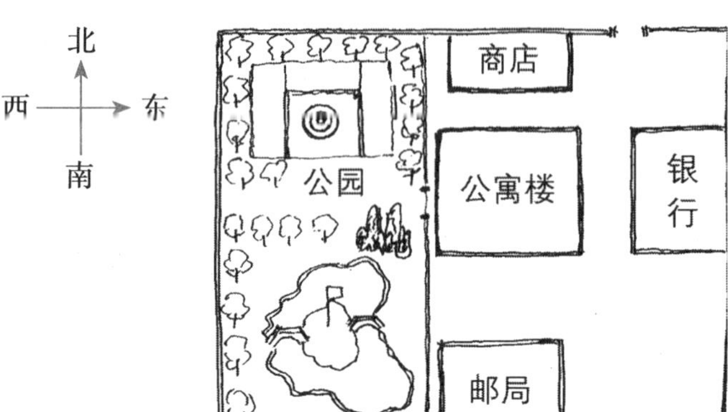

❶ 我住的楼前边有＿＿＿＿＿＿。东边是＿＿＿＿＿＿＿＿，西边是＿＿＿＿＿＿＿＿，＿＿＿＿＿＿在＿＿＿＿＿＿。

❷ 客厅在厨房＿＿＿＿＿＿＿＿，卫生间在客厅＿＿＿＿＿＿＿，房子里有两个＿＿＿＿＿＿＿，大卧室在＿＿＿＿＿＿＿＿＿，小卧室在＿＿＿＿＿＿＿＿＿，＿＿＿＿＿＿还有一个阳台。

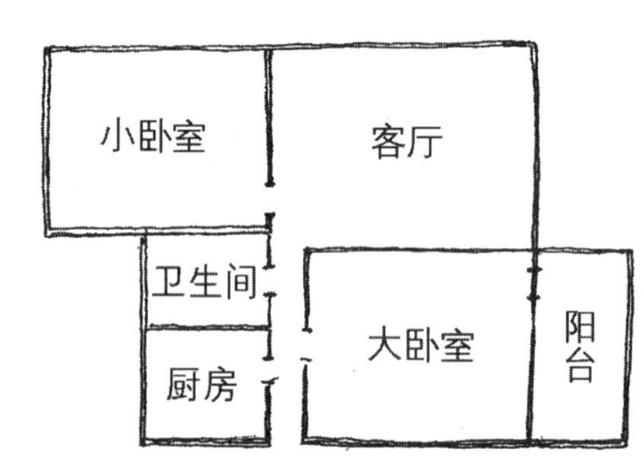

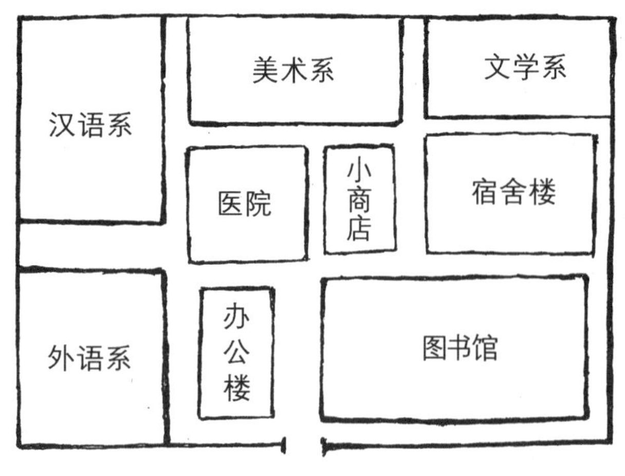

❸ 我们学校不太大，一共有＿＿＿＿＿＿＿个系。汉语系在外语系＿＿＿＿＿＿，文学系在美术系＿＿＿＿＿＿。办公楼＿＿＿＿＿＿有一个图书馆。宿舍楼＿＿＿＿＿还有＿＿＿＿＿和＿＿＿＿＿＿＿＿。

6. 交际练习 Communication exercises

(1) You heard that one of your classmates went to Europe, so you ask the other students about the specific details concerning his or her departure.

(2) Inquire about the birthdays and birthplaces of at least 5 of your friends.

(3) You become acquainted with a new friend. You invite him or her to your home and describe the surroundings and layout of your residence to your guest.

阅读与复述 Reading Comprehension and Paraphrasing

28 南方的花园

中国人常说："上有天堂（tiāntáng），下有苏杭（Sū Háng）。"意思是苏州和杭州这两个城市跟天堂一样美。它们都在中国的南方，是中国南方的"花园"。它们的美在哪儿呢？——杭州的山水（shānshuǐ）和苏州的园林（yuánlín）。苏州的园林非常有名。那些园林是过去一些有钱人请人修建（xiūjiàn）的。园林里边有山、有水、有花儿，真是一幅幅美丽（měilì）的山水画。中国的园林跟西方的园林很不一样。中国的园林好像中国画，是用水和墨画的；西方的园林好像油画，是用油彩画的。因为中国古典（gǔdiǎn）的园林常常是画家和诗人（shīrén）设计（shèjì）的，西方的园林常常是建筑师（jiànzhùshī）设计的，所以它们的美很不一样。

苏州

杭州

三、语法 Grammar

1 "是……的"句 The construction "是……的"

The construction "是……的" can be used to emphasize the time and location of past events, and the manner in which they have occurred. The word "是" is placed before the part to be emphasized (sometimes it can be omitted), and the "的" is placed at the end of the sentence. The negative form is "不是……的".

Subject	是	Word(s) indicating time, place or manner	V	O	的
他	是	去年	来		的。
你们	是	在语言学院	比赛		的吗?
我们的队员	是	从不同国家	来		的。
你	是	怎么	知道	这件事儿	的?
我们	不是	坐出租车	去	大为家	的。

A sentence with a verb as the predicate to indicate that something has happened in the past is different in meaning from a sentence with "是……的" as the predicate. Compare the following:

他是去年来的。(It emphasizes that the time that he came was last year.)

去年他来了。(It just tells what happened last year.)

The sentence with "是……的" can also be used to emphasize purpose, function and origin. For example:

我今天是来问你们问题的。

我是听朋友说的。

2 方位词 Location words

The words "里边", "外边", "左边", "右边", "上边", "下边", "前边", "后边", "东边", "西边", "南边", and "北边" are all nouns expressing direction and location, and can function as the subject, object, or attributive. They can also be modified by attributives. For example:

里边有什么？

邮局在前边。

左边的床是我的。

图书馆外边有很多人。

Note:

❶ When a location word functions as an attributive, it must be followed by the word "的". For example: "上边的报纸", "前边的花园". When a location word functions as a central word, "的" is usually not used before it. For example: "厨房里边", "银行北边".

❷ The word "里边" cannot be used after the name of a country, a place or a workplace. For example, one may only say "在中国/北京", but we cannot say "在中国/北京里边"; one may only say "我在中国银行工作", but we cannot say "我在中国银行里边工作".

3 表示存在的句子　Sentences indicating existence

We have learned that the word "在" is often used as the main verb of the predicate to indicate somebody or something exists somewhere. The subject of this kind of sentence is usually a person or thing that exists; the object is usually a noun expressing direction or location.

S (Phrase indicating the existence of somebody or something)	V "在"	O (Phrase indicating somewhere)
我	在	他右边。
大为的房子	在	八号楼九层吗？
厨房	不在	客厅的北边。

"有" or "是" is usually used as the main verb of the predicate to indicate somebody or something exists somewhere. The subject of such a sentence is usually a noun or phrase indicating somewhere; the object is usually a phrase indicating somebody or something.

S (Phrase indicating somewhere)	V "有/是"	O (Phrase indicating somebody or something)
卧室外边	有	一个大阳台。
办公室里边	没有	老师。
前边	有没有	一个小花园?
图书馆后边	是	英语系。
阳台东边	不是	卫生间。
你前边	是	谁?

Notes:

There are two differences between a sentence using "是" and a sentence using "有" when indicating existence:

❶ A sentence with "有" only denotes somebody or something exists somewhere, while a sentence with "是" not only indicates that somebody or something exists somewhere, but also further specifies what it is.

❷ The object of a sentence indicating existence with "有" is usually of a general reference, while the object of a sentence indicating existence with "是" is usually of a specific reference. Therefore, we can say "图书馆前边有一个学院", but not "图书馆前边有我们学院". "图书馆前边是我们学院" or "我们学院在图书馆前边" should be used instead.

四、汉字 Chinese Characters

1 汉字的构字法(7) Methods of constructing Chinese characters (7)

The pictophonetic method（形声法）(3)

In this method, a character is formed by placing the semantic component on the top, and the phonetic component at the bottom. For example: 花, 寄, 蕉, 篇, 苹, 舍, 药.

2 认写基本汉字　Learn and write basic Chinese characters

(1) 凡　　丿 几 凡
fán　　every　　3 strokes

(2) 臣　　一 丅 𠃋 五 亐 臣
chén　　official under a feudal ruler　　6 strokes

3 认写课文中的汉字　Learn and write the Chinese characters in the texts

(1) 不同 bùtóng

同 → 冂 + 一 + 口　　6 strokes

(2) 赢 yíng（赢）

赢 → 亡 + 口 + 月 + 贝 + 凡　　17 strokes

𡗗 (hánzìyāo, the middle part of the character "寒(hán)")
一 二 三 丰 𡗗　　5 strokes

(3) 比赛 bǐsài（比賽）

赛 → 宀 + 𡗗 + 八 + 贝　　14 strokes

(4) 学校 xuéxiào（學校）

校 → 木 + 交　　10 strokes

(5) 以后 yǐhòu（以後）

后 → 厂 + 一 + 口　　6 strokes

(6) 提高 tígāo

提 → 扌 + 是　　12 strokes

(7) 踢 tī

踢 → 𧾷 + 易 15 strokes

(8) 左边 zuǒbian（左邊）

左 → 𠂇 + 工 5 strokes

(9) 右边 yòubian（右邊）

右 → 𠂇 + 口 5 strokes

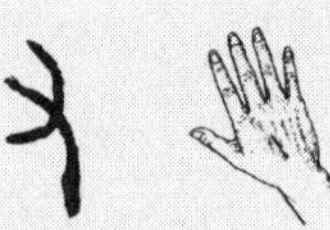

(10) 离 lí（離）

离 → 亠 + 凶 + 内 10 strokes

(11) 远 yuǎn（遠）

远 → 元 + 辶 7 strokes

(12) 拐 guǎi

拐 → 扌 + 口 + 力 8 strokes

(13) 卫生间 wèishēngjiān（衛生間）

卫 → 卩 + 一 3 strokes

(14) 卧室 wòshì

卧 → 臣 + 卜 8 strokes

(15) 阳台 yángtái（陽臺）

阳 → 阝 + 日 6 strokes

台 → 厶 + 口 5 strokes

文化知识 Cultural Note

Sports in China

China has traditional sports such as martial arts, wrestling, qigong, and playing on a swing. Martial arts are also known as "Chinese gongfu" by foreigners, which help people be fit and healthy.

Modern sports started late in China; however, it enjoys a rapid development. China's first world record was made by the weightlifter Chen Jingkai in 1956. Table tennis, badminton, gymnastics, diving, middle and long distance races are all what Chinese teams are good at. Chinese players won all the first and second-place titles in the World Table Tennis Championships 1982. Chinese Women's National Volleyball Team won five straight championships in the Women's Volleyball World Cup and other international games in 1980s. Chinese people, who were not good at sports in 1950s, ranked the third place in Sydney 2000 Olympic Games in terms of the total number of gold medals and the total number of medals.

Chinese teams ranked the first place in terms of the total number of gold medals, only second to America in terms of the total number of medals in the 29th Olympic Games held in Beijing in 2008. Sports are booming in China.

你看过越剧没有

Have you watched a Shaoxing opera?

Do you know that in addition to Beijing opera there are diverse regional operas, such as Shaoxing opera? Do you know the renowned classical Chinese novel, *Dream of the Red Chamber*? In this chapter, Song Hua and Lin Na will tell you about these subjects. You will also learn how to comment on your past experiences, how to make an appointment with somebody, and how to express your opinions on various topics.

一、课文　Text

29（一）

谈过去的经历
Talking about a past experience

宋　华：林娜，你看过越剧没有？①

林　娜：没有。来中国以后，我听过两次音乐会，看过一次京剧。我虽然去过南方，但是没有看过越剧。昨天的报上说，南方的一个越剧团到北京来了。②

宋　华：是啊，越剧是中国有名的地方戏。这个剧团是从上海来的，现在在长安大戏院上演《红楼梦》。③

林　娜：上演《红楼梦》吗？太好了！我知道《红楼梦》是中国有名的古典小说，我看过一遍，是用英文翻译的。

宋　华：你觉得这部小说怎么样？

林　娜：我觉得小说里的爱情故事非常感人。

宋　华：你想不想再看一次越剧的《红楼梦》？我有两张票。

林　娜：当然想看。是什么时候的票？

约会
Making an appointment or a date with somebody

宋　华：是明天晚上七点一刻的。座位很好，

楼下五排八号和十号。

林 娜：我没去过长安大戏院。这个戏院在哪儿？

宋 华：我去过啊，长安大戏院离建国门不远，就在建国门的西边。咱们一起打的去。

林 娜：好，明天见。

生词 New Words

*1. 过	guo	AsPt	(*indicating a past experience*) 看过，听过，去过，写过，试过，踢过
2. 越剧	yuèjù	N	Shaoxing opera 看过越剧，看过一次越剧，一场越剧，两张越剧票

	剧	jù	N	opera, theatrical work, play
3.	虽然	suīrán	Conj	although, though
4.	但是	dànshì	Conj	but, whereas, yet
5.	剧团	jùtuán	N	opera troupe, theatrical group 越剧团，京剧团，一个剧团，南方的剧团
6.	地方戏	dìfāngxì	N	regional opera 有名的地方戏，地方戏剧团
	戏	xì	N	drama, play, show 看戏，听戏，唱戏，一场戏，南方的戏
7.	上演	shàngyǎn	V	to stage a show, to perform 上演越剧，上演京剧，上演地方戏
*	演	yǎn	V	to act, to perform, to play 演电影，演大学生，演记者，演戏
8.	古典	gǔdiǎn	A	classical 古典音乐，古典乐曲，古典音乐会，古典文学
9.	小说	xiǎoshuō	N	novel, fiction 看小说，写小说，看过一遍小说，古典小说
*10.	遍	biàn	M	(*a measure word for actions*) 一遍，几遍，多少遍，看过一遍，听过一遍
11.	部	bù	M	(*a measure word for films, works of literature, etc.*) 一部小说，一部电影
12.	爱情	àiqíng	N	love 爱情小说，爱情戏，他们的爱情
13.	故事	gùshi	N	story 爱情故事，足球队的故事，租房子的故事，有意思的故事
14.	感人	gǎnrén	A	touching, moving 感人的故事，感人的爱情，非常感人，演得很感人
15.	座位	zuòwèi	N	seat 好座位，有座位，一个座位
*16.	排	pái	M	line, row 五排，八排，几排

17. 西边	xībian	N	the west (side) 厨房西边，医院西边，在公园西边，西边的书店
18. 打的	dǎdī	VO	to take a taxi 一起打的，打的去，是打的来的
*19. 见	jiàn	V	to see, to meet 见过，再见，明天见，下星期见，什么时候见
20. 长安大戏院	Cháng'ān Dà Xìyuàn	PN	the Chang'an Theater
戏院	xìyuàn	N	theater
21.《红楼梦》	Hónglóu Mèng	PN	*Dream of the Red Chamber* 上演《红楼梦》，看一次越剧的《红楼梦》
梦	mèng	N	dream 做梦，好梦，一个梦，我的梦

注释 Notes

① 林娜，你看过越剧没有？

"Lin Na, have you ever seen a Shaoxing opera?"

Shaoxing opera is a regional opera from Zhejiang Province. It is derived from local folk songs, and is mainly popular in areas such as Jiangsu Province and Zhejiang Province, as well as in Shanghai. It is a well-known regional opera in China, characterized by sweet and beautiful melodies.

② 昨天的报上说，南方的一个越剧团到北京来了。

"It was announced in yesterday's newspaper that a Shaoxing opera troupe from south China has come to Beijing."

When combined with a preceding noun, some location words such as "上边" and "里边", usually omit the character "边". For example, "报上, 书上, 头上, 小说里, 家里, 楼里, 系里, 国外".

When "上" follows a noun, it indicates the surface of an object, for example, "头上, 身(体)上"; it may also indicate an abstract or figurative location, i.e. in the scope of something, for example, "书上, 报上".

③ 现在在长安大戏院上演《红楼梦》。

"*Dream of the Red Chamber* is now playing at the Chang'an Theatre."

Dream of the Red Chamber is one of the most famous four classical Chinese novels. This profound work depicts the rise and fall of the Jia, Wang, Shi, and Xue families; it is an encyclopaedic chronicle of late Chinese feudal society. The love story between the leading male character, Jia Baoyu, and the female character, Lin Daiyu, is the main plot of the novel.

评价 Making comments

宋 华：你觉得越剧《红楼梦》怎么样？

林 娜：我从来没有看过这么感人的戏。④两个主角演得好极了。我觉得越剧的音乐特别优美，越剧的风格跟京剧很不一样。

宋 华：你说得很对。你可能还不知道，很早以前，京剧里没有女演员，都是男演员演女角色。越剧跟京剧不同，以前没有男演员，让女演员演男角色。所以越剧的风格跟京剧很不一样。

林 娜：听说中国地方戏的种类很多，每个地方都有吧？

宋 华：是啊，每种地方戏都有自己的风格，每个地方的人都习惯看自己的地方戏，但是京剧是全中国的，喜欢京剧的人特别多。

林 娜：中国京剧团两年以前到英国访问演出过，我跟爸爸妈妈一起去看过一次。他们都觉得京剧很美。

宋 华：很多外国朋友都喜欢中国京剧，一些外国留学生还到北京来学京剧。现在，他们有的人会唱京剧，有的人还会演京剧。⑤

林 娜：我有一个朋友，也是英国留学生，他就会演京剧。

宋 华：我还从来没听过外国留学生唱越剧。你这么喜欢越剧的音乐，应该学一学越剧。

林 娜：我虽然喜欢越剧的音乐，可是我觉得唱越剧太难了。

宋 华：你的嗓子很好。你可以先多听听，再学唱。⑥

生词 New Words

1. 从来	cónglái	Adv	all along, always 从来没有看过，从来没有见过，从来没有演过，从来没有说过
2. 这么	zhème	Pr	so, such, like this 这么感人，这么有名，这么流利，这么容易，这么喜欢，这么放心，这么着急
3. 主角	zhǔjué	N	leading actor or actress 两个主角，电影主角，男主角，女主角
4. 特别	tèbié	Adv	extraordinarily, especially, particularly 特别感人，特别高兴，特别远，特别愿意，特别喜欢，特别想
5. 优美	yōuměi	A	beautiful, fine 特别优美，这么优美，优美的音乐，优美的故事
6. 风格	fēnggé	N	style, manner 越剧的风格，小说的风格，不同的风格
7. 以前	yǐqián	N	before, ago, previously, formerly 两年以前，三天以前，上课以前，开学以前，认识你以前
8. 演员	yǎnyuán	N	actor or actress, performer 越剧演员，电影演员，一位男演员
9. 角色	juésè	N	character, role 演一个角色，电影角色
10. 种类	zhǒnglèi	N	kind, sort, type, variety 地方戏的种类，语言的种类，乐曲的种类，不同的种类，别的种类
种	zhǒng	M	kind, sort, type 每种地方戏，这种照相机，一种乐器
11. 地方	dìfang	N	place, region 每个地方，这个地方，很多地方，什么地方
12. 访问	fǎngwèn	V	to visit, to call on 访问过，访问过一次，访问英国，访问上海，访问中国京剧团，访问老画家

↳ formal visit; certain etiquette required.
Not used to describe visits to friends → 看
or educational trips to places → can guan

13. 演出	yǎnchū	V	to play, to perform 京剧演出，演出过，去英国演出
14. 有的	yǒude	Pr	some 有的人，有的学生，有的演员，有的剧团，有的故事，有的特别优美，有的非常感人
15. 难	nán	A	difficult, hard 太难了，特别难，这么难，难学，难唱，难演，难极了

补充生词 Supplementary Words

1. 顿	dùn	M	(*a measure word for meals*)
2. 便饭	biànfàn	N	a simple meal
3. 太太	tàitai	N	wife, Mrs.
4. 不怎么样	bù zěnmeyàng	IE	not so good
5. 研究	yánjiū	V	to study, to research
6. 悲伤	bēishāng	A	sad, sorrowful
7. 贾宝玉	Jiǎ Bǎoyù	PN	(name of the leading male character in *Dream of the Red Chamber*)
8. 林黛玉	Lín Dàiyù	PN	(name of the leading female character in *Dream of the Red Chamber*)
9. 诗	shī	N	poem, poetry
10. 相爱	xiāng'ài	V	to fall in love
11. 结婚	jiéhūn	VO	to get married
12. 骗	piàn	V	to cheat, to trick
13. 烧	shāo	V	to burn
14. 哭	kū	V	to cry, to weep
15. 死	sǐ	V	to die
16. 回忆	huíyì	V	to reminisce, to recollect, to recall
17. 离开	líkāi	V	to leave, to depart from

注释　Notes

④ 我从来没有看过这么感人的戏。

"I have never seen such a moving opera."

The demonstrative pronoun "这么", which is often pronounced "zème" in spoken Chinese, denotes manner, status, method or degree. It is often used to modify adjectives or verbs. In this sentence, it indicates degree. Additional examples are: "这么好的课本" and "这么美的油画". In cases such as "这么写", "这么念", and "这么做", "这么" demonstrates manner of the action.

⑤ 现在，他们有的人会唱京剧，有的人还会演京剧。

"Now some of them can sing the Beijing opera, while some of them can perform it on stage."

When the pronoun "有的" functions as a modifier, it often refers to only part of the group of people or objects that it modifies. It can be used singly, or it can appear two or three times in consecutive clauses within a sentence. For example:

有的人喜欢看小说，有的人喜欢听音乐。

有的书是中文的，有的书是英文的，有的书是日文（Japanese）的。

If the noun which "有的" modifies is used in the previous sentence, it can be omitted in the following sentences starting with "有的". For example:

这些衣服有的太长，有的太短。

Note: A noun with "有的" as its modifier usually doesn't follow a verb as its object. For example, people seldom say "我不太喜欢有的地方戏", they say "有的地方戏我不太喜欢" instead.

⑥ 你可以先多听听，再学唱。

"You can listen to it first, and then learn how to sing it."

In this Chinese sentence, the object "越剧" is omitted. The complete sentence is:

你可以先多听听越剧，再学唱越剧。

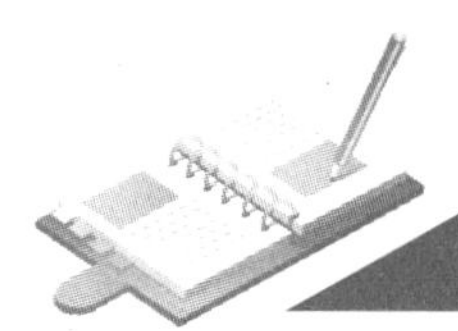

二、练习 Exercises

练习与运用 Drills and Practice

核心句 KEY SENTENCES

1. 你看过越剧没有？
2. 来中国以后，我听过两次音乐会，看过一次京剧。
3. 我虽然去过南方，但是没有看过越剧。
4. 你想不想再看一次越剧的《红楼梦》？
5. 我觉得小说里的爱情故事非常感人。
6. 我从来没有看过这么感人的戏。
7. 现在他们有的人会唱京剧，有的人还会演京剧。
8. 我虽然喜欢越剧的音乐，可是我觉得唱越剧太难了。

1. 熟读下列词组 Read the following phrases until you learn them by heart

（1）报上　书上　课本上　本子上　词典上　电影上　名片上　光盘上
照片上　护照上　借书证上　明信片上　包裹通知单上　你填的表上

（2）没有去过　没有学过　没有送过　没有拿过　没有写过
从来没听说过　从来没进去过　从来没参加过　从来没打扫过
从来没见过他　从来没有访问过画家　从来没赢过足球比赛
从来没有穿过旗袍　从来没有看过《红楼梦》

（3）这么容易　这么难　这么热　这么冷　这么早　这么晚
这么快　这么慢　这么新　这么旧
这么放心　这么爱　这么习惯　这么着急　这么愿意

这么喜欢　这么想

从来没有看过这么好的小说　从来没翻译过这么难的句子

从来没听过这么优美的音乐

（4）特别贵　特别便宜　特别多　特别少　特别年轻　特别长　特别短

特别愿意　特别喜欢　特别想　特别放心　特别习惯　特别着急

（5）有的朋友　有的角色　有的同学　有的队员　有的司机　有的语言

有的专业　有的乐曲　有的文章　有的课本　有的中学　有的民族

有的职业　有的地方　有的时候

有的特别优美　有的非常流利　有的合适极了

有的锻炼身体　有的演奏民乐

（6）回答过问题　开过车　唱过越剧　画过中国画　查过词典　借过书

上过课没有　演过京剧没有　坐过火车没有　参观过兵马俑没有

（7）听过一次　开过一次玩笑　去过一次西安　换过一次人民币

看过一遍　念过一遍课文　写过一遍汉字　听过一遍生词

（8）虽然合适，但是太贵了　虽然有意思，可是特别难

虽然从来没去过英国，但是很喜欢英国文学

虽然从来没有学过京剧，可是觉得京剧的音乐特别优美

2. 句型替换 Pattern drills

（1）A：你看过京剧吗？

B：我看过京剧。

A：你是在哪儿看的京剧？

B：我是在北京看的京剧。

学	汉语	美国
听	中国民乐	上海
吃	北京烤鸭	加拿大
喝	中国红葡萄酒	宋华家

（2）A：你知道《红楼梦》吗？

B：我知道，我看过这部小说。

A：你是什么时候看的？

B：我是二年以前看的。

徐悲鸿	看	他画的马	来中国以后
兵马俑	参观	那个地方	去西安旅行的时候
《春江花月夜》	听	这个曲子	来中国以前
建国门	去	那儿	取包裹的时候

（3）A：你去过长安大戏院没有？

B：我没有去过，我很想去。

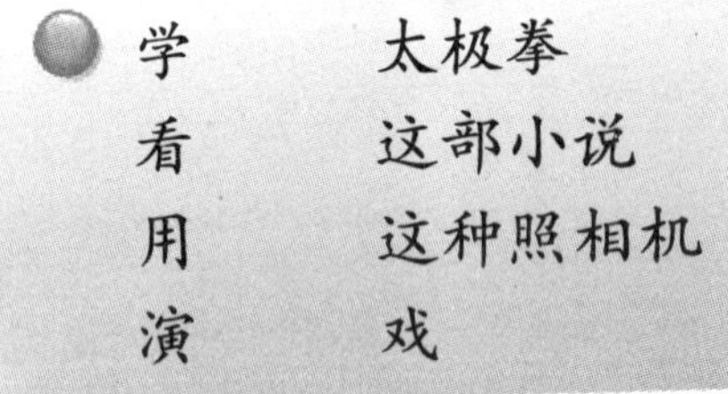

学	太极拳
看	这部小说
用	这种照相机
演	戏

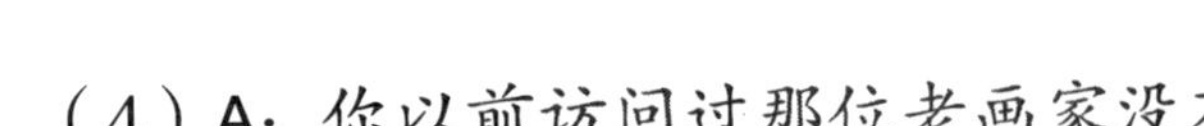

（4）A：你以前访问过那位老画家没有？

B：我访问过（那位老画家）。

A：你访问过他几次？

B：我访问过他两次。

见	那位演员
找	那位经理
麻烦	那位师傅
问	张教授
帮助	你同学

（5）A：这课汉字你写过几遍了？

B：我写过两遍了，我要再写一遍。

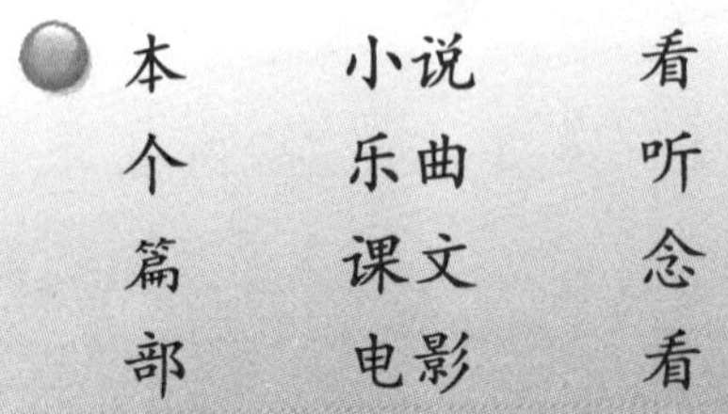

本	小说	看
个	乐曲	听
篇	课文	念
部	电影	看

（6）A：剧院里有什么人？
B：剧院里有中国大学生，也有外国留学生。

包裹里	书	小说	词典
书店里	课本	大学课本	中学课本
楼上	房间	卧室	卫生间
课本里	课文	故事	小说

（7）A：过新年的时候你的同学做什么？
B：有的人去看京剧，有的人去听音乐会。

过生日的时候	吃蛋糕	吃寿面
过圣诞节的时候	旅行	回家
下午四点以后	踢足球	去打太极拳
星期天	看朋友	去商场买东西

（8）A：今天天气这么不好，别去公园玩儿了。
B：虽然天气不好，可是我女朋友一定要去。

排队的人这么多	在这儿换钱	现在我就要用钱
衣服这么贵	在这儿买	衣服的样子好
他们队的水平这么高	跟他们比赛	我们应该试试
公共汽车这么多	打的	坐车的人也多

3. 课堂活动 Classroom activity

A asks B a question, and B answers; then B asks C a question, and C answers....

（1）林娜看过越剧没有？

（2）来中国以后，林娜听过音乐会吗？

（3）她听过几次音乐会？

（4）来中国以前，林娜听说过京剧没有？

（5）中国京剧团到英国演出过没有？

（6）林娜在英国看过京剧吗？

（7）来中国以后，林娜看过京剧没有？

（8）林娜看过小说《红楼梦》没有？

（9）她看过几遍？

（10）林娜看过中文的《红楼梦》没有？

（11）林娜以前去过长安大戏院没有？

（12）宋华去过吗？

（13）林娜去过中国南方没有？

（14）林娜看过越剧吗？

（15）宋华听过外国留学生唱越剧没有？

（16）你学习过中国美术吗？

（17）你以前看过中文小说没有？

（18）你听过中国地方戏没有？

（19）你买过中国音乐光盘没有？

（20）你听过《春江花月夜》没有？

4. 会话练习 Conversation exercises

【谈过去的经历 Talking about a past experience】

（1）A：你去过欧洲没有？

B：我去过三次。

A：______________________？

B：（虽然）我去过很多欧洲国家，可是我还没去过英国。

A：下次你到英国，一定给我打电话。

（2）A：你访问过那位老画家没有？

B：________________。

A：你是在哪儿访问他的？

B：________________。

A：________________？

B：我访问过他两次。

A：你来中国以前听说过他没有？

B：我很早以前就听说过他。

（3）A：啊，王明，你刚才去哪儿了？

B：我________________了。有事儿吗？

A：你老同学来找过你三次，你都不在。

B：糟糕，上星期四我给他打过一次电话，让他今天下午来我这儿，可是我把这事儿________。

A：你可以去他那儿找他。

B：不行，我从来没有去过他那儿，我不知道他住哪儿。

【约会 Making an appointment or a date with somebody】

（1）A：你还没有来过我的新家呢，星期六晚上到我家来玩儿，一起吃顿（dùn）便饭（biànfàn），好吗？

B：我很想来，可是这个星期六我有点事儿。

A：____________？

B：星期天可以，我一定来。几点？

A：________________。你太太（tàitai）能一起来吗？

B：我想没问题。

A：那太好了。

（2）A：（打电话）喂，请问田小姐在家吗？

B：我就是。您是哪一位？

A：________________。田小姐，你看过电影《爱情故事》吗？

B：没有看过，可是我听说过，好像是一部很好的电影。

A：是啊，大家都说这部电影好。________________？

B：想看。什么时候演啊？

A：________________，不知道你有没有时间。

B：我看看。可以，明天晚上我没有事儿。

A：我已经买了两张电影票，座位是十二排一号和三号。

B：好极了！________________？

A：咱们一起打的去吧。七点半我在你家东边的商场等你。

B：好，明天七点半见。

【评价 Making comments】

A：《爱情故事》这部电影太感人了，我已经看了两遍，以后还想再看一遍。你觉得____________？

B：我觉得不怎么样（bù zěnmeyàng）。

A：为什么？你知道吗？女主角和男主角都____________。

B：演员虽然有名，但是这次他们演得不好。

A：我觉得这部电影的音乐________________。

B：可是这部电影的故事太没有意思了，我也不喜欢它的风格。

【找工作 Looking for a job】

（1）A：张先生，您想来我们公司工作，是吗？

B：是的。

A：您以前学过什么？

B：我的专业是________，我还学习过________。

A：张先生，您学过电脑没有？

B：我没有正式学习过，但是我看过很多关于电脑的书，也常常用电脑。

A：很好。请下星期五再来见我们一次。

（2）A：我的朋友很愿意来你们学院工作，她想在英语系工作，可以吗？

B：________？

A：不，她是美国人。

B：她以前做过什么工作？

A：她一年以前在美国一个大学教过语言课，去年到中国以后教过英语语法。

B：________？

A：她会说一点儿汉语。上大学的时候她学过汉语。

B：谢谢您的介绍，我们研究（yánjiū）一下再告诉您。

5. 看图说话 Describe the following pictures

❶ A：你吃过北京烤鸭没有？

B：我________。

A：你________？

B：我吃过九次北京烤鸭。

❷ A：你们________？

B：我们跟中国大学生队比赛过足球。

A：你们比赛过几次？

B：我们________。

③ A：力波看过这篇文章没有？

B：他____________________。

A：他看过几遍？

B：______________________。

④ A：大为____________________？

B：他复习过那篇课文。

A：______________________？

B：________________三遍课文。

6. 交际练习 Communication exercises

(1) Talk to your classmate about an interesting experience you had last week.

(2) You bought two movie tickets and invite your friend to see the movie with you.

(3) After watching the movie, you discuss it with your friend. (the story, music, style, actors, performance, make-up, etc.)

阅读与复述 Reading Comprehension and Paraphrasing

32《红楼梦》里的爱情故事

中国古典小说《红楼梦》里讲了一个优美、悲伤（bēishāng）的爱情故事。

故事里的男主角叫贾宝玉（Jiǎ Bǎoyù），是在有钱的人家里出生的。他很聪明。故事里的女主角是一个非常漂亮的姑娘，叫林黛玉

（Lín Dàiyù），她从南方来到贾家生活。她比贾宝玉小一岁，看过很多书，写诗（shī）写得很好，还会画画儿。他们每天一起吃饭、看书，一起写诗、画画儿。他们很相爱（xiāng'ài）。可是贾宝玉的奶奶和爸爸妈妈不让他们结婚（jiéhūn）。贾宝玉生病的时候，奶奶骗（piàn）了他，让他跟别的姑娘结了婚。就在贾宝玉结婚的时候，林黛玉在自己的卧室里把她写给贾宝玉的诗都烧（shāo）了，把他送给她的礼物也烧了。她哭（kū）了一天，悲伤而死（sǐ）。林黛玉死了以后，贾宝玉到她住的地方去过很多次，每次都悲伤极了。他回忆（huíyì）他们的每一次相聚，回忆他们有过的快乐。他不愿意和那个跟他结婚的姑娘一起生活。所以，最后他离开（líkāi）了家。

三、语法　Grammar

1　过去的经验或经历　Past experience

The aspect particle “过”, which occurs immediately after a verb, denotes that an action took place in the past. It is often used to emphasize someone had such an experience in the past. For example:

他来过北京，他知道怎么坐车去王府井。

我朋友足球踢得很好，他参加过很多比赛。

The negative form of “过” is “没（有）……过”. For example:

没有来过，没有参加过.

The V/A-not-V/A question with “过” is “……过……没有”. For example:

来过没有？

参加过比赛没有？

V + 过 (+O+没有)

Subject	Predicate				
	Adverbial	V	过	O	没有
她		看	过	越剧《红楼梦》。	
丁力波	在加拿大	学	过	中国画。	
我	没有	开	过	车。	
他	从来 没有	用	过	电脑。	
我们	以前	去	过。		
你		唱	过	京剧	没有?

Note:

❶ “过” must be placed right after the verb. “过” must be followed by an object if it has one. For example, one does not say: “我看那部电影过”, but rather “我看过那部电影”.

❷ “过” is usually placed after the second verb in a sentence with serial verb phrases to indicate one's experience. For example:

他去西安参观过兵马俑。

(It is incorrect to say: 他去过西安参观兵马俑。)

我们去花园小区看过大为的新房子。

(It is incorrect to say: 我们去过花园小区看大为的新房子。)

2 动量补语 The complement of frequency

The action-measure word “次” or “遍” is often combined with a numeral and placed after a verb as the complement of frequency to express the frequency of an action. In addition to signifying the number of times, “遍” also denotes the whole process of an action from the beginning to the end. For example:

我上星期六打扫过一次。

这部小说我又看了两遍。

When the object of the verb is a noun, the complement of frequency is usually placed before the object. When the object is a pronoun, the complement often comes after the object.

Subject	Predicate					
	Adverbial	V	过	O(Pr)	Nu + action-measure word	O(N/NP)
林娜		去	过		两次	上海。
丁力波	今天下午/又	写	过		一遍	课本上的汉字。
我	以前	来	过	这儿	三次。	
王小云	到学院以后	找	过	她	几次。	

Besides indicating the frequency of an action, the complement of frequency "一下" is also used to indicate a short or casual action. For example, "介绍一下，等一下" (please refer to Note 1 in Lesson 7).

3 "虽然……但是/可是……" The construction "虽然……但是/可是……"

"虽然……但是/可是……", meaning "although", is used to link two contradictory statements. "虽然" may go either before or after the subject of the first clause, while "但是" (or "可是") is always placed at the beginning of the second clause. For example:

虽然他从来没有看过这部小说，但是他很早就听说过。

我虽然喜欢西方的油画，可是不会画油画。

"虽然" can also be omitted. For example:

他（虽然）学汉语的时间不长，但是学得很好。

四、汉字 Chinese Characters

1 汉字的构字法(8) Methods of constructing Chinese characters (8)

The pictophonetic method（形声法）(4)

In this method, a character is formed by placing the semantic component at the bottom, and the phonetic component on the top. For example: 帮, 婆, 华, 照, 您, 愿.

2 认写基本汉字 Learn and write basic Chinese characters

(1) 旦 丨 冂 日 日 旦
dàn dawn, daybreak 5 strokes

(2) 戉 一 𠂉 戈 戉 戉
yuè battle-axe used in ancient China 5 strokes

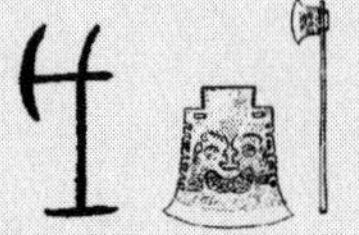

3 认写课文中的汉字 Learn and write the Chinese characters in the texts

(1) 越剧 yuèjù（越劇）

越 → 走 + 戉 12 strokes

(2) 虽然 suīrán（雖然）

虽 → 口 + 虫 9 strokes

(3) 但是 dànshì

但 → 亻 + 旦 7 strokes

(4) 剧团 jùtuán（劇團）

团 → 囗 + 才 6 strokes

(5) 地方戏 dìfāngxì（地方戲）

戏 → 又 + 戈 6 strokes

(6) 遍 biàn

遍 → 户 + 冊 + 辶 12 strokes

(7) 部 bù

部 → 立 + 口 + 阝　　10 strokes

(8) 爱情 àiqíng（愛情）

情 → 忄 + 青　　11 strokes

(9) 故事 gùshi

故 → 古 + 攵　　9 strokes

(10) 座位 zuòwèi

座 → 广 + 坐　　10 strokes

(11) 红楼梦 Hónglóu Mèng（紅樓夢）

梦 → 林 + 夕　　11 strokes

(12) 主角 zhǔjué

角 → ⺈ + 用　　7 strokes

(13) 特别 tèbié

特 → 牜 + 土 + 寸　　10 strokes

(14) 优美 yōuměi（優美）

优 → 亻 + 尤　　6 strokes

(15) 风格 fēnggé（風格）

格 → 木 + 夂 + 口 10 strokes

(16) 种类 zhǒnglèi（種類）

种 → 禾 + 中 9 strokes

类 → 米 + 大 9 strokes

(17) 访问 fǎngwèn（訪問）

访 → 讠 + 方 6 strokes

(18) 难 nán（難）

难 → 又 + 隹 10 strokes

Classical Chinese Poetry, Prose and Novels

Classical Chinese literature has a history as long as the literary histories of Greece, Arab, and India. Poetry is the most developed genre of classical Chinese literature. The earliest collection of Chinese poetry, *The Book of Songs*, contains three hundred and five poems dating from the eleventh century B.C. to the sixth century B.C.. The golden age of Chinese poetry was during the Tang and Song dynasties. The poems of Qu Yuan, Li Bai, Du Fu, Bai Juyi, and Su Shi represent the highest achievements in this genre.

Chinese prose has a history just as long as Chinese poetry. The earliest prose consists of historical texts dating back to the eleventh century B.C.. These are followed by prose pieces representing various schools of thought. During the Tang and Song dynasties, as well as in the Ming and Qing dynasties, a great number of excellent works were produced.

Novels, especially those written by famons authors, appeared fairly late in China. *The Romance of the Three Kingdoms*, *Journey to the West*, *Water Margin*, and *Dream of the Red Chamber* are the most famous four classical Chinese novels.

我们爬上长城来了

We have ascended the Great Wall.

People in Beijing like ascending the Great Wall. Ding Libo and his friends ascended the Great Wall again with their teacher, Ms. Chen, before the holiday. Let's go to the Great Wall with them and learn how to discuss plans, make suggestions, and talk about the scenery and the weather.

一、课文　Text

33（一）

陈老师：要放假了，同学们有什么打算？

林　娜：有的同学去旅行，有的同学回家。

谈计划
Talking about plans

陈老师：小云，你呢？

王小云：我打算先去泰山，再回家看我爸爸妈妈。[①] 林娜，你去过泰山没有？

林　娜：泰山我去过一次了。这次我想去海南岛旅行。

王小云：你跟宋华一起去吧？

林　娜：是啊，去海南岛旅行就是他提出来的。[②]

王小云：你们坐飞机去还是坐火车去？

林　娜：坐飞机去。机票已经买好了。[③]

力波呢？去不去泰山？

王小云：去。他说他要从山下爬上去，

再从山顶走下来。他还说，

先爬泰山，再去参观孔子教书的地方。④

提建议
Making suggestions

林　娜：对了，大为想去哪儿？⑤

王小云：小燕子建议大为也去海南岛。她说现在那儿天气好，气温合适，能去游泳，还可以看优美的景色。现在北京是冬天，可是在海南岛还可以过夏天的生活，多有意思啊！⑥

林　娜：小燕子是导游，旅行的事儿她知道得很多，应该听她的。大为可以跟我们一起去。

王小云：大为还建议放假以前咱们一起去长城。陈老师，您能不能跟我们一起去？

陈老师：行。我很愿意跟你们一起去爬一次长城。

生词 New Words

1. 爬	pá	V	to climb 爬上来，爬上去，爬一次
2. 放假	fàngjià	VO	to have a holiday or vacation 要放假了，开始放假，放假的时候，放假以前，放假以后
假	jià	N	vacation, holiday 请假
3. 打算	dǎsuan	N / V	plan; to plan, to intend 我的打算，放假的打算，有什么打算；打算去看越剧，打算去旅行

*4. 提	tí	V	to put forward, to raise 提出，提出来，提问题
5. 飞机	fēijī	N	airplanc 坐飞机，开飞机，上飞机，下飞机
飞	fēi	V	to fly 飞到北京，飞回加拿大
*机	jī	N	airplane
6. 机票	jīpiào	N	air ticket
7. 山	shān	N	hill, mountain 高山，山上，山下，山里，爬山，爬上山来，爬上山去
8. 顶	dǐng	N	peak, top 山顶，楼顶，头顶
9. 教书	jiāoshū	VO	to teach
10. 建议	jiànyì	V / N	to make a suggestion; advice, suggestion 建议去爬山，建议坐飞机；提建议，有一个建议
11. 气温	qìwēn	N	air temperature 气温合适，气温不太高，气温这么高，气温怎么样，今天的气温，北京的气温
12. 景色	jǐngsè	N	scene, scenery, landscape 优美的景色，山顶的景色，看景色
景	jǐng	N	view, scenery 美景，全景，远景
色	sè	N	view, scene, scenery 景色，夜色
*13. 游泳	yóuyǒng	V	to swim 去游泳，打算游泳，建议游泳，游泳队，游泳教练
14. 冬天	dōngtiān	N	winter 在冬天，冬天的气温，冬天的景色，冬天的时候
15. 夏天	xiàtiān	N	summer 喜欢夏天，夏天的生活，夏天的天气，夏天的衣服
16. 导游	dǎoyóu	N	tour guide 一位导游，女导游，男导游
导	dǎo	V	to guide, to lead
*游	yóu	V	to travel

17. 行	xíng	V	to be OK
18. 长城	Chángchéng	PN	the Great Wall 爬一次长城，参观长城
19. 泰山	Tài Shān	PN	Mount Tai 爬泰山，去泰山，爬上泰山去
20. 海南岛	Hǎinán Dǎo	PN	Hainan Island 去海南岛旅行，海南岛的景色
21. 孔子	Kǒngzǐ	PN	Confucius
22. 小燕子	Xiǎo Yànzi	PN	(name of a Chinese tour guide)

注释 Notes

① 我打算先去泰山，再回家看我爸爸妈妈。

"I plan to go to Mount Tai first, and then go home to see my parents."

Mount Tai is a famous mountain in Shandong Province. It is one of the great tourist attractions of China. It is also known as the "Eastern Mountain" among China's five famous mountains.

② 是啊，去海南岛旅行就是他提出来的。

"That's right. It is his idea to travel to Hainan Island."

Hainan Island is in Hainan Province of China. It attracts many tourists for its tropical scenery.

③ 机票已经买好了。

"I have already bought the plane ticket."

Used as a resultative complement, "好" can sometimes indicate the completion of an action. For example:

他已经画好这幅画儿了。

你什么时候能洗好这些衣服?

④ 他还说，先爬泰山，再去参观孔子教书的地方。

"He also said that he would climb Mount Tai first, and then visit the place where Confucius used to teach."

Confucius was a famous philosopher and educator in the Spring and Autumn Period of ancient China. As a leading exponent of Confucianism, his philosophy and educational thoughts have influenced generations of Chinese people.

⑤ 对了，大为想去哪儿?

"By the way, where does Dawei want to go?"

"对了" is used as an interruption or to start a new topic. It is commonly used to indicate that the speaker has suddenly thought of something or is going to correct or add to his previous comments. For example:

对了，你刚才说你想买什么？

对了，他是昨天上午来的，不是昨天下午来的。

⑥ 多有意思啊！

"How interesting!"

"多 + A/V + 啊！" is commonly used in exclamatory sentences that express strong feelings. The adverb "多" is usually used as an adverbial in front of adjectives or certain verbs. The modal particle "啊" is often used at the end of the sentence. For example:

她的汉字写得多漂亮啊！

《红楼梦》这部小说多感人啊！

我多喜欢长城的景色啊！

"太……了", which was learned before, is also a form of exclamatory sentence.

34（二）

王小云：陈老师、林娜，加油！快上来！

陈老师：力波、大为他们呢？⑦

王小云：他们已经爬上去了。咱们也快要到山顶了。

陈老师：别着急。我觉得有点儿累，林娜也累了，咱们就坐下来休息一会儿吧。⑧ 先喝点儿水再往上爬。

林　娜：这儿的景色多美啊！长城好像一条龙。⑨ 看，下边都是山，火车从山里开出来了。我要多拍些照片寄回家去。

王小云：你来过这儿吗？

林　娜：来过。是秋天来的。那时候长城的景色跟现在很不一样。

王小云：是啊。现在是冬天，今天还是阴天，要下雪了。

林　娜：在长城上看下雪，太美了。

陈老师：今天这儿的气温是零下十度。可是你们知道吗？广州今天是零上二十度。

谈天气
Talking about weather

林　娜：中国真大。北方还是这么冷的冬天，可是春天已经到了南方。你们看，力波怎么走下来了？

丁力波：喂，你们怎么还没上来？要帮忙吗？⑩

王小云：不用。你不用跑过来，我们自己能上去。陈老师，您休息好了吗？

陈老师：休息好了。小云，你帮我站起来……

*　　*　　*　　*

林　娜：啊！我们爬上长城来了！

生词 New Words

1.	加油	jiāyóu	VO	to make an extra effort, to cheer sb. on 给我们加油，给男同学加油
	加	jiā	V	to increase, to add
2.	累	lèi	A	tired 有点儿累，特别累，这么累，从来不累，觉得很累
3.	条	tiáo	M	strip, long narrow piece (*a measure word for something long, narrow or thin, like rivers, dragons, trousers*) 一条龙
4.	龙	lóng	N	dragon 好像龙，画龙，龙的故事
5.	拍	pāi	V	to take (a picture) 拍照片，拍一张照片，拍山顶的景色，给他们拍照片
6.	秋天	qiūtiān	N	autumn 在秋天，喜欢秋天，北京的秋天，秋天的天气
7.	阴天	yīntiān	N	cloudy day, overcast day 今天阴天，阴天的时候
8.	下雪	xià xuě	V O	to snow 要下雪了，可能下雪，下雪天
	雪	xuě	N	snow 雪人，雪景，一场大雪，雪花
9.	气温	qìwēn	N	air temperature 今天的气温，气温高，气温低
	温	wēn	N	temperature 气温，体温，高温，水温
10.	零下	líng xià		below zero

11. 度	dù	M	degree (*a measure word for temperature*) 十度，零下五度，气温是多少度
12. 北方	běifāng	N	north 在北方，到北方，北方人，北方话
13. 春天	chūntiān	N	spring 春天到了，春天的时候，南方的春天，春天的气温
14. 帮忙	bāngmáng	VO	to help 要帮忙，不用帮忙，请帮(个)忙，常常帮忙
帮	bāng	V	to help, to assist 请帮我一下，帮同学
*15. 站	zhàn	V	to stand
*16. 起	qǐ	V	to rise, to get up 起来，起床，站起来，坐起来
17. 广州	Guǎngzhōu	PN	Guangzhou (capital of Guangdong Province)

补充生词 Supplementary Words

1. 天气预报	tiānqì yùbào		weather forecast
2. 晴天	qíngtiān	N	fine day
3. 中国国航	Zhōngguó Guóháng	PN	Air China (CA)
4. 起飞	qǐfēi	V	to take off
5. 街	jiē	N	street
6. 停车场	tíngchēchǎng	N	parking lot
7. 菜单	càidān	N	menu
8. 渴	kě	A	thirsty
9. 只	zhī	M	(*a measure word for cats, sheep, birds and bears, etc.*)
10. 熊	xióng	N	bear
11. 害怕	hàipà	V	to be afraid, to fear

12. 棵	kē	M	(*a measure word for plants*)
13. 树	shù	N	tree
14. 装	zhuāng	V	to pretend to be sth./sb.
15. 动	dòng	V	to move
16. 危险	wēixiǎn	A	dangerous

注释 Notes

⑦ 力波、大为他们呢？

"Where are Libo and Dawei?"

"力波、大为他们" is an appositive phrase. "力波、大为" is equivalent to "他们". For example: 小云她们，我们大家. "张介元教授", a phrase which was learned before, is also an appositive phrase.

⑧ 我觉得有点儿累，林娜也累了，咱们就坐下来休息一会儿吧。

"I feel a little tired. Lin Na is tired, too. Let's sit down to rest for a while."

The adverb "就" (3) links the previous statement and its conclusion. For example:

爬上山以后，他们都觉得有点儿累，就坐下来休息。

王贵觉得很不好意思，就问张才："刚才它跟你说什么了？"

⑨ 长城好像一条龙。

"The Great Wall looks like a dragon."

The dragon is a magical creature in ancient Chinese legends. It has a long body, scales, horns, and feet. It can walk, fly, swim, and summon cloud and rain. As the feudal age came to an end, the dragon was no longer the symbol of imperial emperor. However, Chinese people all over the world still consider themselves as the "Descendants of the Dragon." Images of dragon and "dragon culture" can be seen everywhere across China.

⑩ 喂，你们怎么还没上来？要帮忙吗？

"Hi, why haven't you come up? Do you need any help?"

Please note the difference between "帮忙" and "帮助": the verb "帮助" may be followed by an object (for example: 帮助我，帮助他们); whereas "帮忙" cannot be followed by an object. For example,"要帮忙" or "来帮忙" is correct, but "帮忙我" is not.

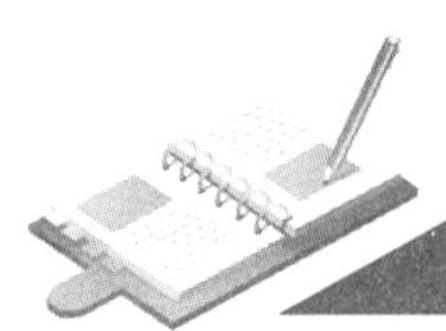

二、练习 Exercises

练习与运用 Drills and Practice

核心句 KEY SENTENCES

1. 我们爬上长城来了。
2. 要放假了。
3. 机票已经买好了。
4. 他说他要从山下爬上去，再从山顶走下来。
5. 咱们也快要到山顶了。
6. 我觉得有点儿累，林娜也累了，咱们就坐下来休息一会儿吧。
7. 这儿的景色多美啊！
8. 我要多拍些照片寄回家去。

1. 熟读下列词组 Read the following phrases until you learn them by heart

（1）有一个打算　有什么打算　说说你的打算
打算拍照片　打算游泳　打算爬山　打算去长城　打算踢足球
打算锻炼身体

（2）建议去打工　建议多练习　建议听音乐会　建议访问老演员
建议去看越剧
提建议　有一个建议　好建议　新建议　合适的建议

（3）写好汉字　画好画儿　复习好课文　做好练习　拍好照片
化好妆　填好表　办好借书证　借好书　打好电话
买好衣服　换好钱　租好房子

（4）多好啊　多漂亮啊　多流利啊　多帅啊　多便宜啊　多合适啊
多热啊　多高啊　多远啊　多优美啊　多难啊　多累啊
多高兴啊　多可爱啊　多感人啊　多容易啊

（5）林娜她们　陈老师他们　爸爸妈妈他们　姐姐她们

（6）要开学了　要复习了　要考试了　要放假了　要过圣诞节了
快要上课了　快要开始了　快要开门了　快要爬上山顶了
快要到广州了

（7）爬上来　走上去　坐下来　送下去　提出来　开出去　拐过来
游过去　站起来　爬上长城来　走下楼去　跑回学院来
寄回家去　提出问题来　送出国去

（8）西安我去过　电影票买好了　太极拳学过　汉字写过一遍
生词念过两遍

2. 句型替换 Pattern drills

（1）A：现在几点？
B：七点五十。
A：要上课了，快走吧。
B：等一下儿，我就来。

8:45	出发
9:10	上车
11:55	吃饭
4:20	去游泳
3:25	踢足球
5:12	拍照片

（2）A：他们快要去泰山了吧？
B：他们明天就要去泰山了。
A：他们去过泰山没有？
B：他们没有去过。

来北京	下星期
去访问广州	下个月
来参观花园小区	星期五
到山顶	一会儿

（3）A：谁从长城上走下来了？
B：大为他们从长城上走下来了。

山下	爬上来
楼里	走出来
外边	走进来
前边	跑过来

（4）A：宋华他们呢？
B：他们爬上山去了。

陈老师	走进	饭馆
你朋友	跑下	楼
你同学	住进	宿舍楼
你外婆	走回	家

（5）A：他从邮局寄出一些照片去了吗？
B：他没有从邮局寄出一些照片去。

商场	买回	两件旗袍	来
右边	踢进	一个球	去
海关	取回	一个包裹	来
老师那儿	拿回	本子	来
楼下	拿上	一些书	来
外边	带回	烤鸭	来

（6）A：机票已经买好了吗？
B：还没有买好呢。
A：（春节）买机票多难啊！

课文	复习	不容易
客厅	打扫	累
文章	写	难
饭	做	累

（7）A：圣诞节过得怎么样？
B：圣诞节过得很好。

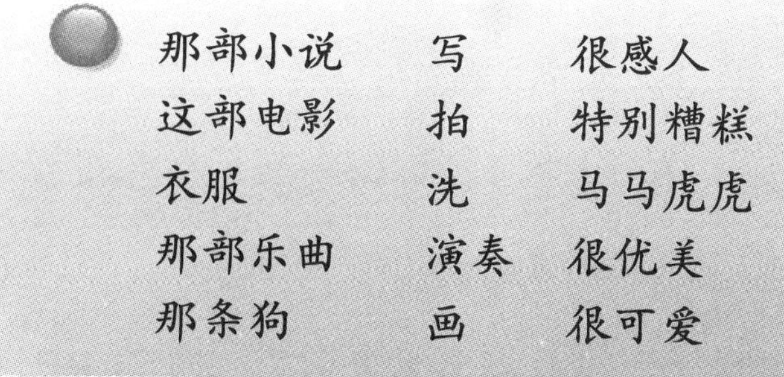

那部小说	写	很感人
这部电影	拍	特别糟糕
衣服	洗	马马虎虎
那部乐曲	演奏	很优美
那条狗	画	很可爱

（8）A：旅行的事儿她知道得多不多？
B：旅行的事儿她知道得不多。

汉语语法	考	好
生活口语	说	流利
学过的汉字	写	漂亮
老师的问题	回答	快
这一课的生词	用	对

3. 课堂活动　Classroom activity

Have a conversation with your classmate: A says he/she is planning to do something, and then B uses “可是要……了” to explain why this cannot be done. For example:

A：我打算从现在开始在系办公室打工。

B：可是要放假了……

4. 会话练习　Conversation exercises

【谈计划　Talking about plans】

（1）A：快要放假了，你有什么打算？

B：我打算________________________。你呢？

A：去年我去过一次上海，今年我想先__________，再__________。

B：你打算在家里住多长时间？

A：我想住十天。

（2）A：要开学了！

B：是啊。________________________？

A：上次我的汉语语法考得糟糕极了，我打算用一个星期的时间先复习一下。

B：你打算怎么复习？

A：我去图书馆借了____________________，我想在这个星期看一遍。

B：要我帮忙吗？

A：你能帮助我，当然好极了。

【提建议 Making suggestions】

（1）A：你要提高汉语水平，我有一个好建议。

B：____________________？快说说。

A：我建议你放假的时候到北京去旅行一次，在那儿学习一个月汉语。

B：______________________________。

（2）A：新年你打算去哪儿？

B：我还没有想好呢。你帮我提提建议吧。

A：我打算去广州旅行，看看那儿的花儿。我建议你也______________。

B：太好了！咱们一起去吧！我特别喜欢花儿。

【谈天气 Talking about weather】

（1）A：今天多冷啊，你听天气预报（tiānqì yùbào）了没有？

B：__________________，天气预报说今天是阴天，中午以后还要下雪。

A：气温是多少？

B：气温是零下十二度。这儿的冬天________________？

A：这么冷，我有点儿不习惯，可是我很想看下雪的景色。

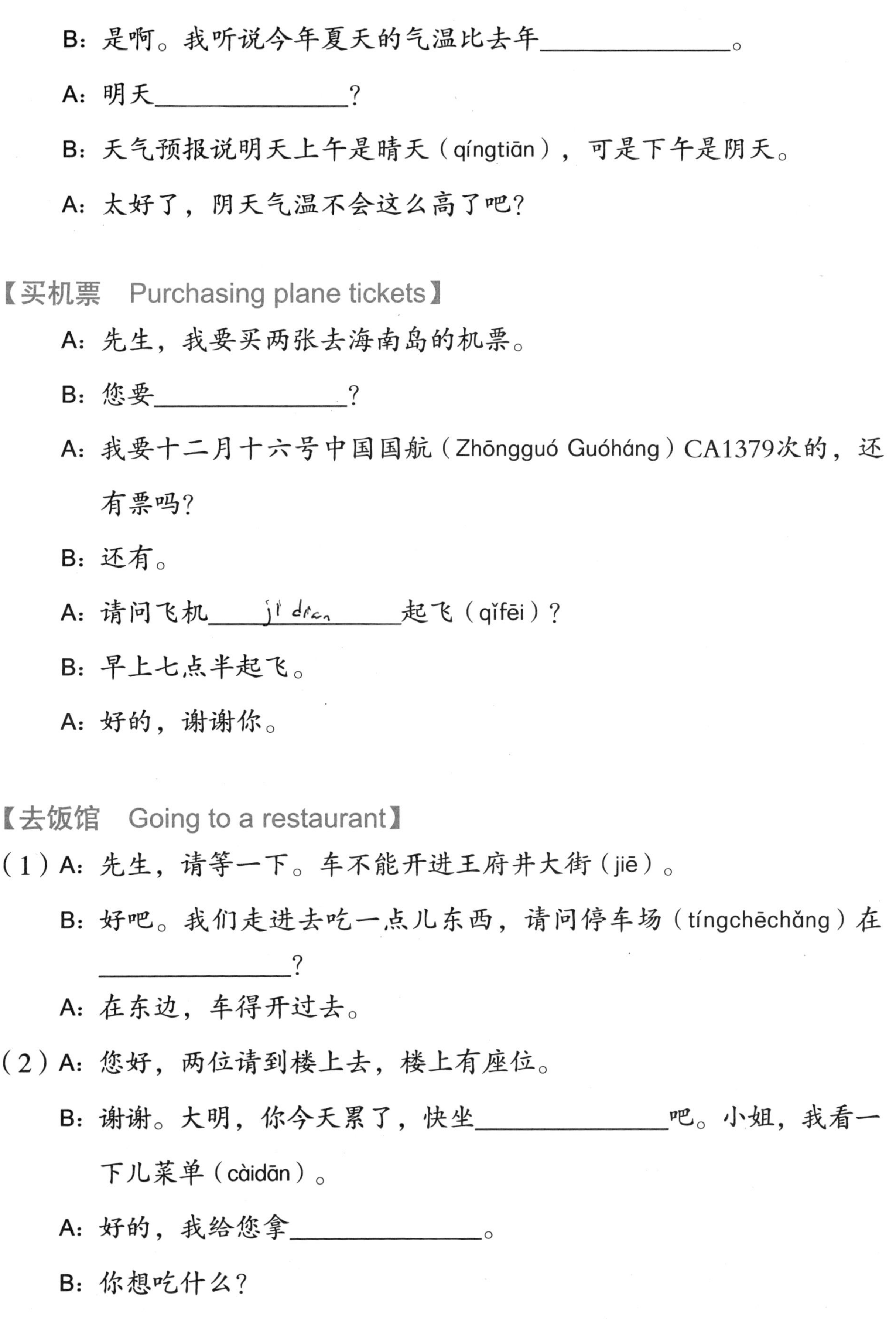

（2）A：今年夏天太热了！我每天都得去游泳。

B：是啊。我听说今年夏天的气温比去年______________。

A：明天______________？

B：天气预报说明天上午是晴天（qíngtiān），可是下午是阴天。

A：太好了，阴天气温不会这么高了吧？

【买机票　Purchasing plane tickets】

A：先生，我要买两张去海南岛的机票。

B：您要______________？

A：我要十二月十六号中国国航（Zhōngguó Guóháng）CA1379次的，还有票吗？

B：还有。

A：请问飞机____ji dian______起飞（qǐfēi）？

B：早上七点半起飞。

A：好的，谢谢你。

【去饭馆　Going to a restaurant】

（1）A：先生，请等一下。车不能开进王府井大街（jiē）。

B：好吧。我们走进去吃一点儿东西，请问停车场（tíngchēchǎng）在______________？

A：在东边，车得开过去。

（2）A：您好，两位请到楼上去，楼上有座位。

B：谢谢。大明，你今天累了，快坐______________吧。小姐，我看一下儿菜单（càidān）。

A：好的，我给您拿______________。

B：你想吃什么？

C：先来点儿水吧，我渴（kě）极了。

B：好，请先来两杯水。咱们吃饺子，______________？

C：没问题。小姐，我们要一斤饺子。能不能快点儿？

A：行，一会儿就给您送上来。

5. 看图说话 Describe the following pictures

❶ 爬上去

❷ 走过来

❸ 跑下楼来

❹ 寄回英国去

6. 交际练习 Communication exercises

(1) Summer holiday is coming soon. You and your friends are discussing your respective plans for it.

(2) Give your classmate three suggestions and try to convince him / her to take your advice.

(3) Talk about the weather in each of the four seasons in your city .

阅读与复述 Reading Comprehension and Paraphrasing

36 大黑熊（xióng）跟你说什么了

很早以前，有两个年轻人，一个叫王贵，一个叫张才。王贵比张才大。因为他们常在一起玩儿，是很好的朋友，大家都说王贵、张才两个人就好像哥哥弟弟一样。

一天，他们上山去玩儿。爬上山以后，他们都觉得有点儿累，就坐下来休息。这时候，他们看见一只（zhī）大黑熊走过来了。他们都很害怕（hàipà）。旁边有一棵（kē）大树（shù），王贵很快就爬上去了。张才不会爬树，非常着急。可是他听奶奶说过，熊不吃死人，他就装（zhuāng）成死人。大黑熊在张才旁边走过来走过去，看他不动（dòng），它想这一定是个死人，就走了。王贵看见大黑熊走远了，就从树上爬下来，张才也站了起来。王贵觉得很不好意思，就问张才："刚才大黑熊跟你说什么了？"

张才有点儿不高兴，他说："大黑熊刚才跟我说：年轻人，我告诉你，在危险（wēixiǎn）的时候，就能知道谁是你的真朋友！"

三、语法 Grammar

1 动作即将发生 An action that is going to take place soon

"要……了" indicates that an action or situation is going to take place soon. The adverb "要" indicates "be going to" or "will". "就" or "快" can be used in front of "要" as an adverbial to indicate urgency. The subject can often be omitted in this type of sentence.

要 + V/A (+O) + 了

Subject	Predicate				
	Adverbial	要	V / A	(O)	了
		要	开学		了。
(天气)		要	热		了。
他们	明天 就	要	去	泰山	了。
我们	快	要	到	山顶	了。

This type of sentence can be transformed into a question simply by adding “吗” at the end. A negative response can be formed by using the negative adverb “没有” or “还没有呢”. For example:

A：火车要开了吗?

B：没有。

A：我们就要到海南岛了吗?

B：还没有呢。

Note:

❶ A time adverbial can be added in front of “要……了” or “就要……了”, for example, “他们明天要走了” or “他们明天就要走了”. However, time adverbials cannot be added before “快要……了”. For example, one cannot say “他们明天快要走了”.

❷ “要……了” can be changed to “快……了”, without changing the meaning of the sentence. For example: “要放假了” = “快放假了”.

2 复合趋向补语 The complex directional complement

A directional verb (“上”, “下”, “进”, “出”, “回”, “过”, “起”), followed by a simple directional complement (“来” or “去”), can be used as a complement to other verbs. This kind of directional complement indicates the direction of the action, thus forming a compound directional complement to give a detailed description of the action. For example:

我从山上跑下去。

他们从外边走进来了。

Common compound directional complements are as follows:

	上	下	进	出	回	过	起
来	上来	下来	进来	出来	回来	过来	起来
去	上去	下去	进去	出去	回去	过去	X

The basic meanings of these compound directional complements:

上来 —— to come up　　上去—— to go up

下来 —— to come down　　下去—— to go down

进来 —— to come in　　进去—— to go in

出来 —— to come out　　出去—— to go out

回来 —— to come back　　回去—— to go back

过来 —— to come over　　过去—— to go over

起来 —— to get up

The relationship between the direction of the action and the speaker (or the topic being discussed), which is indicated by "来" or "去", is the same as in the case of a simple directional complement (please refer to Lesson 16).

If an object is used after the verb of a compound directional complement, and the object is a word or phrase which indicates location or place, then the object must be placed before "来" or "去". For example:

我们爬上长城来了。

我要多拍些照片寄回家去。

3 无标志被动句 Notional passive sentences

In some Chinese sentences, the subject itself is the object of an action. Structurally, it is not different from a sentence in which the subject is the doer of an action, except that it has obviously a passive notion. The notional passive sentence is often used to emphasize the explanation of the object of an action. The subject of the sentence usually refers to something which is definite. For example:

越剧票已经买好了。

那部小说看过没有?

饭已经做好了，还没有拿进去。

旅行的事儿她知道得很多。

四、汉字 Chinese Characters

1 汉字的构字法(9) Methods of constructing Chinese characters (9)

The pictophonetic method (形声法) (5)

In this method, a character is formed by placing the semantic component inside and the phonetic component outside. For example: 问, 闷, 闻. There are very few characters of this type.

2 认写基本汉字 Learn and write basic Chinese characters

(1) 山 丨 山 山
shān hill, mountain 3 strokes

(2) 飞(飛) ⺄ ⺄ 飞
fēi to fly 3 strokes

(3) 义(義) 丶 ㇒ 义
yì meaning 3 strokes

(4) 龙(龍) 一 ナ 九 龙 龙
lóng dragon 5 strokes

(5) 雨 一 ㄏ 冂 币 雨 雨 雨 雨
yǔ rain 8 strokes

(6) 成 一 厂 万 成 成 成
chéng to accomplish 6 strokes

3 认写课文中的汉字 Learn and write the Chinese characters in the texts

(1) 爬 pá

爬 → 爪 + 巴 8 strokes

叚 jiǎ ㇇ ㇇ ㇏ 𠂆 𠃜 𠃜 𠬝 𠬞 叚

(Pay attention to the difference from "段 (duàn)".) 9 strokes

(2) 放假 fàngjià

假 → 亻 + 叚 11 strokes

廾 (nòngzìdǐr, the bottom part of the character "弄 (nòng)")

一 ナ 廾 3 strokes

(3) 打算 dǎsuan

算 → ⺮ + 目 + 廾 14 strokes

(4) 顶 dǐng（頂）

顶 → 丁 + 页 8 strokes

(5) 建议 jiànyì（建議）

议 → 讠 + 义 5 strokes

(6) 气温 qìwēn（氣溫）

温 → 氵 + 日 + 皿 12 strokes

(7) 景色 jǐngsè

景 → 日 + 京 12 strokes

(8) 游泳 yóuyǒng

泳 → 氵 + 永 8 strokes

(9) 冬天 dōngtiān

冬 → 夂 + ⺀ 5 strokes

(10) 夏天 xiàtiān

夏 → 一 + 自 + 夂　　10 strokes

(11) 导游 dǎoyóu（導游）

导 → 巳 + 寸　　6 strokes

(12) 长城 Chángchéng（長城）

城 → 土 + 成　　9 strokes

(13) 泰山 Tài Shān

泰 → 夫 + 氺　　10 strokes

乌 (niǎozìtóur, the top of "鸟(niǎo)")　′ ⺈ 勺 乌　　4 strokes

(14) 海南岛 Hǎinán Dǎo（海南島）

岛 → 乌 + 山　　7 strokes

(15) 孔子 Kǒngzǐ

孔 → 子 + 乚　　4 strokes

(16) 小燕子 Xiǎo Yànzi　　16 strokes

燕 → 廿 + 口 + 丬 + 匕 + 灬

(In the ancient form of the character "燕 (swallow)", "廿" represents the head of the swallow; "口" represents the body; "北" is separated by "口" to indicate the wings; and the bottom four dots make up the tail.)

(17) 累 lèi

累 → 田 + 糸　　11 strokes

(18) 条 tiáo（條）

条 → 夂 + 朩　　7 strokes

(19) 拍 pāi

拍 → 扌 + 白　　8 strokes

(20) 秋天 qiūtiān

秋 → 禾 + 火　　9 strokes

(21) 阴天 yīntiān（陰天）

阴 → 阝 + 月　　6 strokes

(22) 下雪 xià xuě

雪 → 雨 + 彐　　11 strokes

(23) 零（下） líng（xià）

零 → 雨 + 令　　13 strokes

(24) 度 dù

度 → 广 + 廿 + 又　　9 strokes

文化知识 Cultural Note

Eastern and Western China

China is a country with a vast territory. Its land area measures 9.6 million square kilometers, ranking the third in the world and only after Russia and Canada.

In general, China's physical structure is higher in the east and lower in the west. There are many mountainous areas and few plains. Its mountainous areas cover two-thirds of the total area; plains account for less than one-third and mainly in the east.

Comparatively speaking, Eastern China enjoys a better geological and weather condition. In addition to historical reasons, the majority of Chinese population live in the east. Eastern China is also the hub of China's agriculture, industry, commerce and finance. As a result, Eastern China is much more developed than Western China.

In 1999, China set out to launch the full-scale development program for the western regions, including Chongqing, Sichuan, Guizhou, Yunnan, Tibet, Shaanxi, Gansu, Ningxia, Xinjiang, Inner Mongolia, and Guangxi. With vast area and rich resources, Western China promises an even better future.

东部

广东

北京

上海

西部

云南

西藏

重庆

你舅妈也开始用电脑了

Your aunt began to use a computer, too.

Xiaoyun and Libo went to the railway station to pick up Xiaoyun's uncle and were told great changes have taken place in the lives of Shanghai farmers. In this lesson, you will learn how to talk about ongoing actions and changing circumstances.

一、课文 Text

37

接人和送行
Picking someone up and seeing someone off

丁力波：小云，火车快到了吧？

王小云：从上海到北京的D308次七点十九分到，[1] 现在七点，快到了。

丁力波：你舅舅是农民吗？

王小云：是。他过去是上海郊区的农民，现在当蔬菜公司的经理了。

丁力波：他来过北京吗？

谈正在进行的动作
Talking about an action in progress

王小云：他来过两次，可是我都不在。上次他来的时候，我正在南方旅行呢。

丁力波：看，那个人正在问路呢。我们过去看看，那是不是你舅舅？

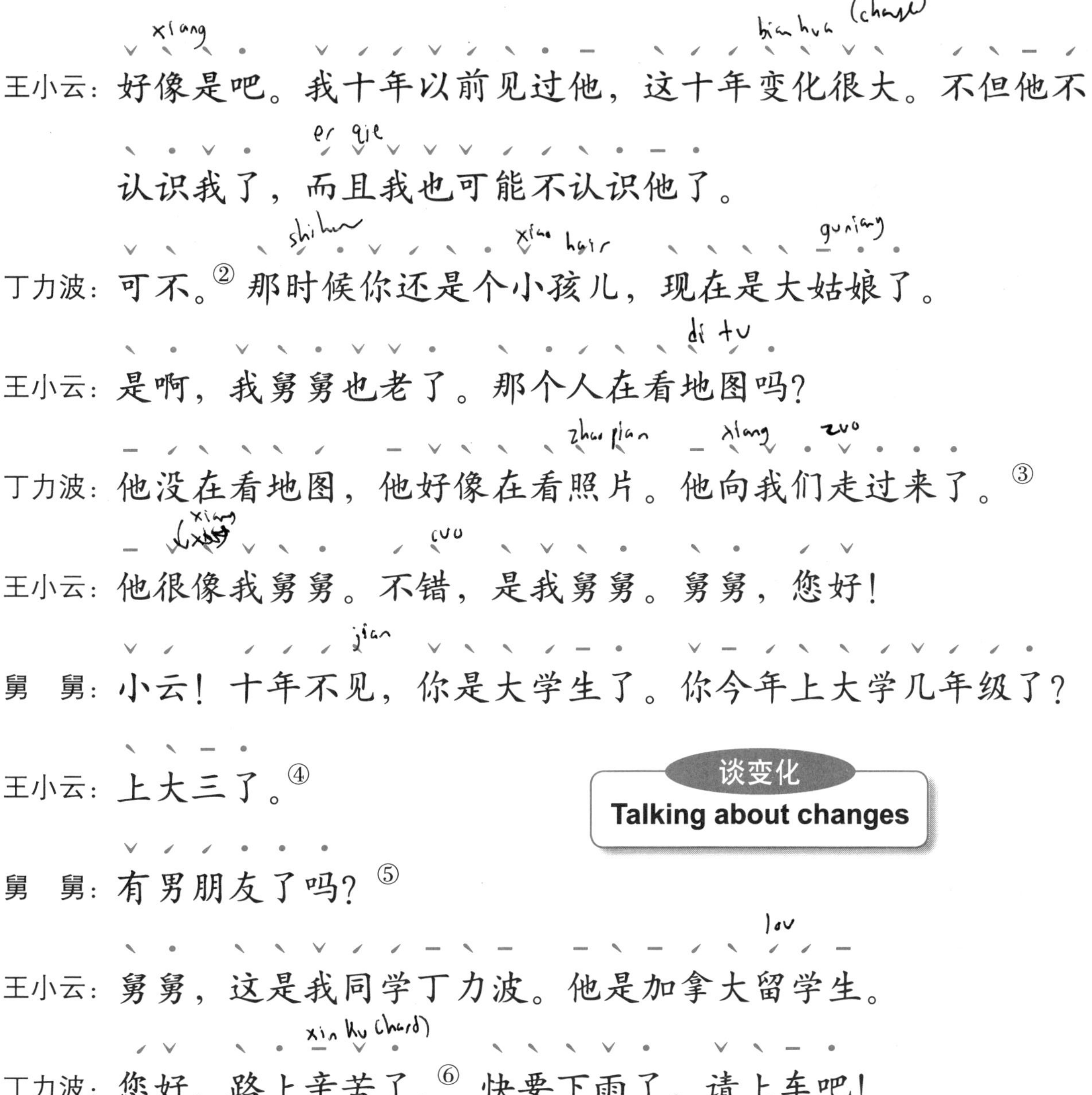

王小云：好像是吧。我十年以前见过他，这十年变化很大。不但他不认识我了，而且我也可能不认识他了。

丁力波：可不。[②] 那时候你还是个小孩儿，现在是大姑娘了。

王小云：是啊，我舅舅也老了。那个人在看地图吗？

丁力波：他没在看地图，他好像在看照片。他向我们走过来了。[③]

王小云：他很像我舅舅。不错，是我舅舅。舅舅，您好！

舅　舅：小云！十年不见，你是大学生了。你今年上大学几年级了？

王小云：上大三了。[④]

谈变化
Talking about changes

舅　舅：有男朋友了吗？[⑤]

王小云：舅舅，这是我同学丁力波。他是加拿大留学生。

丁力波：您好，路上辛苦了。[⑥] 快要下雨了，请上车吧！

生词 New Words

1. 舅妈	jiùmā	N	aunt (wife of mother's brother) 你舅妈，舅妈家，叫舅妈
2. 舅舅	jiùjiu	N	uncle (mother's brother) 你舅舅，是我舅舅，等舅舅，有两个舅舅
3. 农民	nóngmín	N	farmer, peasant 郊区的农民，一个农民

4. 当	dāng	V	to serve as, to be 当经理，当老师，当导游，当演员，当教练，当售货员，当司机，当医生
5. 蔬菜	shūcài	N	vegetable 蔬菜公司，一些蔬菜，买一斤蔬菜，吃一点儿蔬菜
菜	cài	N	vegetable 白菜，买菜，种菜
6. 正在	zhèngzài	Adv	in the process of, in the middle of (*used as a key word of a progressive construction*) 正在南方旅行，正在等舅舅，正在上课，正在考试，正在爬山
*在	zài	Adv	(*used to indicate an action in progress*) 在访问，在比赛，在化妆，在看照片，在等舅舅
7. 问路	wèn lù	VO	to ask for directions, to ask the way 正在问路，在问路，去问路，应该问路
8. 变化	biànhuà	N	change 变化很大，变化不多，有一个小变化
9. 不但	búdàn	Conj	not only
10. 而且	érqiě	Conj	but also, and
11. 可不	kěbù	Adv	exactly, right, that's just the way it is
12. 小孩儿	xiǎoháir	N	kid, child 是个小孩儿，有小孩儿，一个小孩儿
13. 地图	dìtú	N	map 看地图，查地图，买地图，一张地图，中国地图
14. 向	xiàng	Prep	towards, to 向我们走过来，向他跑过去，向你问好，向她介绍
*15. 像	xiàng	V	to be alike, to take after 像我舅舅，很像那部电影的女主角，有点儿像售票员，不太像工作人员
*16. 上	shàng	V	to be engaged in (work, study, etc.) at a fixed time 上小学，上中学，上大学，上大三
17. 大学	dàxué	N	university, college 上大学，念大学，北京大学，有名的大学，大学生活，大学的变化

18. 年级	niánjí	N	grade 三年级，大学四年级，上一年级，二年级同学
19. 辛苦	xīnkǔ	A	hard, toilsome 路上辛苦了，特别辛苦，这么辛苦，辛苦极了
20. 下雨	xià yǔ	V O	to rain 要下雨了，可能下雨，下雨的天气
雨	yǔ	N	rain 一场大雨，下小雨

注释　Notes

① 从上海到北京的D308次七点十九分到。

"Train D308 from Shanghai to Beijing will arrive at 19:19."

In the construction "从……到……", "从" and "到" may be followed by words indicating either location or time to express distance or duration. For example:

从美国到中国很远。

从广州到海南岛不太远。

他从去年9月到今年6月在语言学院学习中国文学。

我每天从下午1点到3点去锻炼身体。

There are many train numbers in China. They are classified based on the running speed. The train number is generally formed by an English letter and a number. The trains without an English letter are normal speed trains or slow trains, for example, Train 4442. Fast trains are indicated by the capital letter "K", for example, Train K1117, while express trains are indicated by the capital letter "T", for example, Train T190. Direct express trains start with the capital letter "Z", ie., nonstop trains, for instance, Train Z11. Bullet trains start with the capital letter "D", which are the fastest trains at the present time, for example, Train D308. Besides, during the Spring Festival and summer vacation when an extremely large number of people are on the move, there are additional temporary trains, the number of which begin with the capital letter "L", for example, Train L7737.

② 可不。

"Exactly!"

"可不" indicates one's agreement with what another person said. It is interchangeable with "可不是". For example:

A：您有七十岁了吧？

B：可不（是），今年五月就到七十岁了。

③ 他向我们走过来了。

"He is walking towards us."

The preposition "向" denotes the direction of an action, for example: 向东看, 向图书馆走去, 向他问好.

④ 上大三了。

"上大三了" means "上大学三年级了(be a college junior)", "大学几年级" is usually abbreviated as "大几", for example, "大一", "大二", "大三", "大四". Therefore, "你上大学几年级了？" can be abbreviated as "你上大几了？"

⑤ 有男朋友了吗？

"Do you have a boyfriend?"

In China, when a senior family member, especially an elder relative, asks a younger member of the family about his / her age, occupation, income, family situation and marital status, it is not meant to pry into the privacy of the younger one, but shows the elder's concern for his junior. Therefore, such questions shouldn't be perceived as nosey or offensive. Of course, the younger one does not need to give direct, exhaustive answers, either.

⑥ 您好，路上辛苦了。

"How are you? Did you have a good trip? (literally: You must have had a tiring journey.)"

"路上辛苦了" is a common expression used to greet and show concern for someone who has just returned from a trip. It is equivalent to expressions such as "一路辛苦", "路上一定很辛苦吧？" or "辛苦了".

38（二）

王小云：舅妈呢？怎么没有来？她说过要跟您一起来北京。

舅　舅：你舅妈在种温室蔬菜呢。她现在很忙，这次不来了。

王小云：现在你们种蔬菜的收入怎么样？

舅　舅：我们种温室蔬菜，收入比以前好多了。

王小云：家里的生活怎么样？⑦

谈生活情况
Talking about living conditions

舅　舅：生活还可以。⑧ 前年我们盖了一座两层的小楼，去年还买了一辆汽车。现在我们去别的城市也方便了。

丁力波：您的生活水平比城里人的还高。⑨

舅　舅：我们村吃的、穿的、住的都不比城里差。问题是我们农民的文化水平还比城里人的低一些。⑩

王小云：现在农民没有文化真不行。

舅　舅：你说得很对，农民也都要学习新技术。温室蔬菜是用电脑管理的。你舅妈也开始用电脑了。

王小云：今年我一定要去看看你们。

生词 New Words

1. 种	zhòng	V	to grow, to plant 种菜，种蔬菜，种花儿，正在种，打算种，建议种
2. 温室	wēnshì	N	greenhouse 温室蔬菜，郊区的温室，种温室蔬菜
*温	wēn	A	warm 温水
3. 收入	shōurù	N	income, earnings 种蔬菜的收入，农民的收入，一些收入，主要收入，别的收入，提高收入
收	shōu	V	to accept, to receive 收入，收衣服
入	rù	V	to enter 入口，出入，入学
4. 前年	qiánnián	N	the year before last 前年的收入，前年的生活
5. 盖	gài	V	to build 盖楼，盖房子，盖温室，盖商店，盖宿舍，盖医院

6. 座	zuò	M	(*a measure word for mountains, buildings and other similar immovable objects*) 一座楼，一座山，一座两层的小楼，盖一座大楼
7. 辆	liàng	M	(*a measure word for vehicles*) 一辆车，一辆出租车，一辆公共汽车
8. 城市	chéngshì	N	city 城市的生活，城市里的人，一个大城市
城	chéng	N	city 城里，城外，去城里买东西
9. 方便	fāngbiàn	A	convenient 很(不)方便，不太方便，方便的时候
10. 村	cūn	N	village 村里，村里的农民，向村里走去
11. 文化	wénhuà	N	culture, education, literacy 中国文化，民族文化；文化水平，大学文化，有文化，没有文化，学文化
12. 低	dī	A	low 水平低，收入低，气温低，房租低
13. 技术	jìshù	N	technology, skill 新技术，电脑技术，有技术，懂技术，学习技术，发展技术，提高技术水平
14. 管理	guǎnlǐ	V	to manage, to administer 用电脑管理，管理大学，管理银行，提高管理水平
管	guǎn	V	to manage, to discipline 管这件事，管学生

补充生词 Supplementary Words

1. 暖和	nuǎnhuo	A	warm
2. 凉快	liángkuai	A	cool
3. 机场	jīchǎng	N	airport
4. 接(人)	jiē (rén)	V	to pick up (someone)
5. 行李	xíngli	N	baggage, luggage
6. 箱子	xiāngzi	N	box, case, trunk
7. 一路平安	yílù píng'ān	IE	to have a safe journey, bon voyage

8. 停	tíng	V	to stop, to cease
9. 爱人	àiren	N	husband or wife, spouse
10. 士兵	shìbīng	N	soldier
11. 将军	jiāngjūn	N	general
12. 站岗	zhàngǎng	VO	to stand guard
13. 冻	dòng	V	to freeze
14. 发抖	fādǒu	V	to shake, to tremble, to shiver
15. 生火	shēnghuǒ	VO	to make a fire
16. 正常	zhèngcháng	A	normal, regular
17. 声	shēng	N	sound, voice

注释 Notes

⑦ 家里的生活怎么样?

"How is the living condition at home?"

⑧ 生活还可以。

"It's OK."

The family of Wang Xiaoyun's uncle lives in the outskirts of Shanghai, one of the most economically developed regions in China; therefore, his family's standard of living is fairly high. However, to be modest, he said "生活还可以".

⑨ 您的生活水平比城里人的还高。

"Your living standard is even higher than that of city dwellers."

Here the adverb "还" (3) in a comparative sentence is used to indicate a higher degree. For example:

今天比昨天还冷。 (Yesterday was already very cold.)

您的生活水平比城里人的还高。(The city dwellers' living standard is already very high.)

⑩ 问题是我们农民的文化水平还比城里人的低一些。

"The problem is that the education level of we farmers is still a bit lower than that of city dwellers."

"文化水平" refers to the level of education in this case.

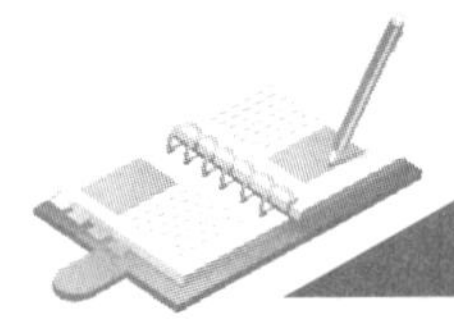

二、练习 Exercises

练习与运用 Drills and Practice

核心句 KEY SENTENCES

1. 你舅妈也开始用电脑了。
2. 从上海到北京的D308次七点十九分到。
3. 看，那个人正在问路呢。
4. 他现在当蔬菜公司的经理了。
5. 不但他不认识我了，而且我也可能不认识他了。
6. 我舅舅也老了。
7. 你是大学生了，你今年上大学几年级了？
8. 你舅妈在种温室蔬菜呢。

1. 熟读下列词组 Read the following phrases until you learn them by heart

（1）当演员　当教授　当售票员　当导游　当画家　当记者　当男主角
当出租车司机　当商场售货员　当公司经理

（2）从中国到欧洲　从前门到王府井　从花园小区到长安大戏院
从东边到西边　从汉语系到英语系　从山顶到山下　从城里到村里
从阳台到客厅　从银行到邮局　从八点到十点　从上午到下午
从昨天到今天　从圣诞节到新年　从前年到去年　从春天到秋天
从去年冬天到今年夏天　从早到晚

（3）向他走过去　向我们跑过来　向山顶爬去　向他学习　向她介绍

（4）老了　热了　高了　难了　累了　低了　对了　合适了　便宜了
上四年级了　上大学了　当教授了　租新房子了
是大学生了　是蔬菜公司经理了　是越剧团演员了

是有名的画家了　是足球队教练了

有女朋友了　有孙女儿了　有小孩儿了　有变化了　有电脑课了

（5）在说　在想　在用　在喝　在找　在查词典　在看地图　在打电话

在打扫房子　在买东西

正在听　正在唱　正在演　正在办　正在等人　正在练习汉字

在写呢　在画呢　在游泳呢　在上课呢　在问路呢　在爬山呢

正在念呢　正在睡觉呢　正在填表呢　正在寄包裹呢

正在种蔬菜呢　正在拍照片呢

（6）不但旧而且脏　不但对而且快　不但感人而且优美　不但年轻而且漂亮

不但喜欢音乐，而且喜欢美术　不但学习汉语，而且学习中国文化

不但盖了新楼，而且买了汽车　不但种温室蔬菜，而且用电脑管理

2. 句型替换　Pattern drills

（1）A：现在是冬天了。

B：是啊，天气冷了。

春天　暖和（nuǎnhuo）
夏天　热
秋天　凉快（liángkuai）
十月　很舒服

（2）A：已经两点了，怎么还不开始呢？

B：我们在等小燕子呢。

A：她有事儿，今天不来了。

出发　病了　去
开车　有点儿累　去参观
比赛　去郊区了　能来参加

（3）A：他正在做什么？

B：他正在种蔬菜。

A：他跟谁一起种蔬菜？

B：他跟村里的农民一起种蔬菜。

看电视　他朋友
看球赛　他同学
听音乐　他舅舅
游泳　教练
拍照片　导游

（4）A：他们在唱歌吗？

B：他们没在唱歌，他们在唱京剧呢。

（没有，他们唱京剧呢。）

比赛	练习
参观	工作
复习	写汉字
散步	打太极拳

（5）A：他们正在哪儿盖楼呢？

B：他们正在城里盖楼呢。

A：你去过他们那儿吗？

B：我没有去过。

吃饭	饭馆里	那个饭馆
访问	村里	他们村
玩儿	花园里	那个花园
演奏	戏院里	那个戏院

（6）A：你给她打电话的时候，

她正在做什么呢？

B：我给她打电话的时候，

她正在看地图呢。

去看她	睡觉
找车站	问路
到她家	给朋友写信
走进办公室	用电脑

（7）A：你们下午从几点到几点上课？

B：我们从两点到四点 上课。

办公	1:30	5:30
锻炼	4:00	6:00
参观	1:00	5:00
比赛	3:45	6:00

（8）A：你弟弟上几年级了？

B：他上二年级了。

A：他学习好吗？

B：他不但学习好，而且身体也很好。

会打太极拳	会游泳
喜欢看电影	喜欢看戏
学习汉语	学习中国文化
常常踢足球	参加足球赛

3. 课堂活动　Classroom activity

A asks B a question and B replies; then B asks C a question, and C replies; ...

（1）D308次是从哪儿到哪儿的火车？
（2）火车快到了吗？
（3）小云的舅舅是上海人吗？
（4）舅舅现在是种蔬菜的农民吗？
（5）舅舅来过北京吗？
（6）那个中年人正在做什么？
（7）小云什么时候见过舅舅？
（8）舅舅还认识小云吗？小云呢？
（9）舅舅有什么变化？
（10）那个中年人在看地图吗？
（11）小云今年上大学几年级了？
（12）小云的舅妈来北京了吗？
（13）舅妈在做什么？
（14）现在舅舅他们种蔬菜的收入怎么样？
（15）舅舅家里的生活怎么样？
（16）现在的温室蔬菜是用什么管理的？
（17）舅妈有什么变化？
（18）（问你的中国朋友）你今年上大学几年级了？

4. 会话练习　Conversation exercises

【接人和送行　Picking someone up and seeing someone off】

（1）A：请问，从北京来的飞机到了没有？

B：________________，还有十分钟。

A：谢谢。

A：啊，张先生，您来了。

C：你好！谢谢你来机场（jīchǎng）接（jiē）我。

A：____________，张先生。您的行李（xíngli）都到了吗？

C：两个箱子（xiāngzi）都到了。

A：您在这儿等一等，我去叫出租车。

C：______________________________。

（2）A：雨平，我在这儿呢！

B：小白！怎么样？路上辛苦吧？

A：还可以。你等了____________？

B：可不，火车晚了半个小时。

A：我也非常着急，想早点儿到北京。

B：来，把箱子给我，我帮你拿。

（3）A：这次在______________的时间太短了，以后我一定再来。

B：我有时间也一定去北京看你。火车六点十分就要开了，上车吧。

A：好，我到了北京就给你打电话。

B：别忘了，我等你的电话。祝你一路平安（yílù píng'ān）！

A：谢谢。______________！

B：____________！

【谈变化 Talking about changes】

（1）A：糟糕，下雪了。

B：是吗？我们不能去长城了。

A：下雪的时候长城________________，我们应该去拍些照片。

B：可是外边真冷。

A：可不，到零下十度了。咱们等雪停（tíng）了再去吧。

（2）A：不下雨了吧？

B：还在下呢。但是雨小点儿了。

A：现在已经九点半了，我们该走了。

B：好吧。这儿的冬天____________。

A：你不____________吧？

B：开始我觉得太冷，现在已经有点儿习惯了。

【谈生活情况　Talking about living conditions】

A：王先生，好久不见！还在大学____________吗？

B：我前年就不当老师了，现在开了一家翻译公司。

A：啊，当经理了。自己开公司一定不错吧？

B：还可以。公司跟大学很不一样，我开始不太习惯，现在______了。

A：听说你买了新房子？

B：是去年刚买的，在建国门。有时间你和你爱人（àiren）到我家去坐坐。

A：好，有时间____________。

5. 看图说话　Describe the following pictures

❶ 以前他不忙，现在他____________。

❷ 虽然现在刚到五月，但是天气已经____________。

③ 去年他学习音乐，今年他__________。

④ 他以前是游泳队队员，可是现在他__________。

⑤ 看

⑥ 考

6. 交际练习 Communication exercises

(1) You go to the airport to see off a friend who is leaving for the United States. Then, you rush off to the train station to pick up your younger brother.

(2) Tell your classmate about the changes you have experienced in the last couple of years.

(3) Discuss your present living conditions, and then compare it to that of your close friends.

阅读与复述 Reading Comprehension and Paraphrasing

40 士兵（shìbīng）和将军（jiāngjūn）的故事

一个冬天的晚上，天气非常冷，不但风很大，而且雪也很大。路上已经没有人了，可是有一个士兵正在外边站岗（zhàngǎng）。从下午到现在他还没有吃一点儿东西。他穿得又很少，胳膊和腿都冻(dòng)得发抖(fādǒu)。

这时候，就在离他不远的客厅里，将军在喝酒呢。桌上有很多吃的、喝的，士兵还给他生了火(shēngle huǒ)，客厅里非常暖和。将军喝了很多酒，觉得非常热，有点儿不舒服。他很不高兴，说："已经十二月了，应该冷了，可是现在还这么热，天气真不正常(zhèngcháng)！"

外边站岗的士兵听到了这些话，就大声(shēng)说："将军，您那儿的天气不正常，可是我这儿的天气很正常。您喜欢正常的天气，咱们就换一换地方，请您到外边来站一站吧。"

三、语法 Grammar

1 情况的变化(1) The change of circumstances(1)

The particle "了" (or: "了"②) is employed at the end of a sentence to indicate the change of circumstances or the emergence of some new situation or condition. "了" is often used in this way in a sentence with an adjectival predicate or a sentence with "是" or "有". For example:

你舅舅也老了。 (以前不老)

现在天气冷了。 (以前不冷)

雪大了。 (以前不大)

你是大学生了。 (以前不是)

我有男朋友了。 (以前没有)

In a sentence with a verbal predicate, the particle "了" (2) often confirms the completion or realization of some event or situation (please refer to Lesson 15). Sometimes it can also indicate the change of a circumstance. For example:

现在他当蔬菜公司的经理了。 (以前没当)

你舅妈也开始用电脑了。 (以前没用)

(她)上大学二年级了。 (以前没上)

Also, in a sentence with the negative adverb “不” preceding a verbal predicate, the particle “了” at the end of the sentence often indicates a change. For example:

她这次不来了。 （以前打算来）

他不认识我了。 （以前认识）

2 动作的进行 The progression of an action

To indicate an action in progress, either use the adverb “在” or “正在” before a verb, or “呢” at the end of a sentence. “正在” further emphasizes the progression of an action at a certain time. “在” or “正在” can also be used together with “呢”.

正在 / 在 + V + O (+呢)

Subject	Predicate			
	正在 / 在	V	O	呢
你	在	做	什么？	
我	在	写	汉字。	
力波	（现在）正在	念	课文。	
林娜她们	正在	看	越剧《红楼梦》	呢。
你舅妈		种	温室蔬菜	呢。

To indicate negation, “没有” can be used by itself. The structure “没在 + V” or “没(有) + V” may also be used. For example:

A：他在看地图吗？

B_1：没有，他在看照片。

B_2：没有。

B_3：他没在看地图，他在看照片。

B_4：他没（有）看地图，他在看照片。

An ongoing action may take place in the present, the past, or the future time. For example:

A：小云，你在写什么呢？

B：我在写文章呢。 (in the present)

昨天下午他给我打电话的时候，我正在看报。 (in the past)

下星期六晚上你去找他的时候，他一定在复习语法呢。 (in the future)

3 "不但……而且……" The construction "不但……而且……"

"不但……而且……" generally occurs in compound progressive sentences. If the two clauses share the same subject, the subject usually appears in the the first clause, and "不但" is usually placed after the subject. If the two clauses have different subjects, "不但" and "而且" are normally placed before their respective subjects. For example:

张教授不但是我的汉语老师，而且也是我的中国朋友。

我们不但盖了一座小楼，而且还买了一辆汽车。

不但他不认识我了，而且我也可能不认识他了。

不但中国人喜欢《红楼梦》，而且外国人也很喜欢这部小说。

In the second clause, "而且" is often used together with the adverb "也" or "还".

四、汉字 Chinese Characters

1 汉字的构字法(10) Methods of constructing Chinese characters (10)

The pictophonetic method (形声法) (6)

In this method, a character is formed by placing the semantic component outside, and the phonetic component inside. For example: 园, 房, 府, 厅, 进, 历, 座, 裹.

2 认写基本汉字 Learn and write basic Chinese characters

(1) 农(農)
nóng — agriculture — 6 strokes

(2) 而
ér — and; as well as — 6 strokes

(3) 入 丿 入
rù — to enter — 2 strokes

(Pay attention to the difference between "入" and "人".)

3 认写课文中的汉字 Learn and write the Chinese characters in the texts

臼 ノ 𠃊 𦥑 臼 臼 臼

jiù 6 strokes

(1) 舅妈 jiùmā（舅媽）

舅 → 臼 + 男 13 strokes

𤴓 (shūzìpángr, the left component of the character "疏(shū)")

乛 了 𠄐 𤴓 𤴓 5 strokes

(2) 蔬菜 shūcài

蔬 → 艹 + 𤴓 + 㐬 15 strokes

菜 → 艹 + 采 11 strokes

亦 (biànzìtóur, the top of the character "变")

丶 亠 亣 亣 亦 亦 6 strokes

(3) 变化 biànhuà（變化）

变 → 亦 + 又 8 strokes

(4) 小孩儿 xiǎoháir（小孩兒）

孩 → 子 + 亥 9 strokes

(5) 向 xiàng

向 → ノ + 同 6 strokes

(6) 年级 niánjí（年級）

级 → 纟 + 及 6 strokes

(7) 辛苦 xīnkǔ

辛 → 立 + 十 7 strokes

苦 → 艹 + 古　　8 strokes

(8) 收入 shōurù

收 → 丩 + 攵　　6 strokes

(9) 盖 gài（蓋）

盖 → 𦍌 + 皿　　11 strokes

(10) 辆 liàng（輛）

辆 → 车 + 两　　11 strokes

(11) 城市 chéngshì

市 → 亠 + 巾　　5 strokes

(12) 村 cūn

村 → 木 + 寸　　7 strokes

氐　㇒ ㇇ 𠂆 氏 氐
dī　　5 strokes

(13) 低 dī

低 → 亻 + 氐　　7 strokes

(14) 技术 jìshù（技術）

技 → 扌 + 十 + 又　　7 strokes

(15) 管理 guǎnlǐ

管 → ⺮ + 官　　14 strokes

文化知识 Cultural Note

Administrative Divisions of China

Division	Place	Abbreviation	Administration Centre
Municipality Directly Under the Central Government	北京市 Běijīng Shì	京 Jīng	北京 Běijīng
	上海市 Shànghǎi Shì	沪 Hù	上海 Shànghǎi
	天津市 Tiānjīn Shì	津 Jīn	天津 Tiānjīn
	重庆市 Chóngqìng Shì	渝 Yú	重庆 Chóngqìng
Province	河北省 Héběi Shěng	冀 Jì	石家庄 Shíjiāzhuāng
	山西省 Shānxī Shěng	晋 Jìn	太原 Tàiyuán
	辽宁省 Liáoníng Shěng	辽 Liáo	沈阳 Shěnyáng
	吉林省 Jílín Shěng	吉 Jí	长春 Chángchūn
	黑龙江省 Hēilóngjiāng Shěng	黑 Hēi	哈尔滨 Hā'ěrbīn
	江苏省 Jiāngsū Shěng	苏 Sū	南京 Nánjīng
	浙江省 Zhèjiāng Shěng	浙 Zhè	杭州 Hángzhōu
	安徽省 Ānhuī Shěng	皖 Wǎn	合肥 Héféi
	福建省 Fújiàn Shěng	闽 Mǐn	福州 Fúzhōu
	江西省 Jiāngxī Shěng	赣 Gàn	南昌 Nánchāng
	山东省 Shāndōng Shěng	鲁 Lǔ	济南 Jǐnán
	河南省 Hénán Shěng	豫 Yù	郑州 Zhèngzhōu
	湖北省 Húběi Shěng	鄂 È	武汉 Wǔhàn
Province	湖南省 Húnán Shěng	湘 Xiāng	长沙 Chángshā
	广东省 Guǎngdōng Shěng	粤 Yuè	广州 Guǎngzhōu
	海南省 Hǎinán Shěng	琼 Qióng	海口 Hǎikǒu
	四川省 Sìchuān Shěng	川 Chuān	成都 Chéngdū
	贵州省 Guìzhōu Shěng	黔 Qián	贵阳 Guìyáng
	云南省 Yúnnán Shěng	滇 Diān	昆明 Kūnmíng
	陕西省 Shǎnxī Shěng	陕 Shǎn	西安 Xī'ān
	甘肃省 Gānsù Shěng	甘 Gān	兰州 Lánzhōu
	青海省 Qīnghǎi Shěng	青 Qīng	西宁 Xīníng
	台湾省 Táiwān Shěng	台 Tái	台北 Táiběi
Autonomous Region	内蒙古自治区 Nèiměnggǔ Zìzhìqū	内蒙古 Nèiměnggǔ	呼和浩特 Hūhéhàotè
	广西壮族自治区 Guǎngxī Zhuàngzú Zìzhìqū	桂 Guì	南宁 Nánníng
	西藏自治区 Xīzàng Zìzhìqū	藏 Zàng	拉萨 Lāsà
	宁夏回族自治区 Níngxià Huízú Zìzhìqū	宁 Níng	银川 Yínchuān
	新疆维吾尔自治区 Xīnjiāng Wéiwú'ěr Zìzhìqū	新 Xīn	乌鲁木齐 Wūlǔmùqí
Special Administrative District	香港特别行政区 Xiānggǎng Tèbié Xíngzhèngqū	港 Gǎng	香港 Xiānggǎng
	澳门特别行政区 Àomén Tèbié Xíngzhèngqū	澳 Ào	澳门 Àomén

司机开着车送我们到医院

The driver drove us to the hospital.

Sometimes, unpleasant incidents occur in our lives, like Lin Na collided with a car on her bike, and Dawei had his bike stolen. In this lesson, you will learn how to use Chinese language to give an account of an incident, show your concern when you visit a patient, and make a complaint to others.

一、课文 Text

41（一）

王小云：宋华，你来帮我们一下，好吗？

宋　华：你们怎么了？[①] 现在你在哪儿？

王小云：林娜被撞伤了，正在第三医院检查呢。[②]

宋　华：她伤了哪儿了？伤得重吗？

王小云：还没有检查完呢。你带点儿钱来。

宋　华：好的，你们等着，我马上就来。

（在第三医院）

宋　华：林娜，你怎么样？伤得重不重？

林　娜：伤得不太重。我的胳膊被撞伤了，右腿也有点儿疼。

宋　华：你是怎么被撞伤的？

叙述事情的经过
Talking about an incident

林　娜：怎么说呢？③ 下午我和小云看完电影，骑着自行车回学院。我们说着、笑着，往右拐的时候没有注意，撞到了车上。那辆车停在路边，司机正在从车上拿东西。

宋　华：你们是怎么到医院来的？④

林　娜：那位司机看到我被撞伤了，就马上开着车送我们到医院。

宋　华：那位司机真不错。

林　娜：我们带的钱不多，医药费都是他帮我们交的。他还给了我一张名片。

宋　华：真应该谢谢那位司机，明天我去把钱还他。刚才我还以为你被汽车撞了。⑤

林　娜：还好，汽车被我撞了。⑥ 如果我被汽车撞了，就糟糕了。

生词 New Words

1.	着	zhe	Pt	(*used to indicate a continuous aspect*) 说着，笑着，等着，开着车，带着花儿，穿着旗袍
*2.	送	sòng	V	to take someone somewhere, to see someone off 送我回家，开着车送我们到医院，送我到门外（边），送我到火车站
3.	被	bèi	Prep	by (*used to indicate the passive voice*) 被问，被踢，被罚款
4.	撞	zhuàng	V	to bump against, to knock down 被车撞，撞车，撞人
5.	伤	shāng	V	to hurt, to wound 被撞伤，撞伤人
6.	第	dì	Pref	(*used to indicate ordinal numbers*) 第二十五课，第一，第十二，第三医院
7.	检查	jiǎnchá	V	to examine 检查身体，检查电脑，检查汽车，检查练习
8.	重	zhòng	A	serious, heavy 伤很重，伤不重；衣服很重，包裹不重，工作不重
9.	胳膊	gēbo	N	arm 胳膊被撞伤，胳膊疼
10.	腿	tuǐ	N	leg 撞伤腿，腿有点儿疼
11.	完	wán	V	to finish, to run out of 看完电影，做完练习，用完钱，吃完饭
12.	骑	qí	V	to ride 骑马，骑车
13.	自行车	zìxíngchē	N	bicycle 骑自行车，买自行车
14.	笑	xiào	V	to laugh, to smile 笑着，笑着说，别笑了，喜欢笑，大笑
15.	注意	zhùyì	V	to pay attention to 没注意，注意语法，注意听，注意看

16. 停	tíng	V	to stop, to park 停在路边，停车，停课
17. 马上	mǎshàng	Adv	right away, immediately 马上就来，马上去，马上看完，马上出发
18. 医药费	yīyàofèi	N	medical expenses 交医药费
19. 以为	yǐwéi	V	to think 我以为，别以为，都以为
20. 如果	rúguǒ	Conj	if

注释 Notes

① 你们怎么了？

"What's happened to you?"

"怎么了" is used to ask about what has happened to somebody or something, which the speaker doesn't know yet. For example:

他怎么了？今天没有来上课。

A：你的车怎么了？

B：昨天被撞坏了。

② 林娜被撞伤了，正在第三医院检查呢。

"Lin Na got injured and she is now having a medical examination at Hospital No. 3."

A cardinal number can be changed into an ordinal number by putting the prefix "第" before it. For example: "第一课", "第三医院", "第十天", "第十五个月". Sometimes, a cardinal number can be used as an ordinal number without "第", for example, "一楼", "四〇二号", and "二年级", as we have learned in previous lessons.

③ 怎么说呢？

"How should I put it?"

It means "it's not easy to explain".

④ 你们是怎么到医院来的？

"How did you come to the hospital?"

The construction "到 + PW + 来 / 去" is equivalent to "来 / 去 + PW". For example: "到学院来"(= "来学院"), "到上海去" (= "去上海").

⑤ 刚才我还以为你被汽车撞了。

"Just now I thought that you had been knocked down by a car."

The word "以为" means "想", but it is often used to show that the fact is not what somebody thought. For example:

我以为他不会来，可是他已经来了。

快下雪了，我还以为今天是好天气。

⑥ 还好，汽车被我撞了。

"Fortunately, I was the one who bumped against the car."

Here, "还好" means "fortunately". For example:

还好，排队的人不多。

还好，我们没有坐错车。

42（二）

看望病人
Visiting a patient

陆雨平：大为，林娜宿舍的门开着，她躺着看电视呢。

林　娜：啊，陆雨平、大为，快进来。

马大为：林娜，你怎么样？好点儿了吗？⑦

林　娜：好多了。你们这么忙，还带着花儿来看我，谢谢你们。这束花儿真漂亮，放在桌（子）上吧。

马大为：检查的结果怎么样？

林　娜：医生说没有大的问题，他让我躺在床上休息休息。大为，你把电视关了吧，咱们说会儿话。

陆雨平：现在胳膊还疼不疼？

林　娜：不疼了。可是胳膊这么弯着，写字很不方便。上星期我汉字没有考好，现在又撞伤了胳膊，真倒霉！[8] 这两天都是坏消息。

抱怨
Making a complaint

马大为：别着急，我有一个好消息。

林　娜：什么好消息？

马大为：上星期六晚上，我的自行车被小偷偷走了。

林　娜：自行车被偷了，这是什么好消息？

马大为：你听着，来你这儿以前，派出所给我打了一个电话，让我去一下。[9]

林　娜：你去派出所做什么？

马大为：小偷被抓到了，我丢的车也找到了，现在在派出所呢。你说，这是不是好消息？

林　娜：是个好消息。

陆雨平：真应该祝贺你！

生词 New Words

1. 躺	tǎng	V	to lie (down)	躺着看书，躺在床上，躺一会儿，躺一躺
2. 电视	diànshì	N	TV	看电视，开电视，买电视，用电视，上电视
视	shì	V	to look at	视力，近视，远视
3. 束	shù	M	(*a measure word for flowers*)	一束花儿
4. 放	fàng	V	to put, to place	放下，放东西，放衣服，放在床上，放在包裹里
5. 桌子	zhuōzi	N	table, desk	一张桌子，桌子上，放在桌子上
6. 结果	jiéguǒ	N	result, outcome	检查的结果，考试的结果，比赛的结果
7. 关	guān	V	to close, to turn off	关门，关电视
8. 弯	wān	V	to bend	弯着胳膊，弯着腿，弯着身体
9. 倒霉	dǎoméi	A	bad luck	真倒霉，特别倒霉，倒霉极了，倒霉的事儿
10. 坏	huài	A	bad, broken	坏苹果，坏人，电视坏了，自行车坏了，撞坏，考坏，用坏
11. 消息	xiāoxi	N	news	好消息，一个坏消息，有消息，没有消息，听到消息，看到消息
12. 小偷	xiǎotōu	N	thief	一个小偷，被小偷偷走
偷	tōu	V	to steal	偷钱，偷东西，偷汽车，偷电视，偷自行车

13. 派出所	pàichūsuǒ	N	local police station 去派出所
14. 抓	zhuā	V	to clutch, to catch, to arrest 抓住，抓小偷
15. 丢	diū	V	to lose 丢钱，丢东西，丢自行车，丢电视

补充生词 Supplementary Words

1. 型号	xínghào	N	model, type
2. 补	bǔ	V	to mend, to make up
3. 挂失	guàshī	VO	to report the loss of something
4. 项链	xiàngliàn	N	necklace
5. 警车	jǐngchē	N	police car, police van
6. 手机	shǒujī	N	cell phone
7. 突然	tūrán	Adv	suddenly
8. 刀	dāo	N	knife
9. 警察	jǐngchá	N	policeman
10. 吓	xià	V	to scare, to frighten
11. 手	shǒu	N	hand
12. 掉	diào	V	to drop, to fall
13. 地上	dìshang	N	ground, floor

注释　Notes

⑦ 你怎么样？好点儿了吗？

"How are you? Are you feeling better?"

This is an expression used to ask a patient about his / her condition.

⑧ 上星期我汉字没有考好，现在又撞伤了胳膊，真倒霉！

"Last week I did badly in the Chinese character test, and now I have hurt my arm. What bad luck!"

The adverb "又", used here in the sense of "furthermore, in addition", indicates that an event is not a repetition of the previous one, but is an additional occurrence. For example:

他昨天去了王府井，又看了电影。

司机送林娜到医院，又帮她交了医药费。

⑨ 派出所给我打了一个电话，让我去一下。

"I got a call from the local police station, telling me to go over there."

"派出所" (local police stations) are police stations operating at the grass-roots level in Chinese communities, which manage residence booklets and ensure public security within a neighbourhood.

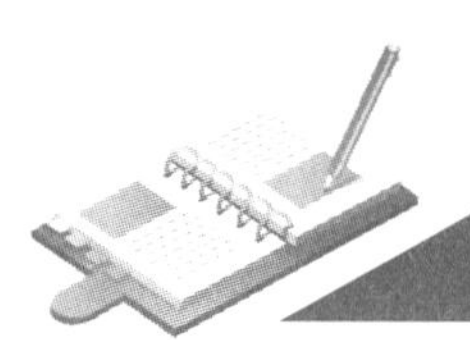

二、练习 Exercises

练习与运用 Drills and Practice

43

核心句 KEY SENTENCES

1. 我的胳膊被撞伤了。
2. 我和小云骑着自行车回学院。
3. 我们说着、笑着。
4. 如果我被汽车撞了，就糟糕了。
5. 林娜宿舍的门开着，她躺着看电视呢。
6. 他让我躺在床上休息休息。
7. 我的自行车被小偷偷走了。
8. 小偷被抓到了，我丢的车也找到了。

1. 熟读下列词组 Read the following phrases until you learn them by heart

（1）听着　写着　笑着　用着　住着　想着　放着　等着　试着
注意着　发展着　变化着
说着话　睡着觉　排着队　打着电话　拍着照片　踢着足球

开着汽车　唱着越剧　种着蔬菜　盖着大楼
门开着　商场开着　电视开着　电脑关着　车停着
坐着说话　躺着休息　骑着车去学校　带着花儿看朋友
穿着旗袍参加聚会　看着课文回答问题

（2）被介绍　被罚款　被检查　被访问　被忘了
被（自行车）撞伤　被（小偷）偷走　被（大为）记错　被（人）借去
被（同学）拿走　被（农民）请去　被（大家）吃完

（3）第一次　第二天　第二十五课　第三遍　第一部电影　第一本小说
第二语言　第一外语　第一件事儿　第五篇文章　第四场戏

（4）到学校去　到书店去　到饭馆去　到郊区去　到派出所去
到城里去　到长城去　到北方去

（5）看到山　见到小云　抓到小偷　拿到借书证　买到中药　找到导游
租到房子　学习到第二十课　送到医院　撞到汽车上
上到四年级　翻译到晚上　睡到十点　放假放到九月　游泳游到中午

（6）躺在床上　站在阳台上　坐在客厅里　睡在卧室里　住在郊区
排在前边　停在楼前　放在桌上　写在本子上　画在纸上
种在温室里

（7）打完电话　喝完咖啡　复习完生词　回答完问题　检查完身体
办完借书证　办完事儿　拍坏了照片　穿坏了衣服　用坏了乐器

2. 句型替换　Pattern drills

（1）A：他拿着什么？
B：他拿着照相机。

穿	一件新衬衫
洗	衣服
吃	寿面
带	书和本子

（2）A：宿舍的门开着没有？
B：宿舍的门没开着，我把它关了。

汽车的门
卫生间的门
办公室的电脑
客厅里的电视

（3）A：他们在做什么呢？
B：他们在站着 说话呢。

坐着	演奏乐器
等着	买音乐会票
笑着	拍照片
看着书	回答问题
喝着咖啡	听音乐

（4）A：你的自行车在吗？
B：不在。我的自行车被我同学借走了。

照相机	拿去
练习本	拿错
汽车	开走
词典	丢

（5）A：胳膊被撞伤了没有？
B：胳膊没有被撞伤。

头	撞疼
腿	撞坏
球	踢进
钱	偷去
他	罚款

（6）A：他们听到这个消息没有？
B：他们听到这个消息了。

复习	第二十三课
买	那套西服
拿	包裹通知单
见	那位演员
爬	山顶
拍	长城的景色

（7）A：那束花儿你放在哪儿了？
B：我放在桌（子）上了。

那些生词	写	本子上
那张明信片	放	书里
那件中式衣服	放	客厅
那些音乐光盘	放	办公室
你的车	停	楼前

（8）A：他们看完那个电影了没有？
B：他们没有看完那个电影。

吃	饭
学	这本书
赛	足球
参观	美术馆
办	护照
交	医药费

3. 课堂活动　Classroom activity

This game is to be played by two groups of students. The students in Group A make up ten conditional clauses using "如果", and the students in Group B are required to complete the sentences by making up ten corresponding clauses with "就". The scoring method is as follows: if Group B gives the correct answer, it gets one point; if it gives an incorrect answer and Group A can provide the correct one, then Group A gets the point. When the game is over, the two groups reverse roles and play it again, using the same scoring method. The group that gets the higher score wins.

4. 会话练习　Conversation exercises

【叙述事情的经过　Talking about an incident】

（1）A：先生，＿＿＿＿＿＿不见了。

B：你的＿＿＿＿＿＿是什么型号（xínghào）的？

A：是飞龙黑色男车。

B：车号是多少？

A：060809742。

B：是什么时候丢的？

A：昨天下午。

B：你的＿＿＿＿＿＿是在哪儿放着的？

A：在图书馆前边放着的。下午两点，我骑车到图书馆以后，车就放在那儿。四点钟我从图书馆出来，＿＿＿＿＿＿＿＿＿＿。

B：你先等着。如果有消息，我们马上告诉你。

（2）A：老先生，您看到一个＿＿＿＿＿＿没有？

B：什么样儿的小男孩？

A：他穿着一件红衬衫，手里拿着一个小球。他是跟我们一起来公园玩儿的，刚才我们说着话，没有注意，他就＿＿＿＿＿＿。

B：红衬衫？刚才我看到＿＿＿＿＿＿，他往东边跑过去了。你们快去看看。

A：谢谢。

【看望病人 Visiting a patient】

A：听说你住院了，大家都不放心，让我们来看看你。

B：你们学习这么忙，还跑来看我，真谢谢你们。

A：＿＿＿＿＿＿＿＿＿＿＿＿？

B：好多了，已经不发烧了，头也不太疼了。

C：吃东西＿＿＿＿＿＿？

B：还是不太想吃东西，这儿的饭菜我也不习惯。

A：睡觉还好吗？

B：很好。可是我不愿意这么躺着，我想早点儿回学校去。现在咱们该学第二十四课了吧？

C：第二十四课已经学完了，这个星期正在学第二十五课。你别着急，以后我们帮你补（bǔ）这两课。

A：我们该走了，你＿＿＿＿＿＿。

【抱怨 Making a complaint】

A：真倒霉！

B：＿＿＿＿＿＿＿？

A：我的钱包被＿＿＿＿＿＿＿。

B：丢了多少钱？

A：五百块人民币，还有三百美元。学生证、借书证和信用卡也都丢了。

B：真糟糕！你得马上到银行挂失（guàshī），还得去办新证。

5. 看图说话 Describe the following pictures

① 着

② 着

③ 被

④ 被

6. 交际练习 Communication exercises

(1) Your teacher fell ill and was hospitalized. What should you say to her when you see her in the hospital?

(2) You rode your bike and knocked down an elderly person. What should you do?

(3) Your notebook computer was stolen from your room. How do you report it to the local police station?

阅读与复述 Reading Comprehension and Paraphrasing

44 张大力的故事

昨天是张大力女儿的生日，他买了一条很漂亮的项链（xiàngliàn）做礼物。他知道女儿喜欢看越剧，还买了两张晚上的越剧票。

他们在饭馆吃了饭以后，就去看戏。回家的时候，已经很晚了。天气不好，开始下雪了，路上的人也少了。他们骑着自行车往右拐的时候，一个人从旁边走出来，问他们："请问，这儿有没有派出所？"张大力告诉他："没有。派出所离这儿很远。"那个人又问："现在哪儿可以叫一辆警车（jǐngchē）来？"张大力回答说："可以打110电话。"

"你有没有手机（shǒujī）？"那个人又问。

张大力说："没有。"

张大力正在想那个人为什么要问他这些问题，突然（tūrán），那个人拿出刀（dāo）来，对张大力说："对不起，把你们的项链和钱都给我！"

张大力笑着说："你忘了问一个问题了。我告诉你，这儿虽然没有派出所，可是有一个老警察（jǐngchá），他抓过九十八个像你这样的人，马上要抓第九十九个。"

"老警察在哪儿？"那个人问。

"在这儿！我就是！"

那个人吓（xià）坏了，手（shǒu）里的刀也掉（diào）在地上（dì-shang）。他被张大力送到了派出所。

三、语法 Grammar

1 动作或状态的持续 The continuation of an action or a state

The aspect particle "着" is placed directly after a verb to express the continuation of an action or a state. For example:

我们说着、笑着。

林娜宿舍的门开着。

胳膊这么弯着。

她穿着红色的旗袍。

When used in a sentence with serial verb phrases, in addition to emphasizing that the two actions in the sentence are happening simultaneously, the construction "V + 着" is often used to indicate the manner of the action expressed by the second verb. For example:

我们骑着自行车回学院。

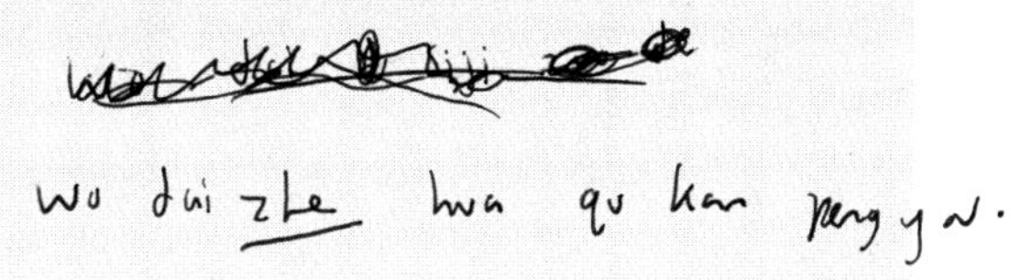

他笑着说："应该祝贺你！"

你们还带着花儿来看我。

The negative form of this construction is "没(有) + V + 着", and its V/A-not-V/A question form is "V + 着 + 没有". For example:

A：电视开着没有？
B：电视没有开着。

A：你带着护照没有？
B：我没带着护照。

他没有躺着看电视，他坐着看电视呢。

The construction "V + 着" is frequently used with words such as "在", "正在", and "呢". For example:

林娜躺着看电视呢。

他正在打着电话呢。

他在开着车呢。

Note that no complements are used after the "V + 着" construction. For example, "他写着汉字写十分钟" is a wrong sentence.

2 "被"字句 The "被" sentence

Besides the notional passive sentences, there is another kind of passive sentence with the preposition "被" (often replaced by "叫" or "让" in spoken Chinese), which is used to introduce the agent of an action, or to emphasize that the subject of the sentence is the recipient of an action.

S (recipient) + 被 + O (agent) + V + Other elements

Subject	Predicate			
	被	O (agent)	V	Other elements
我的自行车	被	小偷	偷	走了。
那本小说	被	我同学	借	去了。
那套西服	被	人	买	走了没有?
她的新照相机	让	她弟弟	撞	坏了。
小偷	叫	谁	抓	到了?

If there is no need to introduce the agent of an action, "被" can be placed right before the verb; however, "叫" or "让" is not used this way in spoken Chinese. For example:

我的胳膊被撞伤了。

自行车被偷了。

Note that a negative adverb or an optative verb must be placed before "被" ("叫", "让"). For example:

这本小说没有被借走。("这本小说被没有借走" is a wrong sentence.)

那套西服明天会被人买走。("那套西服明天被人会买走" is a wrong sentence.)

3 结果补语"到"、"在" The resultative complements "到" and "在"

The verb "到" is often used as a resultative complement to express that something was done. For example:

小偷被抓到了,我丢的车也找到了。

A：你去买那本词典了没有？

B：我去买了，可是我没有买到。

"到" can also be used to show that an action has ended in a certain place (with a noun or noun phrase indicating place used as the object), or that it has continued up to a certain time (with a noun or noun phrase indicating time used as the object). For example:

她撞到了车上。

我们学到第二十五课了。

他晚上写汉字常常写到十点。

"在" is often used as a resultative complement to indicate that somebody or something at somewhere (with a noun or noun phrase indicating place used as the object) as a result of the action. For example:

他让我躺在床上休息休息。

那位司机的车停在路边。

花儿放在桌子上。

他住在二楼。

4 "如果……就……"　The conditional construction "如果……就……"

The first clause introduced by the conjunction "如果" presents a condition, and the second clause denotes the result that is brought about under such a condition. The adverb "就" (3) in the second clause often indicates a conclusion derived from the conditional clause. The word "如果" in the first clause may be omitted. For example:

如果明天天气不好，我们就不去了。

如果有问题，你就打电话找我。

（如果）你昨天来，你就看见他了。

四、汉字　Chinese Characters

1 区分同音字　Differentiating homophones

There are only over 1,300 meaningful phonetic syllables with tones in Mandarin Chinese; howerer, there are 3,500 Chinese characters in common use. As a result, it is not unusual that some characters may have the same pronunciation. For example, the characters "游", "邮", "油" learned before are all pronounced yóu, and they are distinguished from one another only by their written forms. Therefore, when studying homophonetic characters, we must learn to distinguish them by comparing them in terms of form, meaning and word combination. For example, "导游" cannot be written as "导油" or "导邮", and "游泳" cannot be written as "油泳" or "邮泳".

2 认写基本汉字 Learn and write basic Chinese characters

(1) 壬 　　ノ 二 千 壬

rén 　　the ninth of the ten Heavenly Stems 　　4 strokes

(Pay attention to the difference between "壬" and "王".)

(2) 束 　　一 ㄏ 冂 日 中 串 束

shù 　　*a measure word for flowers* 　　7 strokes

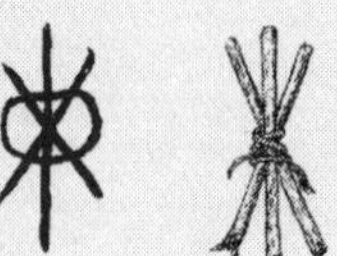

("木" indicates the firewood, and "口" indicates the rope which bundles the firewood.)

3 认写课文中的汉字 Learn and write the Chinese characters in the texts

(1) 被 bèi

被 → 衤 + 皮 　　10 strokes

(2) 撞 zhuàng

撞 → 扌 + 立 + 里 　　15 strokes

(3) 伤 shāng（傷）

伤 → 亻 + ⺈ + 力 　　6 strokes

(4) 第 dì

第 → ⺮ + 弓 + 丨 + ノ 　　11 strokes

(5) 检查 jiǎnchá（檢查）

检 → 木 + 佥　　11 strokes

(6) 完 wán

完 → 宀 + 元　　7 strokes

(7) 胳膊 gēbo

胳 → 月 + 夂 + 口　　10 strokes

膊 → 月 + 甫 + 寸　　14 strokes

(8) 腿 tuǐ

腿 → 月 + 艮 + 辶　　13 strokes

(9) 骑 qí（騎）

骑 → 马 + 大 + 可　　11 strokes

(10) 注意 zhùyì

注 → 氵 + 主　　8 strokes

(11) 停 tíng

停 → 亻 + 亠 + 口 + 冖 + 丁　　11 strokes

(12) 如果 rúguǒ

如 → 女 + 口　　6 strokes

(13) 躺 tǎng

躺 → 身 + 小 + 冋　　15 strokes

(14) 电视 diànshì（電視）

视 → 礻 + 见　　8 strokes

(15) 桌子 zhuōzi

桌 → ⺊ + 木 10 strokes

(16) 结果 jiéguǒ（結果）

结 → 纟 + 吉 9 strokes

(17) 弯 wān（彎）

弯 → 亦 + 弓 9 strokes

(18) 倒霉 dǎoméi（倒黴）

倒 → 亻 + 到 10 strokes

霉 → 雨 + 每 15 strokes

(19) 坏 huài（壞）

坏 → 土 + 不 7 strokes

(20) 消息 xiāoxi

消 → 氵 + ⺌ + 月 10 strokes

(21) 小偷 xiǎotōu

偷 → 亻 + 人 + 一 + 月 + 刂 11 strokes

(22) 派出所 pàichūsuǒ

派 → 氵 + 厂 + 𠂢 9 strokes

(23) 抓 zhuā

抓 → 扌 + 爪 7 strokes

(24) 丢 diū

丢 → 丿 + 去 6 strokes

(Pay attention to the first stroke which is a left falling stroke, not a horizontal one.)

文化知识 Cultural Note

Bikes in China

China, reputed as the "Kingdom of Bikes", has a spectacular torrent of bikes during the rush hours in many cities.

The bike was introduced to China from the West at the end of the 19th century. It served as a toy of the imperial nobles at first. By the 1960s~1970s, it has become one of the "three must-haves for the wedding" together with the sewing machine and wrist watch. After 1980s, the bike has gradually become the most important, popular and ideal means of transport for Chinese people.

Chinese people enjoy a gradual increase in their living standards with the reform and opening up in the past 30 years. Public transportation system such as the subway has developed rapidly; there is also an increase in the number of private cars. However, it doesn't mean that they cast off the bike once for all. Nowadays, the bike, which is diverse in form and zooming about in all corners of cities, is not just an ordinary transportation tool. Out of the considerations of transportation pressure, environmental protection and keeping healthy, going out by bike has become a good way for people to keep fit, spend their pastime, and follow the fashion.

Due to its convenience, the bike is ridden by almost every student on the campuses of Chinese universities.

复习 Review

你快要成“中国通”了

You are almost becoming a China hand.

The protagonists are reviewing what they learned in the past year. We will also review and summarize the main contents that we have studied in Volume Two.

一、课文 Text

45

宋 华：林娜，你来中国已经快一年了吧？你不但学习了汉语，而且还认识了很多中国朋友，中国的情况又知道得不少，你快要成“中国通”了。

林 娜：哪里，哪里，“中国通”真不敢当，还差得远呢。① 说实在的，我越来越喜欢中国文化了。② 中国从南到北，从东到西，每个地方都有自己的特点。③

宋 华：历史博物馆正在举办一个中国文化展览，那儿有很多图片，有的是我们见过的，有的是我们没见过的。你对中国文化这么感兴趣，我建议你去看看。④

林 娜：好极了，我一定去。今天我们有一个结业聚会，力波他们快要来了。你把这个消息告诉他们，我想他们也一定会非常感兴趣。

宋 华：好啊。林娜，你还记得吗？刚来的时候你说过，如果每天都让你吃中餐，你就会饿死。

回忆往事
Recalling past events

现在你不但喜欢吃中餐，而且还学会了做中国菜。

林 娜：可不，现在如果一天不吃中餐，我就会觉得有点儿不舒服。

（丁力波、马大为进宿舍）

马大为：你们在聊什么呢？去哪儿吃中餐？我也去。

宋 华：我们在说，你们这些老外快成“中国通”了。⑤ 力波当然就不用说了。

丁力波：因为我妈妈是中国人，所以我早就有点儿中国化了。林娜爱穿旗袍，爱吃中国菜，还喜欢看越剧、听中国民乐，好像也有点儿中国化了。

林 娜：我是到北京以后才开始中国化的。⑦

马大为：我看这很容易，像有的留学生那样，找个中国姑娘做妻子。⑧你找个长得帅的中国小伙子做丈夫，每天在一起生活，就可以中国化了。

林　娜：别开玩笑。说真的，我现在觉得汉语语法不太难，可是汉字很难。

马大为：声调也不容易，我常常说错。

谈语言学习
Talking about the study of language

宋　华：你们在中国才学习了一年，汉语水平就提高得这么快，主要是因为你们学习都很努力。

丁力波：这儿的老师教得特别认真，朋友们对我们也非常热情，常常帮助我们学汉语，所以我们进步很快。

林　娜：一年的学习时间太短了。我虽然已经能听懂中国人说的一些话，可是自己说汉语还说得不太流利，明年我还要来中国学习。

马大为：林娜，老师和同学们都在等着我们呢，⑨我们走吧。

丁力波：好，明年再“中国化”吧！

林 娜：宋华，明天你陪我去参观中国文化展览，好吗？

宋 华：好，明天见！

林 娜：不见不散！⑩

生词 New Words

1. 成	chéng	V	to become 成妈妈了，成教授了，成大学生了，成主角了
2. 中国通	zhōngguótōng	N	a China expert, a China hand 成中国通了，一位中国通，西方的中国通
3. 情况	qíngkuàng	N	situation 中国的情况，学校的情况，这种情况，情况怎么样
4. 实在	shízài	A / Adv	honest; truly, really 说实在的；实在便宜，实在辛苦，实在不敢当
5. 越来越	yuè lái yuè	IE	more and more 越来越喜欢，越来越习惯，越来越方便
6. 南	nán	N	south 从南到北
7. 特点	tèdiǎn	N	characteristic, feature 有特点，自己的特点，一个特点，很多特点
8. 历史	lìshǐ	N	history 历史故事，中国历史，感人的历史
9. 博物馆	bówùguǎn	N	museum 历史博物馆，文化博物馆，美术博物馆，一座博物馆
10. 举办	jǔbàn	V	to conduct, to hold 举办音乐会，举办足球比赛

11.	展览	zhǎnlǎn	N	exhibition, show 举办展览，参观展览，看展览，油画展览，一个展览
	展	zhǎn	N	exhibition, show 文化展，国画展，美术展
12.	图片	túpiàn	N	photograph, picture 展览图片，历史图片，很多图片，一张图片
13.	对	duì	Prep	to 对中国文化，对汉字，对力波说，对他笑
14.	感兴趣	gǎn xìngqù	IE	to be interested in 非常感兴趣，对中国文化感兴趣，对汉字感兴趣，越来越感兴趣
	感	gǎn	V	to feel, to sense
	兴趣	xìngqù	N	interest 有兴趣，有点儿兴趣，没有兴趣，提高兴趣，有很大的兴趣
15.	结业	jiéyè	VO	to complete a course 结业聚会，快要结业了，结业的时候
16.	记得	jìde	V	to remember, to recall 还记得，不记得他的名字，记得以前的朋友，记得中学生活
17.	中餐	zhōngcān	N	Chinese food (meal) 吃中餐，习惯中餐，越来越喜欢中餐
18.	饿	è	A	hungry 很饿，有点儿饿，越来越饿，饿极了
19.	死	sǐ	V	to die 饿死，忙死，疼死，累死
*20.	菜	cài	N	dish, food 中国菜，南方菜，做菜
21.	聊	liáo	V	to chat 聊什么，聊家里的事儿，聊学校的情况，聊中国历史，喜欢聊，愿意聊
22.	老外	lǎowài	N	foreigner 这些老外，一个老外，像老外，成老外了
23.	中国化	zhōngguóhuà	V	to Sinify, to Sinicize 有点儿中国化，越来越中国化
	*化	huà	Suf	(*used as a suffix to a noun or an adjective to indicate sth. or sb. is becoming or made to have that attribute*) 绿化，美化，老化，西方化

24. 才	cái	Adv	just 才开始，才举办，才学习一年，才聊了一会儿
25. 那样	nàyàng	Pr	such, so, like that 像留学生那样，像中国通那样，像导游那样介绍
26. 妻子	qīzi	N	wife 做妻子，有妻子，他妻子，当妻子了
27. 小伙子	xiǎohuǒzi	N	young man 中国小伙子，帅小伙子，一个小伙子
28. 丈夫	zhàngfu	N	husband 做丈夫，她丈夫
29. 声调	shēngdiào	N	tone 汉语的声调，听声调，练习声调，注意声调，四个声调
30. 努力	nǔlì	A	hard-working 努力学习，努力工作，努力练习声调，越来越努力
31. 认真	rènzhēn	A	earnest, serious 非常认真，越来越认真，教得很认真，认真学习
32. 热情	rèqíng	A	warm, warm-hearted, enthusiastic 很热情，那样热情，热情多了
33. 进步	jìnbù	N / V	progress, advancement; to make progress 有进步，进步不太大，进步很快，进步了
34. 明年	míngnián	N	next year 明年举办，明年结业，明年考试，明年再来
35. 陪	péi	V	to accompany 陪我去看电影，陪妻子去买东西，陪丈夫参观
36. 不见不散	bú jiàn bú sàn	IE	don't leave until we meet
散	sàn	V	to break up, to disperse 散场，散开

补充生词 Supplementary Words

1. 首	shǒu	M	(*a measure word for poems, songs or melodies*)
2. 了解	liǎojiě	V	to understand, to realize
3. 熟悉	shúxī	V	to be familiar with

4. 见面	jiànmiàn	VO	to meet, to see
5. 毕业	bìyè	VO	to graduate, to finish school
6. 经验	jīngyàn	N	experience
7. 方法	fāngfǎ	N	method
8. 艺术	yìshù	N	art
9. 请客	qǐngkè	VO	to feast, to invite sb. to dinner
10. 客人	kèrén	N	guest
11. 意思	yìsi	N	meaning
12. 句	jù	M	(*a measure word for sentences*)

注释 Notes

① 还差得远呢。

"I'm still not that good yet."

This is an expression of modesty that Chinese people often use when being praised. One can also say: "哪里，我还差得很多". Nowadays, Chinese people may also sometimes use "谢谢" to respond to others' compliments.

② 说实在的，我越来越喜欢中国文化了。

"Honestly speaking, I'm becoming more and more fond of Chinese culture."

The phrase "说实在的" is a commonly used expression that reveals the attitude of the speaker in a conversation. It is equivalent to the phrase "说真的".

The phrase "越来越" expresses change in degree with the progression of time. For example:

课文越来越有意思了。

他汉语说得越来越流利。

③ 中国从南到北，从东到西，每个地方都有自己的特点。

"From the south to the north, from the east to the west, every place in China has its own characteristics."

④ 你对中国文化这么感兴趣，我建议你去看看。

"Since you are so interested in Chinese culture, I suggest that you go and take a look."

The object of the preposition "对" often indicates the target of an action. The prepositional phrase "对 + NP" is often used as an adverbial in a sentence. For example:

宋华对她说："你怎么了？"

他对我笑笑，就走了。

老师对我们很热情。

他对中国画很感兴趣。

⑤ 我们在说，你们这些老外快成"中国通"了。

"We are talking about the fact that you foreigners are becoming China hands."

The word "老外" is a casual, yet friendly way of addressing foreigners in spoken Chinese.

⑥ 力波当然就不用说了。

"Libo is certainly one of them."

The phrase "不用说" means "certainly, needless to say". It indicates that a reason is very clear, and that the listener also understands this. For example:

星期二公园里人这么多，星期天就不用说了。

他刚来的时候汉字就写得很好，现在就不用说了。

⑦ 我是到北京以后才开始中国化的。

"I was not Sinicized until I arrived in Beijing."

The adverb "才" is contrary to "就", and is often used to express that something happened late, slowly, or with difficulty. For example:

他六点才来。 (He was late.)

这个故事我听了三遍才听懂。 (I listened to the story too many times.)

我等了半个小时，才上公共汽车。 (I waited for a long time.)

It can also express a small quantity or a short time. For example:

他一个人翻译了三篇文章，我们两个人才翻译了一篇。(We translated too few.)

你们在中国才一年。 (You stayed in China for a short time.)

⑧ 像有的留学生那样，找个中国姑娘做妻子。

"Just do as what some foreign students did: find a Chinese girl to be your wife."

⑨ 老师和同学们都在等着我们呢。

"All the teacher and classmates are waiting for us."

In a sentence expressing that an action is going on, the aspect particle “着” sometimes may be used after verbs. For example:

她正在看着电视呢。

我去找他的时候，他做着练习呢。

⑩ 不见不散！

“Don’t leave until we meet!”

This expression is commonly used to emphasize that the two must meet each other (i.e. one must wait until the other arrives) when making a date before they leave. The listener can also respond with this same expression.

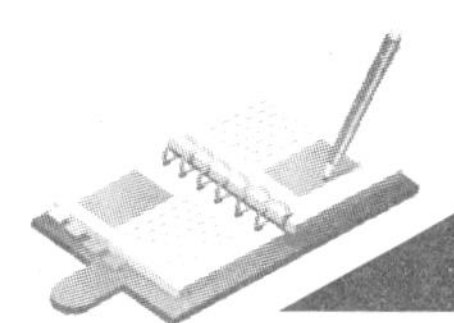

二、练习 Exercises

练习与运用 Drills and Practice

核心句 KEY SENTENCES

1. 哪里，哪里，“中国通”真不敢当，还差得远呢。
2. 说实在的，我越来越喜欢中国文化了。
3. 你对中国文化这么感兴趣，我建议你去看看。
4. 力波当然就不用说了。
5. 我是到北京以后才开始中国化的。
6. 像有的留学生那样，找个中国姑娘做妻子。
7. 你们在中国才学习了一年，汉语水平就提高得这么快。
8. 老师和同学们都在等着我们呢。

1. 熟读下列词组 Read the following phrases until you learn them by heart

（1）成中国通了　成大学教授了　成有名的画家了　成电影演员了

（2）越来越认真　越来越努力　越来越热情　越来越便宜

越来越习惯　越来越感兴趣　越来越喜欢中国文化

越来越注意汉语声调　越来越习惯吃中餐

（3）很感兴趣　特别感兴趣　越来越感兴趣

对汉字感兴趣　对西方音乐感兴趣　对英国足球也感兴趣

对中国历史一定感兴趣　对这部爱情小说非常感兴趣

（4）才五分钟　才三天　才一个月　才两块钱　才三点

才看了一遍　才去过一次

（5）也记得　还记得　不记得　只记得　都记得　一定记得

记得什么时候　记得在哪儿　记得这座城市的历史

记得我们结业的时候　记得上大学三年级的时候

（6）学会课文　学会游泳　学会管理　学会做中国菜　学会骑自行车

（7）像小伙子那样　像导游那样　像记者那样　像我们的朋友那样

像一位中国通那样

（8）如果好就买　如果合适就要　如果喜欢就拿　如果方便就来

如果累就休息　如果你对文化感兴趣，就应该去看看那个展览

如果你想学好汉语，就应该去中国

2. 句型替换 Pattern drills

（1）A：你是什么时候开始学汉语的？

B：我是大学三年级才开始学汉语的。他大学一年级就开始学汉语了。

出发	下午五点	下午三点
去泰山	去年	前年
参观图片展览	今天上午	上星期
认识她	三年以前	五年以前

（2）A：这篇课文难不难？
B：很难，我看了三遍才看懂。
A：我觉得很容易，我看了一遍就看懂了。

（个）故事	听	听懂
（些）汉字	写	写对
（个）声调	练	练会
（课的）语法	复习	复习好

（3）A：为什么他声调念得不太对？
B：他来北京才两个月。

车	开	好	学开车
汉字	写	漂亮	学中文
英语	说	流利	到英国

（4）A：你喜欢这个博物馆吗？
B：我非常喜欢，我对中国历史很感兴趣。

（幅）画儿	西方油画
（部）电影	爱情故事
（首(shǒu)）乐曲	民族音乐
（本）小说	城里的情况

（5）A：你觉得你们经理怎么样？
B：他对我们非常热情。

工作	认真
技术	了解（liǎojiě）
汇率	注意
管理	马虎

（6）A：他为什么明年还要来这儿？
B：他对这儿的生活越来越喜欢了。

天气	习惯
文化	熟悉（shúxī）
变化	感兴趣

3. 课堂活动 Classroom activity

A game to build up a sequence of sentences on the topic of "talking about Chinese language studies": The whole class is divided into two groups. The teacher starts the game with Group A by saying: "我们大家学习汉语". After that, students in Group A must continue to make sentences, one after the other, so that the word at the beginning of each sentence is the same as the last word in the previous sentence. For example: "我们大家学习汉语。" "汉语是中国人说的语言。" "语言学院有很多好老师。"... Group B then takes their turn at the game. At the end, calculate the number of correct sentences made by each group to see who wins.

4. 会话练习 Conversation exercises

【回忆往事 Recalling past events】

（1）A：你是王平吧？

B：是你啊！田元！咱们已经十年没有见面（jiànmiàn）了吧？

A：是啊，老同学，你现在________________工作？

B：我从美国回来以后，在一家公司工作。

A：你是________________去美国的？

B：我是1990年去美国的。你大学毕业（bìyè）后一直在北方吧？

A：不，毕业以后，我去南方了。

（2）A：你还记得那次结业聚会吗？

B：当然记得。那是在夏天，我们______________离开（líkāi）学校了。

A：聚会好像是在宋华家。

B：不对。你记错了，是在________________。

A：对，是在陈老师家。她丈夫给大家做了很多菜。

B：我记得林娜还唱了越剧。

【谈语言学习 Talking about the study of language】

（1）A：咱们学习了一年汉语了，今天大家在一起聊一聊，说说自己的经验（jīngyàn）。

B：我先说吧。我觉得汉语语法________________，但是汉字很难。

C：如果有好的学习方法（fāngfǎ），汉字也不太难。________________，我觉得口语不容易。这次考试我口语考得非常糟糕。

B：口语要多练习、多说。我有一个中国朋友，他每天下午都跟我练习一个小时的口语。

（2）A：快要________________了。你准备（zhǔnbèi）得怎么样？

B：我有点儿不放心，因为我每次语法都考得不好。

A：我想这次你一定会________________。你学习很努力，进步很快。如果认真复习，不会有问题的。

B：老师，我有一些语法上的问题，可以请您帮助我吗？

A：________________。星期三下午我有时间，你到办公室来找我吧。

B：好。谢谢老师。

5. 看图说话 Describe the following pictures

❶ 有、是、在

❷ 被

❸ 了

❹ 正在、着

6. 交际练习 Communication exercises

(1) You and your classmates have been studying Chinese for one year. Talk about your own experience of studying the language.

(2) In a high school reunion party, you meet many old good friends. You all recall and talk about your lives and studies in high school.

阅读与复述 Reading Comprehension and Paraphrasing

47 说话的艺术（yìshù）

说话也是一种艺术。我有一个朋友，他就不会说话。

一天，他在饭馆里请客（qǐngkè）。他一共请了四位客人（kèrén），来了三位，有一位还没有来。他等得有点儿着急了，就说："你看，该来的没来！"有一位客人听了，很不高兴。他想："该来的没来——我是不该来的了？"他走出餐厅去，对工作人员说："如果他们找我，你就告诉他们不用等我了。"

过了一会儿，工作人员走进来问："先生，您要的菜都准备好了，现在拿上来吗？"

"别忙，我们在等人呢。"我朋友问："刚才出去的那位先生怎么还不回来？"工作人员说："他已经走了。"我朋友非常着急，说："不该走的走了！"

这时候还有两位客人在那儿等着。有一位很不高兴，他想："不该走的走了，意思（yìsi）是该走的还没走，好，我是该走的，我现在就走！"他站起来，没有说一句（jù）话就离开了饭馆。

只有一位客人在那儿了。我朋友还在问自己："他们怎么都走了？"这位客人说："您刚才说该来的没来，不该走的走了，他们觉得自己是不该在这儿的了，所以他们都走了。以后您说话要注意点儿。"

"以后我一定注意。"我朋友说，"可是我说的不是他们啊！""什么？那你说的是我啊？！"这位客人也走了。

三、语法复习 Grammar Review

1 动词谓语句（2） Sentences with a verbal predicate (2)

（11）"是……的"句 Sentences with "是……的"

他是2001年来我们学院的。

我们是在上海认识的。

我朋友不是坐火车来的，是坐飞机来的。

力波是来学习美术的。

（12）表示存在的句子 Sentences indicating existence

邮局的旁边是什么地方？

楼后边有一个小花园。

厨房不在客厅右边。

（13）无标志被动句 Notional passive sentences

机票买好了没有？

兵马俑参观过一次。

（14）被动句 Passive sentences

那本小说被借走了。

自行车被我同学骑走了。

门让人撞坏了。

2 动作的态 The aspect of an action

（1）动作或事情的完成 The completion or realization of an action or event

他去书店买了两本书。

他借了我的电脑。

她去上海了。

林娜买了旗袍了。

（2）情况的变化 The change of circumstances

天气越来越冷了。

他是教授了。

她有男朋友了。

小云的舅舅当公司的经理了。

她舅妈也开始用电脑了。

我弟弟上中学三年级了。

老师今天不来了。

（3）动作的持续 The continuation of an action

他们聊着过去的事儿。

我们带着花儿去她家。

宿舍门开着。

他穿着一件中式衣服。

书在桌上放着。

（4）过去的经验或经历 Past experience

林娜以前看过《红楼梦》。

他从来没有骑过自行车。

（5）动作即将发生 An action that is going to take place soon

要开学了。

他们明天就要考试了。

火车快到广州了。

（6）动作的进行 The progression of an action

他正在做什么？

我在看电视呢。

我去他家的时候，他正在画画儿。

她在喝着咖啡呢。

3 几种补语（1） Several kinds of complements (1)

（1）情态补语 The modal complement

你来得真早。

他们（说）普通话说得不太好。

（2）程度补语 The complement of degree

今天冷极了。

这部电影比那部好多了。

（3）趋向补语 The directional complement

她出来了没有？

我们先上楼去。

你带没（有）带照片来？

他们已经走下去了。

我们爬上长城来了。

他从邮局取回包裹来了。

（4）结果补语 The resultative complement

我听懂了，可是记错了。

请写上你的名字。

他还没有看完这本小说呢。

这篇文章已经写好了。

你买到那本词典没有？

这张照片拍坏了。

（5）数量补语 The complement of quantity

这件衣服比那件贵50块钱。

我比他小两岁。

这件衬衫太大，有小一点儿的吗？

（6）时量补语 The complement of duration

他在这儿工作了半年。

你（写）汉字写了多长时间？

我（学）汉语已经学了六年了。

（7）动量补语 The complement of frequency

他去过两次海南岛。

这部小说我又看了一遍。

老师让他念了两遍课文。

四、汉字 Chinese Characters

1 区分形近字 Differentiating characters with similar forms

Many Chinese characters have similar forms. To distinguish them, one must compare the shape, number and combination of strokes, and the position of the component in each character. For example:

(1) 儿——几　石——右　刀——力　入——人

(2) 犬——太　王——壬　土——士　夫——天

(3) 练——炼　孩——该　第——弟　泰——奏

(4) 放——访　明——朋　错——借　请——情

2 认写基本汉字 Learn and write basic Chinese characters

(1) 史　丶 冂 口 史 史

shǐ　history　5 strokes

(2) 歹　一 丆 万 歹

dǎi　evil　4 strokes

(Pay attention to the difference between "歹" and "夕".)

(3) 丈　一 ナ 丈

zhàng　*a unit of length, equall to* $3\frac{1}{3}$ *meters*　3 strokes

(Pay attention to the difference between "丈" and "文".)

(4) 夫　一 二 扌 夫

fū　husband　4 strokes

(Pay attention to the difference between "夫" and "天".)

3 认写课文中的汉字 Learn and write the Chinese characters in the texts

(1) 情况 qíngkuàng

况 → 冫 + 口 + 儿　7 strokes

(2) 历史 lìshǐ（歷史）

历 → 厂 ＋ 力　　4 strokes

(3) 博物馆 bówùguǎn（博物館）

博 → 忄 ＋ 甫 ＋ 寸　　12 strokes

(4) 举办 jǔbàn（舉辦）

举 → 兴 ＋ 丰　　9 strokes

𠂊 (jiānzìtóur, the top of the character “监(jiān)”)

丨 丨丨 丨丨丿 丨丨𠂉 丨丨𠂊　　5 strokes

(5) 展览 zhǎnlǎn（展覽）

览 → 𠂊 ＋ 见　　9 strokes

(6) 感兴趣 gǎn xìngqù（感興趣）

趣 → 走 ＋ 耳 ＋ 又　　15 strokes

(7) 饿 è（餓）

饿 → 饣 ＋ 我　　10 strokes

(8) 死 sǐ

死 → 歹 ＋ 匕　　6 strokes

(9) 聊 liáo

聊 → 耳 ＋ 卯　　11 strokes

(10) 妻子 qīzi

妻 → 一 + 㠯 + 女 8 strokes

(11) 小伙子 xiǎohuǒzi（小夥子）

伙 → 亻 + 火 6 strokes

尸 (méizìkuàngr, the top component of the character "眉(méi)")

4 strokes

(12) 声调 shēngdiào（聲調）

声 → 士 + 尸 7 strokes

调 → 讠 + 冂 + 土 + 口 10 strokes

(13) 努力 nǔlì

努 → 女 + 又 + 力 7 strokes

(14) 陪 péi

陪 → 阝 + 立 + 口 10 strokes

文化知识 Cultural Note

Main Historical Periods of China

Before the foundation of People's Republic of China in 1949

The Historical Period	Years
五帝 (Wǔdì) Five Lords	Around the 30th century B.C. to around the beginning of the 21st century B.C.
夏 (Xià) Xia Dynasty	Around the beginning of the 21st century B.C. to around the 17th century B.C.
商 (Shāng) Shang Dynasty	Around the beginning of the 17th century B.C. to around the 11th century B.C.
周 (Zhōu) Zhou Dynasty	Around the 11th century B.C. to 256 B.C.
秦 (Qín) Qin Dynasty	221 B.C. to 206 B.C.
汉 (Hàn) Han Dynasty	206 B.C. to 220 A.D.
三国 (Sānguó) Three Kingdoms	220 to 280
晋 (Jìn) Jin Dynasty	265 to 420
南北朝 (Nán-Běi Cháo) Northern and Southern Dynasties	420 to 589
隋 (Suí) Sui Dynasty	581 to 618
唐 (Táng) Tang Dynasty	618 to 907
五代 (Wǔdài) Five Dynasties	907 to 960
宋 (Sòng) Song Dynasty	960 to 1279
元 (Yuán) Yuan Dynasty	1206 to 1368
明 (Míng) Ming Dynasty	1368 to 1644
清 (Qīng) Qing Dynasty	1616 to 1911
中华民国 (Zhōnghuá Mínguó) Republic of China	1912 to 1949

After studying 26 lessons, you should have mastered over 800 new words, about 700 Chinese characters and 197 key sentence patterns. You have studied Chinese pronunciation, vocabulary, grammar and Chinese characters at the beginner level. You have also gained some knowledge of Chinese culture. Now, you should be able to converse about daily life in Chinese and read simple Chinese texts.

This is a good beginning. The following volumes of the *New Practical Chinese Reader* will help you to communicate more freely in Chinese and to further understand the Chinese culture.

You must be eager to learn the further adventures of the protagonists in China in the coming year. Let's start a new beginning with them.

附录 Appendices

语法术语缩略形式一览表
Abbreviations for Grammar Terms

Abbreviations	Grammar Terms in English	Grammar Terms in Chinese	Grammar Terms in *pinyin*
A	Adjective	形容词	xíngróngcí
Adv	Adverb	副词	fùcí
AsPt	Aspect Particle	动态助词	dòngtài zhùcí
Conj	Conjunction	连词	liáncí
IE	Idiom Expression	习惯用语	xíguàn yòngyǔ
Int	Interjection	叹词	tàncí
M	Measure Word	量词	liàngcí
MdPt	Modal Particle	语气助词	yǔqì zhùcí
N	Noun	名词	míngcí
NP	Noun Phrase	名词词组	míngcí cízǔ
Nu	Numeral	数词	shùcí
O	Object	宾语	bīnyǔ
Ono	Onomatopoeia	象声词	xiàngshēngcí
OpV	Optative Verb	能愿动词	néngyuàn dòngcí
P	Predicate	谓语	wèiyǔ
PN	Proper Noun	专有名词	zhuānyǒu míngcí
Pr	Pronoun	代词	dàicí
Pref	Prefix	词头	cítóu
Prep	Preposition	介词	jiècí
Pt	Particle	助词	zhùcí
PW	Place Word	地点词	dìdiǎncí
QPr	Question Pronoun	疑问代词	yíwèn dàicí
QPt	Question Particle	疑问助词	yíwèn zhùcí
S	Subject	主语	zhǔyǔ
StPt	Structural Particle	结构助词	jiégòu zhùcí
Suf	Suffix	词尾	cíwěi
TW	Time Word	时间词	shíjiāncí
V	Verb	动词	dòngcí
VC	Verb plus Complement	动补式动词	dòngbǔshì dòngcí
VO	Verb plus Object	动宾式动词	dòngbīnshì dòngcí
VP	Verbal Phrase	动词词组	dòngcí cízǔ

生词索引（简繁对照）
Vocabulary Index

(Simplified Chinese vs Traditional Chinese)

词条	繁体	拼音	词性	英译	课号
A					
爱	愛	ài	V	to love	20
爱好	愛好	àihào	N / V	hobby; to like	19
爱情	愛情	àiqíng	N	love	22
B					
把	把	bǎ	Prep	(*used when the object is the receiver of an action*)	16
白	白	bái	A	white	17
办公	辦公	bàngōng	VO	to handle official business, to work (usu. in an office)	16
办公室	辦公室	bàngōngshì	N	office	16
帮	幫	bāng	V	to help, to assist	23
帮忙	幫忙	bāngmáng	V	to help	23
包	包	bāo	V	to wrap	18
包裹	包裹	bāoguǒ	N	parcel, package	18
北	北	běi	N	north	21
北边	北邊	běibian	N	the north (side)	21
北方	北方	běifāng	N	north	23
被	被	bèi	Prep	by (*used to indicate the passive voice*)	25
比	比	bǐ	Prep	than (*indicating comparison*)	17
比赛	比賽	bǐsài	N/V	match; to compete, to have a match	21
*遍	遍	biàn	M	(*a measure word for actions*)	22

变化	變化	biànhuà	N	change	24
表	表	biǎo	N	form, table, list	16
别	別	bié	Adv	don't	18
别的	別的	biéde	Pr	other	19
兵	兵	bīng	N	soldier, fighter	15
兵马俑	兵馬俑	bīngmǎyǒng	N	ceremonial clay statues of warriors and horses which are buried with the dead	15
博物馆	博物館	bówùguǎn	N	museum	26
不错	不錯	búcuò	A	not bad	16
不但	不但	búdàn	Conj	not only	24
不敢当	不敢當	bù gǎndāng	IE	I really don't deserve this	19
不见不散	不見不散	bú jiàn bú sàn	IE	don't leave until we meet	26
不同	不同	bùtóng	A	different	21
不行	不行	bùxíng	V	to be no way, to be out of the question	16
布	布	bù	N	cloth	19
部	部	bù	M	(*a measure word for films, works of literature, etc.*)	22

C

才	才	cái	Adv	just	26
材料	材料	cáiliào	N	material	19
菜	菜	cài	N	vegetable	24
		cài	N	dish, food	26
参观	參觀	cānguān	V	to visit (a place)	15
查	查	chá	V	to check, to look up	16
差	差	chà	A	not up to standard, poor, bad	17
长	長	cháng	A	long	16
长安大戏院	長安大戲院	Cháng'ān Dà Xìyuàn	PN	the Chang'an Theater	22
长城	長城	Chángchéng	PN	the Great Wall	23
场	場	chǎng	M	(*a measure word for sports, films, performances*)	21
唱	唱	chàng	V	to sing	19

车	車	chē	N	vehicle	18
车站	車站	chēzhàn	N	bus stop	21
衬衫	襯衫	chènshān	N	shirt	17
成	成	chéng	V	to become	26
城	城	chéng	N	city	24
城市	城市	chéngshì	N	city	24
乘	乘	chéng	V	to ride	18
乘客	乘客	chéngkè	N	passenger	18
出	出	chū	V	to go or come out	16
出发	出發	chūfā	V	to set out, to start off	20
出租	出租	chūzū	V	to hire, to rent	20
出租车	出租車	chūzūchē	N	taxi, cab	20
春	春	chūn	N	spring	20
春江花月夜	春江花月夜	Chūn Jiāng Huā Yuè Yè	PN	*Moonlit Night on the Flowery Spring Riverside* (a famous, traditional Chinese music composition)	20
春天	春天	chūntiān	N	spring	23
词典	詞典	cídiǎn	N	dictionary	18
次	次	cì	M	(*a measure word for actions*)	15
从	從	cóng	Prep	from	15
从来	從來	cónglái	Adv	all along, always	22
村	村	cūn	N	village	24
错	錯	cuò	A	wrong, erroneous	18

D

打的	打的	dǎdī	VO	to take a taxi	22
打算	打算	dǎsuan	N / V	plan; to plan, to intend	23
大家	大家	dàjiā	Pr	all, everybody	18
大学	大學	dàxué	N	university, college	24
大学生	大學生	dàxuéshēng	N	university student, college student	21
带	帶	dài	V	to bring	16
单	單	dān	N	sheet, list	18

但是	但是	dànshì	Conj	but, whereas, yet	22
当	當	dāng	V	to serve as, to be	24
导	導	dǎo	V	to guide, to lead	23
导游	導游	dǎoyóu	N	tour guide	23
倒霉	倒黴	dǎoméi	A	bad luck	25
得	得	de	StPt	(*a structural particle*)	15
		děi	V	to need, must, to have to	15
低	低	dī	A	low	24
地方	地方	dìfang	N	place, region	22
地方戏	地方戲	dìfāngxì	N	regional opera	22
地铁	地鐵	dìtiě	N	underground railway, subway	18
地图	地圖	dìtú	N	map	24
第	第	dì	Pref	(*used to indicate ordinal numbers*)	25
电脑	電腦	diànnǎo	N	computer	16
电视	電視	diànshì	N	TV	25
电梯	電梯	diàntī	N	elevator	19
店	店	diàn	N	shop, store	17
顶	頂	dǐng	N	peak, top	23
丢	丢	diū	V	to lose	25
东	東	dōng	N	east	21
东边	東邊	dōngbian	N	the east (side)	21
冬天	冬天	dōngtiān	N	winter	23
懂	懂	dǒng	V	to understand	15
度	度	dù	M	degree (*a measwre word for temperature*)	23
短	短	duǎn	A	short	17
对	對	duì	Prep	to	26
队	隊	duì	N	a row of people, line	15
		duì	N	team	21
队员	隊員	duìyuán	N	team member	21

E

饿	餓	è	A	hungry	26

而且	而且	érqiě	Conj	but also, and	24

F

发展	發展	fāzhǎn	V	to develop	15
罚	罰	fá	V	to punish, to penalize	16
罚款	罰款	fákuǎn	VO/ N	to impose a fine or forfeit; fine	16
翻译	翻譯	fānyì	V	to translate, to interpret	16
饭馆	飯館	fànguǎn(r)	N	restaurant	20
方便	方便	fāngbiàn	A	convenient	24
访问	訪問	fǎngwèn	V	to visit, to call on	22
放	放	fàng	V	to put, to place	25
放假	放假	fàngjià	VO	to have a holiday or vacation	23
放心	放心	fàngxīn	VO	to set one's mind at rest, to be at ease, to feel relieved	18
飞	飛	fēi	V	to fly	23
飞机	飛機	fēijī	N	airplane	23
非常	非常	fēicháng	Adv	very, extremely, highly	15
费	費	fèi	N	fee, expenses, charge	18
风	風	fēng	N	wind	19
风格	風格	fēnggé	N	style, manner	22
幅	幅	fú	M	(*a measure word for paintings, cloth, etc.*)	19

G

该	該	gāi	V	to be sb.'s turn to do sth.	15
盖	蓋	gài	V	to build	24
感	感	gǎn	V	to feel, to sense	26
感人	感人	gǎnrén	A	touching, moving	22
感兴趣	感興趣	gǎn xìngqù	IE	to be interested in	26
刚	剛	gāng	Adv	just, only a short while ago	15
高	高	gāo	A	high, tall	17
胳膊	胳膊	gēbo	N	arm	25

公分	公分	gōngfēn	N	centimeter	17
公共	公共	gōnggòng	A	public, common, communal	18
公共汽车	公共汽車	gōnggòng qìchē		bus	18
恭喜	恭喜	gōngxǐ	V	to congratulate	20
公园	公園	gōngyuán	N	park	17
工作人员	工作人員	gōngzuò rényuán		working personnel, staff member	15
古典	古典	gǔdiǎn	A	classical	22
故事	故事	gùshi	N	story	22
拐	拐	guǎi	V	to turn	21
关	關	guān	V	to close, to turn off	25
馆	館	guǎn	N	term for certain service establishments or places for cultural activities	16
管	管	guǎn	V	to manage, to discipline	24
管理	管理	guǎnlǐ	V	to manage, to administer	24
广州	廣州	Guǎngzhōu	PN	Guangzhou (capital of Guangdong Province)	23
锅	鍋	guō	N	pot, pan	20
国家	國家	guójiā	N	country	21
*过	過	guò	V	to pass	16
		guo	AsPt	(*indicating a past experience*)	22
过期	過期	guòqī	VO	to be overdue	16
过去	過去	guòqu	V	to pass	17
		guòqù	N	past	20

H

海	海	hǎi	N	sea, big lake	18
海关	海關	hǎiguān	N	customhouse, customs	18
海南岛	海南島	Hǎinán Dǎo	PN	Hainan Island	23
海运	海運	hǎiyùn	N	sea transportation, ocean shipping	18
航空	航空	hángkōng	N	aviation	18
好久	好久	hǎojiǔ	A	a very long time	15
好久不见	好久不見	hǎojiǔ bú jiàn	IE	haven't seen (sb.) for a very long time	15
好像	好像	hǎoxiàng	Adv	seem, like	18

合适	合適	héshì	A	suitable, appropriate, right	17
黑	黑	hēi	A	black	17
红	紅	hóng	A	red	17
《红楼梦》	《紅樓夢》	Hónglóu Mèng	PN	*Dream of the Red Chamber*	22
护照	護照	hùzhào	N	passport	18
花儿	花兒	huār	N	flower	20
花园	花園	huāyuán	N	garden	21
花园小区	花園小區	Huāyuán Xiǎoqū	PN	Garden District	21
化	化	huà	V	to change	20
		huà	Suf	(*used as a suffix to a noun or an adjective to indicate sth. or sb. is becoming or made to have the attribute*)	26
化妆	化妝	huàzhuāng	VO	to make up	20
画	畫	huà	V	to paint	19
画家	畫家	huàjiā	N	painter, artist	19
画儿	畫兒	huàr	N	painting	19
话	話	huà	N	dialect, language	15
坏	壞	huài	A	bad, broken	25
还	還	huán	V	to give back, to return	16
换	換	huàn	V	to exchange, to change	15
火	火	huǒ	N	fire, heat	20
火车	火車	huǒchē	N	train	20
火锅	火鍋	huǒguō	N	chafing dish, hotpot	20
或者	或者	huòzhě	Conj	or	20
货	貨	huò	N	goods	17

J

机	機	jī	N	machine, engine	20
		jī	N	airplane	23
机票	機票	jīpiào	N	air ticket	23
极了	極了	jí le		extremely	17
记	記	jì	V	to remember, to bear in mind	18
记得	記得	jìde	V	to remember, to recall	26

技术	技術	jìshù	N	technology, skill	24
记者	記者	jìzhě	N	reporter	21
加	加	jiā	V	to increase, to add	23
加油	加油	jiāyóu	VO	to make an extra effort, to cheer sb. on	23
*家	家	jiā	Suf	(*used as a suffix to indicate sb. is a specialist*)	19
检查	檢查	jiǎnchá	V	to examine	25
*见	見	jiàn	V	to see, to meet	22
建国门	建國門	Jiànguó Mén	PN	Jianguo Men (a place in Beijing)	18
建议	建議	jiànyì	V/ N	to make a suggestion; advice, suggestion	23
江	江	jiāng	N	river	20
交	交	jiāo	V	to hand in, to hand over, to pay (the rent, etc.)	16
郊区	郊區	jiāoqū	N	suburb, outskirts	20
教书	教書	jiāoshū	VO	to teach	23
教练	教練	jiàoliàn	N	coach	21
结果	結果	jiéguǒ	N	result, outcome	25
结业	結業	jiéyè	VO	to complete a course	26
借	借	jiè	V	to borrow	16
借书证	借書證	jièshūzhèng	N	library card	16
进步	進步	jìnbù	N/V	progress, advancement; to make progress	26
*京剧	京劇	jīngjù	N	Beijing opera	19
经过	經過	jīngguò	V	to pass, to go through, to go by	18
景色	景色	jǐngsè	N	scene, scenery, landscape	23
旧	舊	jiù	A	old, used	18
就	就	jiù	Adv	exactly, precisely	15
舅舅	舅舅	jiùjiu	N	uncle (mother's brother)	24
舅妈	舅媽	jiùmā	N	aunt (wife of mother's brother)	24
举办	舉辦	jǔbàn	V	to conduct, to hold	26
剧	劇	jù	N	opera, theatrical work, play	22
剧团	劇團	jùtuán	N	opera troupe, theatrical group	22
角色	角色	juésè	N	character, role	22

觉得	覺得	juéde	V	to feel, to think	17

K

卡	卡	kǎ	N	card	18
开	開	kāi	V	to drive, to operate	20
开车	開車	kāichē	VO	to drive a car	20
开门	開門	kāimén	VO	to open a door, to begin a day's business	19
开始	開始	kāishǐ	V	to start, to begin	17
开玩笑	開玩笑	kāi wánxiào	V O	to crack a joke, to make fun of	19
考	考	kǎo	V	to give or take an examination, to test	16
考试	考試	kǎoshì	V/ N	to give or take an examination; examination, test	16
可不	可不	kěbù	Adv	exactly, right, that's just the way it is	24
客	客	kè	N	visitor, guest	18
客气	客氣	kèqi	A	polite, courteous	18
*客厅	客廳	kètīng	N	living room	21
课本	課本	kèběn	N	textbook	16
空	空	kōng	N	sky, air	18
孔子	孔子	Kǒngzǐ	PN	Confucius	23
空白	空白	kòngbái	N	blank space	19
快	快	kuài	A	fast, quick, rapid	15
款	款	kuǎn	N	a sum of money	16

L

老	老	lǎo	A	old, senior	19
老外	老外	lǎowài	N	foreigner	26
累	累	lèi	A	tired	23
离	離	lí	Prep	away, off, from	21
里(边)	裏(邊)	lǐ(bian)	N	in, inside, within	18
历史	歷史	lìshǐ	N	history	26
辆	輛	liàng	M	(*a measure word for vehicles*)	24

聊	聊	liáo	V	to chat	26
零下	零下	líng xià		below zero	23
流利	流利	liúlì	A	fluent	15
龙	龍	lóng	N	dragon	23
路	路	lù	N	route	18
路上	路上	lùshang	N	on the road, on the way	20
绿	綠	lǜ	A	green	17

M

麻烦	麻煩	máfan	V/A	to bother sb., to trouble sb.; troublesome	17
马虎	馬虎	mǎhu	A	careless	19
马马虎虎	馬馬虎虎	mǎmǎhūhū	A	so-so, passable	19
马上	馬上	mǎshàng	Adv	right away, immediately	25
卖	賣	mài	V	to sell	17
慢	慢	màn	A	slow	16
*没关系	沒關係	méi guānxi	IE	never mind, it doesn't matter	17
美术馆	美術館	měishùguǎn	N	art gallery	19
门	門	mén	N	door, gate, entrance	18
民乐	民樂	mínyuè	N	folk music played with traditional instruments	20
民族	民族	mínzú	N	ethnic group, nation, nationality	20
明年	明年	míngnián	N	next year	26
明信片	明信片	míngxìnpiàn	N	postcard	15
墨	墨	mò	N	Chinese ink	19

N

拿	拿	ná	V	to take, to hold, to get	16
那样	那樣	nàyàng	Pr	such, so, like that	26
南	南	nán	N	south	26
难	難	nán	A	difficult, hard	22
脑	腦	nǎo	N	brain	16
年级	年級	niánjí	N	grade	24

年轻	年輕	niánqīng	A	young	15
农民	農民	nóngmín	N	farmer, peasant	24
努力	努力	nǔlì	A	hard-working	26

P

爬	爬	pá	V	to climb	23
拍	拍	pāi	V	to take (a picture)	23
排	排	pái	V	to arrange, to put in order	15
			M	line, row	22
排队	排隊	páiduì	VO	to form a line, to queue up	15
派出所	派出所	pàichūsuǒ	N	local police station	25
旁边	旁邊	pángbiān	N	side	20
跑	跑	pǎo	V	to run	19
陪	陪	péi	V	to accompany	26
匹	匹	pǐ	M	(*a measure word for horses*)	19
篇	篇	piān	M	(*a measure word for essays and articles*)	20
便宜	便宜	piányi	A	cheap	17
票	票	piào	N	ticket	18
平方	平方	píngfāng	N/M	square; abbreviation for "square meter"	21
平方米	平方米	píngfāngmǐ	M	square meter	21
平米	平米	píngmǐ	M	abbreviation for "square meter"	21
普通	普通	pǔtōng	A	common, general	15
普通话	普通話	pǔtōnghuà	N	the common speech (Mandarin)	15

Q

妻子	妻子	qīzi	N	wife	26
期	期	qī	N	a period of time	16
齐白石	齊白石	Qí Báishí	PN	(name of a well-known Chinese painter)	19
骑	騎	qí	V	to ride	25
旗袍	旗袍	qípáo	N	cheongsam, a long close-fitting dress with a high neck and slit skirt	17

*起	起	qǐ	V	to rise, to get up	23
气温	氣温	qìwēn	N	air temperature	23
汽车	汽車	qìchē	N	automobile, motor vehicle, car	18
器	器	qì	N	utensil	20
千	千	qiān	Nu	thousand	15
前	前	qián	N	front, forward	21
前边	前邊	qiánbian	N	front	21
前门	前門	Qiánmén	PN	Qianmen (a place in Beijing)	18
前年	前年	qiánnián	N	the year before last	24
轻	輕	qīng	A	light	15
情况	情況	qíngkuàng	N	situation	26
秋天	秋天	qiūtiān	N	autumn	23
球	球	qiú	N	ball	21
区	區	qū	N	district, section, area	21
曲	曲	qǔ	N	tune, melody	20
取	取	qǔ	V	to take, to get, to fetch	18
去年	去年	qùnián	N	last year	21

R

热	熱	rè	A	hot	20
热情	熱情	rèqíng	A	warm, warm-hearted, enthusiastic	26
人民	人民	rénmín	N	people	15
人民币	人民幣	rénmínbì	N	Renminbi (RMB)	15
人员	人員	rényuán	N	personnel, staff	15
认真	認真	rènzhēn	A	earnest, serious	26
肉	肉	ròu	N	meat	20
如果	如果	rúguǒ	Conj	if	25
入	入	rù	V	to enter	24

S

赛	賽	sài	N / V	race, match; to compete, to race	21
散	散	sàn	V	to break up, to disperse	26

山	山	shān	N	hill, mountain	23
伤	傷	shāng	V	to hurt, to wound	25
商	商	shāng	N	commerce, business	17
商店	商店	shāngdiàn	N	shop, store	17
*上	上	shàng	V/N	to go up, to get on; last, previous	16
		shàng	N	upper, up	21
		shàng	V	to be engaged in (work, study, etc.) at a fixed time	24
上边	上邊	shàngbian	N	above	21
上演	上演	shàngyǎn	V	to stage a show, to perform	22
*少	少	shǎo	A	few, little	15
声调	聲調	shēngdiào	N	tone	26
生活	生活	shēnghuó	V/N	to live; life	16
实用	實用	shíyòng	A	practical	16
实在	實在	shízài	A/Adv	honest; truly, really	26
式	式	shì	Suf	(*used as a suffix to indicate sth. or sb. belongs to some type, style*)	17
试	試	shì	V	to try on, to have a try	17
视	視	shì	V	to look at	25
室	室	shì	N	room	16
收	收	shōu	V	to accept, to receive	24
收入	收入	shōurù	N	income, earnings	24
售	售	shòu	V	to sell	17
售货员	售貨員	shòuhuòyuán	N	shop assistant, salesclerk	17
售票员	售票員	shòupiàoyuán	N	ticket seller, conductor	18
书店	書店	shūdiàn	N	bookstore	21
蔬菜	蔬菜	shūcài	N	vegetable	24
数	數	shǔ	V	to count	15
束	束	shù	M	(*a measure word for flowers*)	25
刷	刷	shuā	V	to swipe	18
刷卡	刷卡	shuākǎ	VO	to swipe a card	18
帅	帥	shuài	A	handsome	17
涮	涮	shuàn	V	to cook thin slices of meat in boiling water	20

涮羊肉	涮羊肉	shuàn yángròu		thin slices of mutton boiled in water	20
水平	水平	shuǐpíng	N	level	21
丝绸	絲綢	sīchóu	N	silk	17
死	死	sǐ	V	to die	26
*送	送	sòng	V	to take someone somewhere, to see someone off	25
虽然	雖然	suīrán	Conj	although, though	22
所以	所以	suǒyǐ	Conj	so	20

T

它	它	tā	Pr	it	19
它们	它們	tāmen	Pr	they (*referring to things or animals*)	19
太极拳	太極拳	tàijíquán	N	*tai chi*	17
泰山	泰山	Tài Shān	PN	Mount Tai	23
躺	躺	tǎng	V	to lie (down)	25
套	套	tào	M	set, suit, suite	17
特别	特別	tèbié	Adv	extraordinarily, especially, particularly	22
特点	特點	tèdiǎn	N	characteristic, feature	26
踢	踢	tī	V	to play (literally “kick”)	21
提	提	tí	V	to lift	21
		tí	V	to put forward, to raise	23
提高	提高	tígāo	V	to improve, to increase	21
填	填	tián	V	to fill in, to write	16
条	條	tiáo	M	strip, long narrow piece (*a measure word for something long, narrow or thin, like rivers, dragons, trousers*)	23
停	停	tíng	V	to stop, to park	25
通知	通知	tōngzhī	V/ N	to notify, to inform; notification	18
通知单	通知單	tōngzhīdān	N	letter of notice	18
同学	同學	tóngxué	N	classmate, schoolmate	21
偷	偷	tōu	V	to steal	25
图片	圖片	túpiàn	N	photograph, picture	26
图书	圖書	túshū	N	books	16

图书馆	圖書館	túshūguǎn	N	library	16
腿	腿	tuǐ	N	leg	25

W

外边	外邊	wàibian	N	outside	21
弯	彎	wān	V	to bend	25
完	完	wán	V	to finish, to run out of	25
王府井	王府井	Wángfǔjǐng	PN	(name of a famous commercial district in Beijing)	15
往	往	wǎng	Prep	to, toward	18
忘	忘	wàng	V	to forget	16
卫生	衛生	wèishēng	N	hygiene, sanitation	21
卫生间	衛生間	wèishēngjiān	N	washroom, restroom	21
温	温	wēn	N	temperature	23
		wēn	A	warm	24
温室	温室	wēnshì	N	greenhouse	24
文化	文化	wénhuà	N	culture, education, literacy	24
文章	文章	wénzhāng	N	essay, article	20
问路	問路	wèn lù	V O	to ask for directions, to ask the way	24
卧	卧	wò	V	to lie down	21
*卧室	卧室	wòshì	N	bedroom	21

X

西	西	xī	N	west	20
西安	西安	Xī'ān	PN	(name of the capital of Shaanxi Province)	15
西边	西邊	xībian	N	the west (side)	22
西方	西方	xīfāng	N	the West	20
西服	西服	xīfú	N	Western-style clothes, suit	17
习惯	習慣	xíguàn	V/N	to be accustomed to; habit	20
戏	戲	xì	N	drama, play, show	22
戏院	戲院	xìyuàn	N	theater	22
虾	蝦	xiā	N	shrimp	19

*下	下	xià	V/N	to go down, to get off; next	16
		xià	N	below, down	21
下边	下邊	xiàbian	N	below	21
下雪	下雪	xià xuě	V O	to snow	23
下雨	下雨	xià yǔ	V O	to rain	24
夏天	夏天	xiàtiān	N	summer	23
先	先	xiān	Adv	first, before	16
想象	想象	xiǎngxiàng	V	to imagine	19
向	向	xiàng	Prep	towards, to	24
像	像	xiàng	Adv	seem, appear	18
		xiàng	V	to be alike, to take after	24
消息	消息	xiāoxi	N	news	25
小孩儿	小孩兒	xiǎoháir	N	kid, child	24
小伙子	小夥子	xiǎohuǒzi	N	young man	26
小时	小時	xiǎoshí	N	hour	17
小说	小説	xiǎoshuō	N	novel, fiction	22
小偷	小偷	xiǎotōu	N	thief	25
小燕子	小燕子	Xiǎo Yànzi	PN	name of a Chinese tour guide	23
笑	笑	xiào	V	to laugh, to smile	25
些	些	xiē	M	some	18
辛苦	辛苦	xīnkǔ	A	hard, toilsome	24
新	新	xīn	A	new	16
新年	新年	xīnnián	N	new year	20
《新实用汉语课本》	《新實用漢語課本》	Xīn Shíyòng Hànyǔ Kèběn	PN	*New Practical Chinese Reader*	16
信	信	xìn	N	letter	15
行	行	xíng	V	to be OK	23
兴趣	興趣	xìngqù	N	interest	26
性别	性别	xìngbié	N	sex, gender	16
姓名	姓名	xìngmíng	N	name	16
徐悲鸿	徐悲鴻	Xú Bēihóng	PN	(name of a well-known Chinese painter)	19
学校	學校	xuéxiào	N	school	21
雪	雪	xuě	N	snow	23

Y

颜色	顏色	yánsè	N	color	17
演	演	yǎn	V	to perform, to play	20
		yǎn	V	to act, to perform, to play	22
演出	演出	yǎnchū	V	to play, to perform	22
演员	演員	yǎnyuán	N	actor or actress, performer	22
演奏	演奏	yǎnzòu	V	to play a musical instrument in a performance	20
羊	羊	yáng	N	sheep	20
阳台	陽臺	yángtái	N	balcony	21
夜	夜	yè	N	night	20
样子	樣子	yàngzi	N	shape, style, model, pattern	17
医药费	醫藥費	yīyàofèi	N	medical expenses	25
一定	一定	yídìng	Adv	must, surely	17
一会儿	一會兒	yíhuìr	Nu-M	a little while	16
一样	一樣	yíyàng	A	same, alike	19
以后	以後	yǐhòu	N	after, afterwards	21
已经	已經	yǐjīng	Adv	already	17
以前	以前	yǐqián	N	before, ago, previously, formerly	22
以为	以爲	yǐwéi	V	to think	25
因为	因爲	yīnwèi	Conj	because	20
阴天	陰天	yīntiān	N	cloudy day, overcast day	23
音乐会	音樂會	yīnyuèhuì	N	concert	20
银行	銀行	yínháng	N	bank	15
英镑	英鎊	yīngbàng	N	pound sterling	15
英文	英文	Yīngwén	N	English	18
赢	贏	yíng	V	to win	21
用	用	yòng	V	to use	15
优美	優美	yōuměi	A	beautiful, fine	22
邮费	郵費	yóufèi	N	postage	18
油	油	yóu	N	oil	19
油彩	油彩	yóucǎi	N	greasepaint	19

油画	油畫	yóuhuà	N	oil painting	19
游	游	yóu	V	to swim	19
		yóu	V	to travel	23
*游泳	游泳	yóuyǒng	V	to swim	23
有的	有的	yǒude	Pr	some	22
又	又	yòu	Adv	again	20
右	右	yòu	N	right	21
右边	右邊	yòubian	N	the right (side)	21
雨	雨	yǔ	N	rain	24
远	遠	yuǎn	A	far	21
月	月	yuè	N	moon	20
乐器	樂器	yuèqì	N	musical instrument	20
乐曲	樂曲	yuèqǔ	N	musical composition	20
越剧	越劇	yuèjù	N	Shaoxing opera	22
越来越	越來越	yuè lái yuè	IE	more and more	26

Z

*在	在	zài	Adv	(*used to indicate an action in progress*)	24
咱们	咱們	zánmen	Pr	we, us	18
糟糕	糟糕	zāogāo	A	in a wretched state, in a mess, too bad	18
早	早	zǎo	A	early	15
展	展	zhǎn	N	exhibition, show	26
展览	展覽	zhǎnlǎn	N	exhibition, show	26
站	站	zhàn	N	station, stop	18
		zhàn	V	to stand	23
丈夫	丈夫	zhàngfu	N	husband	26
着急	著急	zháojí	A	worried	20
照相	照相	zhàoxiàng	VO	to take a picture, to photograph	20
照相机	照相機	zhàoxiàngjī	N	camera	20
着	著	zhe	Pt	(*used to indicate a continuous aspect*)	25
这么	這么	zhème	Pr	so, such, like this	22
正式	正式	zhèngshì	A	formal	20

正在	正在	zhèngzài	Adv	in the process of, in the middle of (*used as a key word of a progressive construction*)	24
证	證	zhèng	N	certificate, card	16
职业	職業	zhíyè	N	occupation, profession	16
只	祇	zhǐ	Adv	only	19
纸	紙	zhǐ	N	paper	19
中餐	中餐	zhōngcān	N	Chinese food (meal)	26
中国化	中國化	zhōngguóhuà	V	to Sinify, to Sinicize	26
中国画	中國畫	zhōngguóhuà	N	traditional Chinese painting	19
中国通	中國通	zhōngguótōng	N	a China expert, a China hand	26
中式	中式	zhōngshì	A	Chinese style	17
种	種	zhǒng	M	kind, sort, type	22
种类	種類	zhǒnglèi	N	kind, sort, type, variety	22
种	種	zhòng	V	to grow, to plant	24
重	重	zhòng	A	serious, heavy	25
主角	主角	zhǔjué	N	leading actor or actress	22
主要	主要	zhǔyào	A	main	19
注意	注意	zhùyì	V	to pay attention to	25
抓	抓	zhuā	V	to clutch, to catch, to arrest	25
妆	妝	zhuāng	N	make-up	20
撞	撞	zhuàng	V	to bump against, to knock down	25
桌子	桌子	zhuōzi	N	table, desk	25
自己	自己	zìjǐ	Pr	oneself	16
自行车	自行車	zìxíngchē	N	bicycle	25
走	走	zǒu	V	to walk, to go	17
奏	奏	zòu	V	to play a musical instrument	20
足	足	zú	N	foot	21
足球	足球	zúqiú	N	soccer	21
左	左	zuǒ	N	left	21
左边	左邊	zuǒbian	N	the left (side)	21
座	座	zuò	M	(*a measure word for mountains, buildings and other similar immovable objects*)	24
座位	座位	zuòwèi	N	seat	22

补充生词
Supplementary Words

词条	繁体	拼音	词性	英译	课号
A					
爱人	愛人	àiren	N	husband or wife, spouse	24
B					
薄	薄	báo	A	thin	17
悲伤	悲傷	bēishāng	A	sad, sorrowful	22
毕业	畢業	bìyè	VO	to graduate, to finish school	26
便饭	便飯	biànfàn	N	a simple meal	22
*表	表	biǎo	N	watch	17
补	補	bǔ	V	to mend, to make up	25
布	布	bù	N	cloth, fabric	17
不怎么样	不怎么樣	bù zěnmeyàng	IE	not so good	22
C					
菜	菜	cài	N	dish	15
菜单	菜單	càidān	N	menu	23
茶楼	茶樓	chálóu	N	tearoom, tea house	16
城市	城市	chéngshì	N	city	15
出差	出差	chūchāi	VO	to go on a business trip	21
聪明	聰明	cōngming	A	clever, bright	18
D					
打折	打折	dǎzhé	VO	to sell at a discount, to give a discount	17

刀	刀	dāo	N	knife	25
地方	地方	dìfang	N	place	15
地上	地上	dìshang	N	ground, floor	25
电影院	電影院	diànyǐngyuàn	N	cinema	21
掉	掉	diào	V	to drop, to fall	25
动	動	dòng	V	to move	23
冻	凍	dòng	V	to freeze	24
顿	頓	dùn	M	(*a measure word for meals*)	22
多余	多餘	duōyú	A	superfluous, uncalled for, redundant	20

E

*儿子	兒子	érzi	N	son	15

F

发抖	發抖	fādǒu	V	to shake, to tremble, to shiver	24
方法	方法	fāngfǎ	N	method	26
房间	房間	fángjiān	N	room	16
封	封	fēng	M	(*a measure word for letters*)	18

G

钢琴	鋼琴	gāngqín	N	piano	19
公斤	公斤	gōngjīn	M	kilogram (kg.)	18
古典	古典	gǔdiǎn	A	classical	21
挂失	挂失	guàshī	VO	to report the loss of something	25
观点	觀點	guāndiǎn	N	point of view	19
管	管	guǎn	V	to discipline	19
广东	廣東	Guǎngdōng	PN	Guangdong Province	16
国籍	國籍	guójí	N	nationality	16

H

孩子	孩子	háizi	N	child	16
害怕	害怕	hàipà	V	to be afraid, to fear	23
杭州	杭州	Hángzhōu	PN	Hangzhou (capital of Zhejiang Province)	21
后边	後邊	hòubian	N	back, behind	21
护照	護照	hùzhào	N	passport	16
画蛇添足	畫蛇添足	huà shé tiān zú	IE	to draw a snake and add feet to it, meaning to ruin the effect by adding something superfluous	20
回忆	回憶	huíyì	V	to reminisce, to recollect, to recall	22
汇率	匯率	huìlǜ	N	exchange rate	15

J

机场	機場	jīchǎng	N	airport	24
纪念	紀念	jìniàn	N	commemoration	18
加元	加元	jiāyuán	N	Canadian dollar	15
贾宝玉	賈寶玉	Jiǎ Bǎoyù	PN	(name of the leading male character in *Dream of the Red Chamber*)	22
减肥	減肥	jiǎnféi	VO	to lose weight	19
见面	見面	jiànmiàn	VO	to meet, to see	26
建筑师	建築師	jiànzhùshī	N	architect	21
将军	將軍	jiāngjūn	N	general	24
脚	脚	jiǎo	N	foot	20
*教育	教育	jiàoyù	V	to teach, to educate	19
接（人）	接（人）	jiē (rén)	V	to pick up (someone)	24
街	街	jiē	N	street	23
节目	節目	jiémù	N	programme	19
结婚	結婚	jiéhūn	VO	to get married	22
经验	經驗	jīngyàn	N	experience	26
警察	警察	jǐngchá	N	policeman	25
警车	警車	jǐngchē	N	police car, police van	25
句	句	jù	M	(*a measure word for sentences*)	26

K

咖啡馆	咖啡館	kāfēiguǎn	N	coffee bar	21
开始	開始	kāishǐ	V	to start, to begin	16
棵	棵	kē	M	(*a measure word for plants*)	23
渴	渴	kě	A	thirsty	23
客人	客人	kèrén	N	guest	26
哭	哭	kū	V	to cry, to weep	22
裤子	褲子	kùzi	N	trousers, pants	17

L

老人	老人	lǎorén	N	the elderly, the aged, old man or woman	16
离开	離開	líkāi	V	to leave, to depart from	22
凉快	涼快	liángkuai	A	cool	24
辆	輛	liàng	M	(*a measure word for vehicles*)	20
了不起	了不起	liǎobuqǐ	IE	amazing, terrific, extraordinary	17
了解	了解	liǎojiě	V	to understand, to realize	26
料子	料子	liàozi	N	material for making clothes	17
林黛玉	林黛玉	Lín Dàiyù	PN	(name of the leading female character in *Dream of the Red Chamber*)	22

M

美丽	美麗	měilì	A	beautiful, pretty	21
美元	美元	měiyuán	N	U. S. dollar	15
目录	目錄	mùlù	N	catalog, list	16

N

南边	南邊	nánbian	N	the south (side)	21
年龄	年齡	niánlíng	N	age	16
暖和	暖和	nuǎnhuo	A	warm	24

O

欧元	歐元	ōuyuán	N	Euro	15

P

跑步	跑步	pǎobù	VO	to run, to jog	19
骗	騙	piàn	V	to cheat, to trick	22

Q

骑	騎	qí	V	to ride, to sit on the back of	19
起飞	起飛	qǐfēi	V	to take off	23
晴天	晴天	qíngtiān	N	fine day	23
请客	請客	qǐngkè	VO	to feast, to invite sb. to dinner	26

R

然后	然后	ránhòu	Conj	then	18
热闹	熱鬧	rènao	A	lively, bustling with noise and excitement	16

S

山	山	shān	N	hill, mountain	21
山水	山水	shānshuǐ	N	mountains and rivers, scenery with hills and waters	21
烧	燒	shāo	V	to burn	22
设计	設計	shèjì	V	to design	21
生火	生火	shēnghuǒ	VO	to make a fire	24
生气	生氣	shēngqì	VO	to get angry, to take offense	19
声	聲	shēng	N	sound, voice	24
诗	詩	shī	N	poem, poetry	22

诗人	詩人	shīrén	N	poet	21
士兵	士兵	shìbīng	N	soldier	24
手	手	shǒu	N	hand	25
手机	手機	shǒujī	N	cell phone	25
首	首	shǒu	M	(*a measure word for poems, songs or melodies*)	26
瘦	瘦	shòu	A	thin	19
*书店	書店	shūdiàn	N	bookstore, bookshop	19
书法	書法	shūfǎ	N	handwriting, calligraphy	19
输	輸	shū	V	to lose	21
熟悉	熟悉	shúxī	V	to be familiar with	26
树	樹	shù	N	tree	23
双	雙	shuāng	M	pair	17
死	死	sǐ	V	to die	22
苏杭	蘇杭	Sū Háng	PN	Suzhou and Hangzhou	21
苏州	蘇州	Sūzhōu	PN	Suzhou (a city of Jiangsu Province)	21
孙子	孫子	sūnzi	N	grandson	18

T

太太	太太	tàitai	N	wife, Mrs.	22
天气预报	天氣預報	tiānqì yùbào		weather forecast	23
天堂	天堂	tiāntáng	N	heaven, paradise	21
条	條	tiáo	M	(*a measure word for long, narrow objects, such as trousers, skirts, snakes, etc.*)	17
贴	貼	tiē	V	to stick, to paste	18
停	停	tíng	V	to stop, to cease	24
停车场	停車場	tíngchēchǎng	N	parking lot	23
头发	頭發	tóufa	N	hair	17
突然	突然	tūrán	Adv	suddenly	25

W

完	完	wán	V	to finish	20

万事如意	萬事如意	wànshì rúyì	IE	May all your wishes come true.	20
危险	危險	wēixiǎn	A	dangerous	23
问答	問答	wèndá	V / N	to ask and answer questions; questions and answers	16

X

吓	嚇	xià	V	to scare, to frighten	25
现金	現金	xiànjīn	N	cash	15
相爱	相愛	xiāng'ài	V	to fall in love	22
相声	相聲	xiàngsheng	N	comic dialogue, cross talk	17
箱子	箱子	xiāngzi	N	box, case, trunk	24
项链	項鏈	xiàngliàn	N	necklace	25
小学	小學	xiǎoxué	N	primary school	20
鞋	鞋	xié	N	shoes	17
新闻	新聞	xīnwén	N	news	16
信封	信封	xìnfēng	N	envelope	18
信用卡	信用卡	xìnyòngkǎ	N	credit card	15
型号	型號	xínghào	N	model, type	25
行李	行李	xíngli	N	baggage, luggage	24
幸福	幸福	xìngfú	A	happy	20
熊	熊	xióng	N	bear	23
修建	修建	xiūjiàn	V	to build, to construct	21
续借	續借	xùjiè	V	to renew	16

Y

亚洲学系	亞洲學系	Yàzhōuxué xì		Department of Asian studies	15
研究	研究	yánjiū	V	to study, to research	22
钥匙	鑰匙	yàoshi	N	key	16
页	頁	yè	M	page	17
业余	業餘	yèyú	A	amateur	19
一路平安	一路平安	yílù píng'ān	IE	to have a safe journey, bon voyage	24
以前	以前	yǐqián	N	before, formerly, previously	19

艺术	藝術	yìshù	N	art	26
意思	意思	yìsi	N	meaning	26
音乐厅	音樂廳	yīnyuètīng	N	concert hall	20
营业员	營業員	yíngyèyuán	N	staff of a shop, post office and a bank, etc.	19
邮票	郵票	yóupiào	N	stamp	18
预订	預訂	yùdìng	V	to reserve, to book	16
元	元	yuán	M	(*a unit of Chinese currency*)	15
园林	園林	yuánlín	N	garden, park	21
远	遠	yuǎn	A	far	19
阅览室	閱覽室	yuèlǎnshì	N	reading room	16

Z

杂志	雜志	zázhì	N	magazine	16
站岗	站崗	zhàngǎng	VO	to stand guard	24
正常	正常	zhèngcháng	A	normal, regular	24
只	隻	zhī	M	(*a measure word for cats, sheep, birds and bears, etc.*)	23
中国国航	中國國航	Zhōngguó Guóháng	PN	Air China (CA)	23
装	裝	zhuāng	V	to pretend to be sth./sb.	23
准备	準備	zhǔnbèi	V / N	to prepare, to get ready; preparation	18
自行车	自行車	zìxíngchē	N	bike, bicycle	19
总是	總是	zǒngshì	Adv	always	17
足球场	足球場	zúqiúchǎng	N	soccer field	21
最	最	zuì	Adv	most, least, best, to the highest or lowest degree	20

汉字索引
Character Index